GIRTON COLLEGE

2017

# A Century of Fiscal Squeeze Politics

# A Century of Fiscal Squeeze Politics

## 100 Years of Austerity, Politics, and Bureaucracy in Britain

Christopher Hood and Rozana Himaz

OXFORD
UNIVERSITY PRESS

# OXFORD

UNIVERSITY PRESS

Great Clarendon Street, Oxford, OX2 6DP,
United Kingdom

Oxford University Press is a department of the University of Oxford.
It furthers the University's objective of excellence in research, scholarship,
and education by publishing worldwide. Oxford is a registered trade mark of
Oxford University Press in the UK and in certain other countries

First Edition published in 2017
Impression: 1

Published in the United States of America by Oxford University Press
198 Madison Avenue, New York, NY 10016, United States of America

British Library Cataloguing in Publication Data
Data available

Library of Congress Control Number: 2016958130

ISBN 978–0–19–877961–2

Printed and bound by
CPI Group (UK) Ltd, Croydon, CR0 4YY

# Preface and Acknowledgements

This book has taken five years to write and over that time the slippery word 'austerity' has seldom been out of the news. Political battles raged in many countries over how governments should respond to public debt and deficits, what balance should be struck between tax increases and spending restraint, and what should be the proper amount of 'tightness' or 'looseness' in monetary policy (interest rates, quantitative easing) and in fiscal policy (public spending and taxes). The accompanying political journeys often resembled a long-distance roller-coaster ride, with dramatic ups and downs and changes of course. When one of us was interviewed in 2010 over the grant application that financed most of the work that went into this book, one of the members of the panel questioned whether 'austerity' would be all over long before the study was finished. But at the time of writing, there was still fierce dispute over whether austerity was or should be over.

We cannot claim that the subject of fiscal squeeze has been neglected by commentators and scholars. On the contrary, there has been a plethora of writing on the subject, from many different disciplinary and political/economic angles. A few years ago we ourselves produced a collected volume comparing fiscal squeezes in different times and places, and the analytic concepts we developed for that book form the point of departure for this one. But even with all the attention that 'austerity' in one form or another has attracted, there remain at least three important gaps or puzzles that this book aims to address.

First, as we explain in the opening chapter, while there are a number of cross-national comparative studies of fiscal 'consolidation' (or similar words related to fiscal squeeze), there is no study that looks at fiscal squeezes in a single country over a century, comparing cases over time rather than between countries. This book is intended to fill that gap.

Second, as we also explain in the opening chapter, while there are studies that look qualitatively at fiscal squeeze through the prism of political analysis and studies that look at fiscal squeeze through that of econometrics, the former almost never probe published figures critically and the latter almost never look carefully behind the numbers to the qualitative political processes and strategies that produce those reported outcomes. But this book aims to do both, starting with reported financial outcome numbers and then looking at the political choices and processes that lie behind those numbers.

When painting and photography came together for the first time in the nineteenth century, the combination produced new perspectives and pre-occupations, in the form of new angles of vision and new kinds of art. And in a roughly analogous way, when we give equal weight to careful scrutiny of reported numbers and qualitative political process over a long period, as we aim to do in this book, we can identify patterns and puzzles that received theory does not even recognize, let alone explain. As we show in Chapter Two, we identify a long-term shift from 'surgery without anaesthetics' approaches to fiscal squeeze in the earlier part of our study—deep but short-lived episodes of spending restraint or tax increases—towards episodes in which the pain is spread out over a longer period. We also identify a marked reduction if not absence of revenue-led squeezes in the last part of the century discussed here, another observation not readily explicable from standard analysis in political science. Third, by looking at fiscal squeeze both in terms of reported outcomes and of qualitative analysis of loss, cost, and effort, we can show that the latter leads us to a different conclusion about the electoral effects of fiscal squeeze than does the former, and hence to solve a puzzle in the literature about apparently erratic voter 'punishment' of governments that impose fiscal squeezes.

We have many debts to acknowledge. This study would not have been possible without the funding provided by the UK's Economic and Social Research Council, in the form of a three-year Professorial Fellowship which provided time for us to get to grips with the complexities of a hundred years of statistics on the public finances and (just as complex) the politics of a dozen or more fiscal squeezes over a century. We are grateful to those who helped us along the way, particularly to David Heald of the University of Glasgow, who offered valuable help and advice all through the project and read some of the chapters of this book in draft, to Richard Allen, who also read and commented on the draft manuscript, to Andrew Gamble of the University of Cambridge (and Sheffield) for support and encouragement, to Ruth Dixon of Oxford University for help and advice, to Roger Middleton from the University of Bristol, to Ryland Thomas of the Bank of England for help with historical statistics, and to Gillian Hood for compiling the index. We are also grateful to a number of serving or former Treasury staff whom we interviewed about the more recent cases in this book, and who generously gave of their time and experience, but by convention are not named here.

*Oxford,*
*September 2016*

# Contents

*List of Figures*        ix

*List of Tables*        xi

**Part I.  Background and Overview**

1. Setting the Scene: The Politics of Austerity and
   Fiscal Squeeze     3

2. UK Fiscal Squeezes over a Century: A Summary
   Comparison     23

**Part II.  Selected Periods of Fiscal Squeeze over a
Century**

3. World War I and the 1920s: From Tax Squeeze through
   Double Squeeze to Spending Squeeze     41

4. The 1930s Squeeze: From Revenue Squeeze to Spending
   Squeeze via Political Crisis     60

5. World War II and Post-War Labour Austerity     80

6. The 'Stop-Go' Squeezes of the 1950s and 1960s     100

7. The 1970s Fiscal Squeeze: Stagflation, Recession,
   Currency Crisis, and Political Crisis     120

8. Rolling Back the State? Fiscal Squeeze, Thatcher-Style     140

9. Fiscal Squeeze in the 1990s: Tales of the
   Unexpected     160

10. After the 2008 Financial Crash: The Early 2010s     180

# Contents

**Part III.  Patterns and Lessons**

11.  Conclusions: From the Past to the Future
     of Fiscal Squeeze                                    203

Appendix                                                  225

*References*                                              231
*Index*                                                   241

# List of Figures

2.1. Trends in selected disaggregated expenditure categories as a
    percentage of GDP                                                        35
2.2. Trends in disaggregated revenue categories as a percentage of GDP       36
A1. Changes in selected UK tax rates, 1900–2012                             230

# List of Tables

1.1. Some different types of fiscal squeeze based on reported
financial outcomes     16

1.2. A qualitative framework for assessing degrees of squeeze in
terms of voter loss, political cost to incumbents, and state effort     17

2.1. UK fiscal squeeze episodes 1900–2015     27

2.2. Episodes of deficit reductions using various definitions
and data sources 1900–2015     29

2.3. UK fiscal squeeze episodes 1900–2015: Decision-making
features and composition of squeezes     33

3.1. A qualitative classification of imposed loss, political cost, and
state effort associated with World War 1 and 1920s fiscal squeezes     54

4.1. A qualitative classification of imposed loss, political cost,
and state effort associated with 1930s fiscal squeezes     76

5.1. A qualitative classification of imposed loss, political cost,
and state effort associated with 1940s fiscal squeezes     98

6.1. A qualitative classification of imposed loss, political cost, and
state effort associated with 1950s and 1960s fiscal squeezes     116

7.1. A qualitative classification of imposed loss, political cost,
and state effort associated with 1970s fiscal squeezes     136

8.1. A qualitative classification of imposed loss, political cost,
and state effort associated with 1980s fiscal squeezes     157

9.1. A qualitative classification of imposed loss, political cost,
and state effort associated with 1990s fiscal squeezes     176

10.1. A qualitative classification of imposed loss, political cost,
and state effort associated with 2010–15 fiscal squeeze     196

11.1. Fiscal squeeze episodes compared: quantitative type and
qualitative evaluation of loss, cost, and effort involved     205

11.2. UK fiscal squeeze episodes 1900–2015: economic aftermath     215

11.3. UK fiscal squeeze episodes 1900–2015: the political and
constitutional aftermath     218

## List of Tables

A1. Defining expenditure-based episodes using alternative
data sources and definitions of spending                          225

A2. Defining revenue-based episodes using alternative data sources
and definitions of revenue                                        226

A3. Economic conditions at the start of spending squeezes 1900–2015    227

A4. Economic conditions at the start of the revenue squeeze and
spending rises during the squeeze 1900–2015                       228

A5. Change in expenditure disaggregated by policy domain as
percentage of fall in total spending                              229

A6. Revenue changes in three sources of revenue as percentage
of total revenue increases                                        229

# Part I
# Background and Overview

# 1

## Setting the Scene

### The Politics of Austerity and Fiscal Squeeze

Since the 2008 financial crash, 'austerity' has been one of the top two or three issues dominating both practice and analysis of politics and economics in much of the world. Like most highly charged political terms, 'austerity' is rarely defined precisely and means different things to different people. In the past the word was used to mean deprivation or restraints on consumption, for example when governments hold down wages or when the essentials of daily life are scarce, severely rationed, or not available in legal markets.[1] More recently, in Europe and North America at least, it has mostly come to denote government policies aimed at restraining public spending, raising taxes, or both.

Austerity in that sense has dominated practice because so much political conflict has been bound up with those issues of taxing and spending. Political drama related to cuts and squeezes across much of the world and especially in the eurozone over the past decade or so has included riots, strikes, demonstrations, epic election and referendum upsets, and (most notably in Greece) cliff-hanging negotiations between debtor governments and their international creditors over financial bailouts. 'Austerity' has also dominated debate in ways ranging from abstruse discussions among economists over arcane concepts like 'expansionary fiscal contraction' to the billions of words poured into heated social media disputes about who is to blame for high public debt and deficit, who should pay for the necessary corrective measures, and who should be protected.[2] A search on Scopus (the largest abstract and citation database of

---

[1] See, for instance, Morgan (1984: 347), describing the rigours imposed by government food rationing on British consumers in the late 1940s, such as only one egg per adult per week.

[2] Just a few examples of the voluminous literature on this subject over the last few years are t'Hart and Tindall (2009), Mauro (2011), Blyth (2013), Bartels and Bermeo (2013), Streeck and Shäfer (2013), Alesina and Giavazzi (2013), Ban (2015), and Kickert and Randma-Liiv (2015).

peer-reviewed literature, including scientific journals, books, and conference proceedings) using the keywords 'fiscal austerity' reveals a total of 110 publications (roughly 2.2 per year) for the forty-eight years from 1960 to 2008. But for the eight years from 2009 to 2016, the number quadrupled to 414— roughly fifty publications a year, on average.

Austerity poses central questions in politics and economics over how long and how hard it can be practised by democracies without big trouble of one kind or another. A century ago (shortly before the Russian Revolution) a leading British liberal and editor of *The Economist*, Francis Wrigley Hirst, declared, 'There is a limit to human endurance and the economic misery which a state can inflict on its people' (Hirst 1915: 150 quoted in Daunton 2002: 36). Equivalent sentiments today are more often expressed about the effects of public spending cutbacks than about the burdens of increased taxation that most preoccupied Hirst. But the basic issue has not gone away.

So what does this book contribute to an already crowded, long-standing, and heavily politicized debate? It aims to add three things. One, it puts more recent episodes of 'fiscal squeeze' (a term we will define shortly) into a longer-term context by offering for the first time an analysis of the politics of every fiscal squeeze over the course of a century in the United Kingdom, one of the world's leading and longest-established democracies. The era of fiscal squeeze that set in for many countries after the financial crash of 2008 was far from the first time in history when such policies had been practised, and for the UK at least, by no means the most severe on many measures. So to put the 'austerity politics' of that era into perspective, we need to look back at earlier episodes of fiscal squeeze to see what was different and what was the same, for example, in what triggered the squeezes, how the political process worked, what other policies of austerity or expansion accompanied fiscal squeeze, and what the electoral and political aftermath was.

Of course individual periods of austerity have been carefully explored by economic and political historians (such as Robert Skidelsky's (1967) classic study of the UK's 1929–31 Labour Government) and we draw heavily on the work of such scholars in some of the chapters of this book. In a few cases, more or less explicit comparisons have been drawn between the 2010s and a particular earlier episode, for example, in Barry Eichengreen's (2015) comparison of the handling of the financial crises of the 1930s and the 2010s in the United States. But the century-long timescale explored here allows us to bring out longer-term trends and patterns in how austerity politics work. For example, despite beguiling comparisons with the Great Depression of the 1930s, we show that the post-2010 squeeze in the UK in many ways had more in common with the squeezes of the 1980s and 1990s.

Second, this book focuses on three critical political choices that inevitably arise in any fiscal squeeze. One concerns what emphasis should be laid on tax hikes as against spending cuts (which of course also raises the issue of what kinds of taxes should be raised, on what items or groups, and what kinds of spending should be cut). How do democratic governments decide whether to tax more, spend less, or apply some mixture of the two? Another key political choice concerns whether to impose fiscal squeeze in 'short sharp shocks' that are deep but not prolonged, as against cushioning the blow or spreading the pain in smaller doses over a longer period. And a third issue, central to the politics of claiming credit and avoiding blame, concerns how incumbents in government choose to handle the blame for the losses imposed on voters by fiscal squeeze, for example, by sharing responsibility in emergency all-party coalitions or passing the poisoned chalice of proposing squeeze measures to independent experts or technocrats. As this book shows, political choices on each of those issues were quite variable in the UK over a century. So what accounts for that variation and for changes over time?

Finally, this book looks at what fiscal squeeze episodes leave behind them—in particular their electoral, political, and public policy consequences. For example, since the financial crash of 2008, observable changes in the western countries have included a remarkable growth of food banks run by charities as a supplement or substitute for state welfare and the raising of the age at which future retirement pensions are to be paid. In some cases new forms of decision-making have been introduced, such as the use of social media to inform decisions over which potholes to fill in by local authorities too cash-strapped to fix everything. If 'necessity is the mother of invention', as the old proverb has it, what inventions or innovations do fiscal squeezes produce in government or public services? When if ever do such episodes have the effect of dramatically reshaping the state, for example by changing what it does or how it does it, under pressures of 'doing more with less'? How, if at all, do fiscal squeezes change the electoral scene, in the way that political credit and blame plays out afterwards?

Many commentators have argued that there are strong inbuilt political pressures for higher public spending in modern democracies, highlighting the powerful opposition that constituencies created by the development of the welfare state can mobilize against efforts even to restrain the growth of public spending (see, for example, Brittan 1976). Some have claimed that such pressures stem from structural changes, notably urbanization, that accompany modern social development, while others (such as Wildavsky (1980: 231–70)) put them down to a long-term rise in egalitarian attitudes in western countries. And political (and bureaucratic) opponents of austerity are often said to engage in 'shroud-waving' and doom-laden predictions about the effects of cutting public spending to persuade voters to reject such policies. But if there really is something unstoppable about state expansion for any of those reasons, how can the presumed electoral toxicity of fiscal squeezes be minimized or avoided?

As we shall show, the political and electoral consequences of the various fiscal squeezes described in the following chapters are often debatable even many decades later and seem to have been quite varied over this century. We also show that more severe forms of fiscal squeeze tended to be associated with a higher electoral casualty rate in terms of loss of office by incumbent parties at subsequent general elections, but with some notable exceptions. Electoral outcomes after fiscal squeezes ranged from severe election defeats for parties imposing fiscal squeezes to punishments for incumbents who had failed to squeeze and electoral victories for incumbents who had just announced major spending cuts (notably for the Conservative-dominated National Government in 1931, discussed in Chapter Four). But for many of the episodes explored in the chapters that follow, such effects seem to have been less direct, more debatable, and more 'slow-burn'.

To set the scene and frame our study, this chapter starts by explaining what we mean by 'fiscal squeeze' as a type of 'austerity', what different forms fiscal squeeze can take and what its significance is for government and politics. Then we move on to discuss the three key political choices over how to handle fiscal squeeze that were mentioned earlier, as well as the much-debated issue of the electoral and political effects of fiscal squeeze. Following that, we explain how we go about observing and classifying fiscal squeezes in this book, why the UK's experience over a century is instructive for exploring the politics of fiscal squeeze, and how our analysis proceeds in the rest of the book.

## 1.1 What Is Fiscal Squeeze and Why does It Matter?

By fiscal squeeze we mean a type of 'austerity' policy that takes the form of substantial effort and activity by governments to impose absolute or relative losses on at least some people by increasing revenue, restraining spending, or a mixture of the two.

The word 'substantial' is there to signify some threshold—hard to define, of course—that distinguishes the normal, everyday 'getting and spending' politics of the budgetary process from episodes when real effort is exerted to rein in government spending, raise revenue, or both. The point is that the normal politics of budgeting, as many scholars have noted,[3] tends to involve a staged process of cutting down initial bids, ambit claims, or strategically pumped-up expectations, setting the rival claims of different groups and agencies for funding or tax relief against one another to test their relative political support, against some at least implicit budget constraint. For 'fiscal squeeze' to mean

---

[3] Notably Wildavsky 1964; see also Rose 1980: 216.

anything other than that normal process of disappointing or winnowing down initial bids to fit finite resources, it must denote some additional effort to raise revenue or restrain spending.

We discuss later what that threshold might be, but the point at which 'normal' budgetary politics ends and fiscal squeeze begins can never be clear-cut, because political pain thresholds can be subjective and context-dependent. For example, if voters have been promised lower taxes or higher spending, a squeeze that looks slight in recorded statistics might have more political effect than one that is statistically bigger but turns out to be lower than what has been widely expected or trailed by politicians trying to manage down expectations and so comes as a 'reprieve' (Rose (1980): 227–8). Similarly, efforts to reduce public spending or increase revenue in the depths of a recession are likely to be more painful to many individuals than they would be in the midst of an economic boom. Such contextual effects obviously matter.

Further, while we defined fiscal squeeze earlier as involving the imposition of losses on some individuals or groups, those losses may in some cases be accompanied by benefits to the same or other individuals or groups. For instance, in some of our cases government spending was reduced expressly to pay for tax cuts (as happened for instance in 1922, when expansionist policies of post-World War I reconstruction clashed with powerful middle-class demands for income tax reductions), and conversely, in other cases, taxes were raised to pay for higher spending on benefits or services (as happened, for instance, in 1974, which saw a major tax hike by a newly elected Labour Government to fund ambitious social and industrial policy plans). The politics of fiscal squeeze therefore centres on how such loss-imposition works, how losses and benefits play out, and what shapes who gets how much political blame or credit.

As we shall argue throughout this book, 'squeeze' defined as political effort or activity is not necessarily the same as the achievement of lower levels of budget deficit (broadly, the difference between public spending and revenue raised, relative to GDP) in subsequently reported financial data. The latter is what econometricians of fiscal consolidations understandably tend to focus on, but we will show in Chapters Two and Eleven how imperfect a measure it is of the political effort going into fiscal squeezes, the degree of pain experienced by voters and taxpayers, or of the timing of squeeze episodes.

For example, as we will describe in Chapter Four, the early 1930s saw substantial efforts to raise revenue and reduce spending, and in the process also witnessed major party splits, politicians putting their credit on the line, and real pain imposed on many voters, notably by cutting unemployment benefits in the depths of the Great Depression. But if we look at that episode only through the prism of deficit reductions, those efforts are reflected only as a one-year fall in primary budget deficit[4] in 1932/3. Conversely, a government might exert less political effort to restrain spending or to raise taxes (as happened during a period of steady economic growth in the later 1980s and later 1990s), and see deficit fall substantially. Accordingly, to capture properly how much loss was imposed on voters and how much political cost and exertion was expended by politicians and the state machine, we have to look directly at what happened to spending and revenues. And to complement this quantitative analysis we have to look more qualitatively at each episode. We describe that exploration in section 1.3 below.

So why does fiscal squeeze matter? Analysing fiscal squeeze is important in its own right, as a central aspect of the politics of many states today. Just as sociologists find that disasters reveal where power lies in a society (Burns and Thomas 2015: 3), any fiscal squeeze is a 'stress test' of political power and priorities—probing anew the political support for every component of public spending and/or testing political tolerance of new or higher taxes. It is a form of political discovery analogous to the 'discovery' function classically attributed to markets by Friedrich Hayek (1949). Further, given that loss imposition is central to our definition of fiscal squeeze, every fiscal squeeze is also a key test of incumbents' capacity to manage political credit and blame. That is why we aim to look carefully and with hindsight at the aftermath of fiscal squeezes.

As for credit and blame, there is an extensive literature on the electoral politics of welfare state retrenchment, much of it inspired by the work of the Paul Pierson (1994 and 1996) in the 1990s. Starting from Kent Weaver's (1986) classic analysis of blame-avoidance imperatives in politics, Pierson argued that the political logic of welfare state retrenchment is different from that of welfare state expansion, mainly because many welfare programmes are not pure 'public goods' in the language of economics (creating services, such as defence, from which no one can be excluded) but rather tend to involve groups enjoying concentrated and direct benefits that can be mobilized to resist cutbacks. Consequently (echoing Weaver's ideas), Pierson claims, 'almost always, retrenchment is an exercise in blame avoidance rather than in credit claiming'. He argues that radical retrenchment was rarer under the Reagan and Thatcher regimes in the United States and UK than is suggested by popular narratives that portray those regimes as driven wholly by 'conviction politics', and that 'cutbacks in social programs usually raise the risk of electoral retribution'.

The idea that cutbacks in welfare state programmes run the risk of such retribution tends to rest on two main assumptions. First, it assumes maleficiaries of such retrenchment will typically be better organized and motivated to

---

[4] Broadly, the difference between government revenue and expenditure excluding interest payments on debt.

political action than beneficiaries (such as taxpayers or non-users) because welfare retrenchment tends to mean concentrated and direct losses to the former but only diffuse and indirect gains to the latter. Second, it assumes electoral choices typically involve a mixture of 'economic voting' (that is, voters normally cast their ballots mainly on the basis of 'pocketbook' issues affecting themselves),[5] 'retrospective voting' (that is, voters choosing as much on perception of the past records of candidates and parties in office as on the promises those candidates and parties make about the future),[6] and 'negativity bias' (that is, voters more disposed to punish incumbents for losses imposed than to reward them for any corresponding gains). It follows from those assumptions that efforts to impose losses on key voters or well-organized interest groups through welfare state retrenchment will tend to produce elect-oral losses or defeat for political incumbents, and that such efforts will be politically viable only if those incumbents find ways of shifting, sharing, or avoiding blame, for example by all-party national governments.

Like many successful social science ideas, this account of the electoral vulnerability of welfare state retrenchment is elegant, simple, and at first sight eminently plausible. But it is surprisingly hard to validate systematically, as numerous scholars have shown.[7] Economic studies of the impact of austerity on electoral outcomes using data from before the 2008 crash have produced only mixed results.[8] As for more recent studies, one study found austerity in the form of adverse economic indicators was associated with increased electoral volatility (Dassonneville and Hooghe 2015), while the work of Alberto Alesina, Dorian Carloni, and Giampaolo Lecce (2012) found no systematic relationship between fiscal austerity and electoral defeat for incumbents, and no evidence that governments which reduced budget def-icits quickly were systematically voted out of office. And in an earlier study with other colleagues comparing nine different cases of fiscal squeeze cross-nationally, we ourselves found numerous cases where fiscal squeeze did not result in notable electoral punishment and even seems to have, on occasion, acted as a credit-claiming opportunity for incumbents (Hood, Heald, and Himaz 2014). Our study here of a century of fiscal squeezes in the UK also shows variety, but we show later that on the measures used here, more severe squeezes seem to be more associated with electoral losses by incumbents.

There could be several reasons why electoral punishment does not invari-ably follow from fiscal squeeze. First, in circumstances such as those of 1931 (once-in-a-century global crisis), or after major wars, it may not make sense

---

[5] See Anderson (2000); König and Wenzelburger (2014).
[6] See, for example, Fiorina (1978).
[7] See Armingeon and Giger (2008); Schumacher, Vis and van Kersbergen (2012).
[8] See Peltzman (1992); Alesina et al. (1998); and Ansell and Samuels (2010).

even in theory for voters to vote retrospectively rather than prospectively, especially given that the major tax hikes of both the twentieth-century world wars were imposed by war coalitions comprising all the major political parties and with ordinary electoral competition suspended (such that the only way for electors to punish the incumbents was to vote in by-elections for parties outside the war coalition, such as Sinn Féin or the Scottish National Party). Second, it may be that Pierson's original assessment that any electoral credit flowing from tax reductions would tend to be outweighed by blame resulting from spending restraint underestimated the credit-claiming opportunities for those types of fiscal squeeze that involve spending cuts to pay for tax cuts.[9]

And third, it could be that blame avoidance can take more varied forms (in presentational, agency, and policy strategies) than was envisaged in Pierson's original study. For example, a blame-avoidance tactic not much discussed by that study comprises what William Riker termed 'heresthetic'[10]—that is, structuring choices in a way that can shape electoral outcomes, notably by introducing issues such as protectionism that cut across the tax-and-spend dimension and thereby undermining the conventional assumption about 'pocketbook' voting that voters are strung out on a single right–left dimension.

This book focuses mainly on the political aftermath of fiscal squeezes, in terms of electoral outcomes, institutional or constitutional changes, and policy developments. But there is a huge literature in economics and economic history on the short- and medium-term effects of fiscal and monetary policy on output, employment, and growth. 'Keynesians' stress the importance of deficit financing in recessions by cutting taxes and raising government spending, while those of other schools, such as monetarist and other revisionist approaches, take a different or more nuanced view (Konzelmann 2014). The average effect of fiscal austerity on economic output is argued to be expansionary by some economists (for example, Giavazzi and Pagano 1990; Alesina and Ardagna 2010), while others claim it is contractionary (such as Guajardo et al. 2014).

What this book shows is that there were some recurring features in the way fiscal squeeze worked over the century but notable variation in the process by which squeeze decisions were made, in who the winners and losers were, and in the composition and time-pattern of squeezes. It also shows that over a hundred years fiscal squeezes rarely seemed to have dramatically reshaped the state or methods of delivery of public services, though in several cases they left deep political scars that shaped the way subsequent squeezes were handled.

---

[9] For instance, Rose and Peters (1978) suggested that when the tax implications of public spending increases started to cut into voters' take-home pay in a context of low economic growth, support for such public spending increases would tend to fall.
[10] See Riker (1986); McLean (2002); Nagel (1993).

## 1.2 Three Key Political Choices in Fiscal Squeeze and Their Consequences

As mentioned earlier, this book focuses particularly on three key political choices bound up with fiscal squeeze, namely the choice of tax hikes as against spending cuts, the choice of whether to deliver the pain in short sharp shocks or in a more gradual and long drawn-out way, and the choice of how to handle the political blame (central to Pierson's analysis), for example, by sharing or shifting decision-making powers or keeping control in the hands of individual parties or elected politicians.

### 1.2.1 *Tax Hikes or Spending Cuts?*

If cutting public spending is so hard and electorally dangerous for democratic politicians in the face of political and social pressures, as much of the literature about the alleged 'unstoppability' of public spending growth implies, why don't democracies always choose to tax their way out of fiscal difficulties? In Paul Pierson's classic study of 1980s welfare state retrenchment, one of the biggest contrasts between the Reagan and Thatcher administrations lay in the role of taxation. The Reagan Administration chose to cut taxes, thereby increasing the United States' budgetary deficit and putting extra pressure on federal government spending, while (as we show in Chapter Eight) the Thatcher Government ramped up taxes in a deep recession and later presided over a real-terms rise in tax revenue as a result of North Sea oilfields coming on-stream and increased revenue from other sources stemming from economic recovery. And as we show in the next chapter, there are marked variations over the century in the relative weight placed on revenue increases as against spending cuts. Indeed, debate over how much fiscal correction should come from revenue increases and how much from spending cuts often runs hot in politics (as it did after both world wars, in the 1930s and again in the 2010s) and has been much discussed by economists, for example, in preferences expressed for 'spending-led adjustments' by economists such as Hideki Konishi (2006) or Alberto Alesina and Silvia Ardagna (2010) and bodies such as the International Monetary Fund (see IMF (2010) and Pete Devries et al. (2011)).

In political science, there is no clear-cut theory that directly explains how political parties and governments choose between tax hikes and spending cuts. There is an older literature on the political limits of taxation (for example, in the work of Colin Clark (1945)), but modern political science typically explains such choices as an outcome of broader electoral calculations or constraints. One well-established theory is the 'median voter theorem', originally developed by Duncan Black (1958), which assumes that voters on issues of economic policy will ordinarily be arrayed on a left–right spectrum and that political parties aiming for office will therefore compete in the centre ground for what they see as the median voter's preferences on taxing and spending. If that is how parties approach austerity decisions, it follows that median voters will, in effect, decide the balance between tax hikes and spending cuts, that the median voters themselves will experience the least austerity both on the tax side and the spending side (with greater pain being inflicted on the voters at either end of the spectrum, such as the comparatively wealthy and the comparatively poor), and that if they follow this electoral logic, parties of the left will not differ greatly from parties of the right in the austerity they enact.

However, the median voter theorem is by no means unchallenged as an account of how policy emerges from party competition, and different predictions about tax and spending policy on austerity can be drawn from different assumptions. Other theories focus on political tactics to shape preferences (by 'heresthetic' or other means) or on group pressures on political parties and government, in particular on how far concentrated groups, with high stakes in policy outcomes, may be able to press for policy choices from which they themselves receive concentrated benefits, paid for by diffusing the costs among less well-organized groups (Wilson 1980: 357–94). The family of group-based theories includes various accounts of 'capitalist democracy', aiming to explain how democracies are shaped by the interactions between states and markets, and includes Thomas Ferguson's (1994) 'investment theory of politics'. The 'investment theory' argues that what drives party policy preferences is not so much competition for centre-ground voters as the competing interests of the key backers and funders of different political parties and candidates. Applied to fiscal squeeze policies, such an approach would lead us to expect political parties to tailor tax and spending choices to fit the preferences of their key stakeholders, which might mean a bias towards favouring groups other than swing voters, for example in tax treatment of wealthy individuals or spending on services for the benefit of non-median voters.

Further, as we noted in earlier work (Hood, Heald, and Himaz 2014: 6), electoral punishment might be asymmetrical between parties of the right and left, in two different ways. Most straightforwardly, core voters of right-wing parties might be expected to punish those parties more severely for tax increases than for spending cuts, while core voters of left-wing parties might be expected to do the reverse, punishing those parties more severely for spending cuts rather than tax increases.

Against that is the so-called 'Nixon goes to China' phenomenon in politics, based on the famous 1972 *rapprochement* between the United States and China initiated by a Republican US president, Richard Nixon, who had previously maintained a strong anti-communist stance (Cukierman and Tommasi 1998). On that analogy, parties might be expected to experience less punishment from their core voters in going against those voters' preferences (if their core voters have nowhere else to go), suggesting that in some circumstances right-wing parties might experience less electoral punishment for tax rises than spending cuts, and vice versa for left-wing parties. As we shall show, our analysis here provides more support for the first type of 'punishment asymmetry' than the second.

### 1.2.2 'Surgery without Anaesthetics' or 'Boiling Frogs'?

A second key political choice in fiscal squeeze concerns depth and timing. Most commentators on retrenchment politics draw some distinction between 'decremental' and more selective or abrupt approaches, particularly over spending (for instance Dunsire and Hood 1989; Kickert and Randma-Liiv 2015). And, though less often mentioned, exactly the same choice in principle arises over tax hikes. Governments have the option of a 'surgery without anaesthetics' approach, in which speed is of the essence to avoid the patient dying of shock, and the more gradual approach represented by the well-known (but contestable) idea that a frog can eventually be boiled alive if placed in a pan of water that is then heated very slowly.

Again, that choice is central to fiscal squeeze politics, sometimes playing out within a single party in government (as it did for the Conservatives in the 1980s and 1990s) and sometimes dividing competing parties, as in 2010, when the Conservatives proposed a plan to start early and eliminate the post-2008 deficit within five years, while the other major parties offered plans to do so in slower-onset manner over two electoral terms.

In general, issues of length, timing, and sequencing have not been much pronounced upon by economists studying fiscal austerity (Alesina et al. 2015: 383), in contrast to the intense discussions about the rival merits of 'big bang' and 'gradualist' approaches in other contexts, such as the 1990s 'transition' literature on the transformation of former Soviet economies (Tanzi 1993). But politically, a choice between 'surgery without anaesthetics' and 'boiling frogs' involves important trade-offs, as Paul Pierson and others have noted. 'Surgery without anaesthetics' has the potential advantage of concentrating the voters' pain at a politically opportune point in the electoral cycle, linking with the idea of 'political business cycles' in which incumbents hike taxes and cut spending in the aftermath of electoral victories, and do the reverse in the run-up to the following election (Lewin 1991). Such a strategy applied to fiscal squeeze in principle gives incumbent parties a chance to recover in the polls as voters' memories of loss are overlaid by later events before the next key election, but has the corresponding disadvantage of being more likely to mobilize massive resistance by those on whom the losses are imposed. By contrast, the 'boiling frogs' approach has the advantage of making losses less visible and consequently reducing the risk that losers will mobilize to resist them, but again has corresponding disadvantages. Such changes are easier to reverse than radical surgery, their immediate pay-offs are lower, and they provide political opponents with continuing opportunities to alert voters to the losses being imposed on them (Pierson 1994: 20ff.), as happened to the Conservatives in the 1990s after a budget that aimed to spread the pain of tax increases over three years.

So when and why do governments choose the 'surgery without anaes-thetics' approach over the 'boiling frogs' approach, and how can we explain why the balance between the two approaches seems to have shifted between the former in the first third of the century under consideration to the latter in the final third?

### 1.2.3 Handling the Blame

The third key political choice relating to the handling of fiscal squeeze that this book focuses on is how incumbents handle the blame associated with loss imposition, particularly since Paul Pierson argued that 1980s retrenchment policies tended to focus on blame avoidance rather than credit claiming. There are various ways of classifying blame avoidance strategies in the literature on that subject, but most make some distinction between presentational strat-egies (the way policy changes are packaged or announced, for instance by 'stealth taxes' outside the headline rates of the most visible taxes), policy strategies (the way policy content is crafted, for instance in 'inertia strategies' of staying with inherited tax measures so that blame can be directed at predecessors (Rose and Karran 1987)), and agency strategies of shifting or sharing the blame by putting some or all decision-making power in the hands of others, such as technocrats or other politicians in coalition or national governments (Hood 2011).

What this book shows is that approaches to handling the blame were far from uniform over the century considered here. For example the array of agency strategies varied from setting up expert committees to come up with proposals for spending cuts (as happened in 1921 and 1931) to governments operating without any intermediary bodies at all to share the blame, as hap-pened in 1949. 'Stealth taxes' and to some extent also 'stealth spending cuts' (for example through subtle adjustments in price indexes) do seem to have become more salient in the final third of the period considered here, and arguably the same goes for the level of 'creative accounting' on the spending side. In most cases there was rhetorical stress on 'equality of sacrifice' (the slogan of the 1931 emergency National Government), but some policy domains were always more heavily hit than others, and explicit 'ring-fencing' of politically favoured domains become more prominent in later episodes than earlier ones. So what accounts for such variations and trends?

## 1.3 Observing and Classifying Fiscal Squeezes

As we noted at the outset, 'austerity' in the sense of restraints imposed on consumption can take different forms, and the focus here is primarily on austerity in the sense of fiscal squeeze, namely pressures to increase tax revenue or reduce public spending. But as has also been noted, the effect of such squeezes depends on what other kinds of 'austerity'—or the reverse—are in play. For example, in the 1920s public spending restraint was coupled with high interest rates and monetary contraction, while in the early 2010s spending restraint was linked with highly expansionist monetary policy (in the form of official interest rates close to zero and massive quantitative easing, which took the form of purchases of government debt by the central bank, thereby driving spending on debt interest below what it would otherwise have been). We have to take such non-fiscal austerity or the reverse into account in assessing the overall amount of loss imposed on citizens or voters.

Even for fiscal squeeze on its own, there is no clear and accepted metric for comparing levels of austerity. We have already noted that a focus on 'fiscal consolidation' in the sense of achieved reductions in deficit as recorded retrospectively in official statistics will not necessarily indicate how much pain citizens or voters experience, and for that reason we focus on recorded changes in spending and revenue both in absolute (constant-price) terms and relative to Gross Domestic Product (GDP).

Table 1.1 therefore lays out the range of fiscal squeeze outcomes that are observable in this study. It distinguishes fiscal squeezes in terms of whether they involve revenue only, spending only, or a mixture of the two. It also identifies different forms of revenue and spending squeeze. On the revenue side we distinguish cases where revenue rose relative to GDP or in constant-price terms, or both; and likewise, for spending we distinguish cases where expenditure fell relative to GDP or in constant price terms or both. We refer to squeezes where revenue rises or spending falls both in constant-prices and relative to GDP as 'hard', and squeezes where revenue rises or spending falls either in constant price terms or relative to GDP (but not both) as 'soft' (Hood, Heald, and Himaz 2014: 8). That gives us sixteen possible types of squeeze on reported spending and revenue outcomes, as shown in Table 1.1, and the next chapter examines the relative incidence of those different types.

But there are inevitable limitations about looking at fiscal squeezes only through the prism of administrative reported-outcome numbers, so we need to supplement that analysis with more qualitative assessments. Accordingly, Table 1.2, also developed from earlier work (Hood, Heald, and Himaz 2014: 7, Table 1.2), presents a qualitative spectrum of the intensity of fiscal squeeze in three dimensions, namely: the degree of extra loss imposed on citizens or voters; the extent of political capital expended or reputation risked, by

**Table 1.1.** Some different types of fiscal squeeze based on reported financial outcomes

| Revenue | Expenditure | | | |
|---|---|---|---|---|
| | No fall | Fall only in constant prices | Fall only as % of GDP | Fall as % of GDP and in real terms |
| No rise | 1 No squeeze | 2 Single (expenditure) soft squeeze | 3 Single (expenditure) soft squeeze | 4 Single (expenditure) hard squeeze |
| Rise only in constant price terms | 5 Single (revenue) soft squeeze | 6 Double soft squeeze | 7 Double soft squeeze | 8 Hybrid soft/hard squeeze |
| Rise only as % of GDP | 9 Single (revenue) soft squeeze | 10 Double soft squeeze | 11 Double soft squeeze | 12 Hybrid soft/hard squeeze |
| Rise as % of GDP and in real terms | 13 Single (revenue) hard squeeze | 14 Hybrid soft/hard squeeze | 15 Hybrid soft/hard squeeze | 16 Double hard squeeze |

*Source*: Adapted from Hood, Heald, and Himaz (2014, Table 12.3, p. 268)

incumbent party politicians imposing the squeeze; and the degree of effort exerted by the state apparatus to develop fiscal squeeze measures.

For the degree of extra loss imposed on citizens or voters, the lower levels identified in Table 1.2 consist of 'inertia strategies', measures that are like 'victimless crimes' in the sense of imposing losses on diffused, low-stakes victims, and squeezes whose effect is offset by other factors, such as economic growth or easy money policies. The higher levels come when significant and visible losses are imposed on swing voters (those most likely to shift between one party and another) and/or a party's 'core' voters (those who normally vote for it) and when squeezes are exacerbated by other types of austerity. In between those two types come cases where squeezes are neither offset nor exacerbated by other measures, involve 'stealth' spending cuts or tax rises, and when core and/or swing voters are hit only moderately.

For political capital expended or reputation risked, by incumbent party politicians, the lower levels in this scheme consist of cases where squeeze measures have been foreshadowed or even promised before elections, where electoral competition is suspended or all-party coalitions share the blame, where there are readily available scapegoats (such as defeated outgoing governments), and where key decisions are made or at least endorsed by experts who can be blamed when things go wrong. The higher levels come when squeezes break explicit election promises, run counter to the election cycle (for

**Table 1.2.** A qualitative framework for assessing degrees of squeeze in terms of voter loss, political cost to incumbents, and state effort

| | Qualitative Intensity of Squeeze in Voter Loss, Political Cost to Incumbents, and State Effort | | |
| --- | --- | --- | --- |
| | Low | Moderate | High |
| **Amount of extra visible cost imposed on key (median/ core) voters or citizens** | [1] Continuing the status quo (e.g. not reducing taxes or raising spending), [2] focus on diffused, low-stakes victims, [3] fiscal squeeze offset by other factors (e.g. economic growth, non-fiscal largesse) | [1] Imposition of less visible losses through 'stealth' taxes or cuts, [2] concentration of losses on non-key voters (e.g. millionaires, bankers, foreigners), [3] no/little extra losses combined with fiscal squeeze | [1] Imposition of significant and visible losses on key voters by raising taxes or cutting spending, [2] fiscal squeeze exacerbated by other factors, e.g. major recession, [3] significant increases in non-fiscal austerity such as rationing, conscription, wage caps |
| **Political capital expended, or reputation risked, by incumbent politicians** | [1] Squeeze measures foreshadowed before elections, [2] all-party coalitions sharing the blame, [3] electoral competition suspended, [4] readily available scapegoats (e.g. outgoing government), [5] key decisions made or endorsed by experts who can be blamed | [1] Tax rises or spending cuts not mentioned (but not abjured) in election promises, [2] measures timed to fit the electoral cycle (i.e. post-election austerity, pre-election largesse), [3] experts divided or not uniformly hostile | [1] Tax rises or spending cuts that break explicit election promises, [2] run counter to the electoral cycle (e.g. extra squeeze imposed in the run-up to expected elections), [3] no plausible political scapegoats available, [4] measures counter (near) unanimous views of policy experts |
| **Effort exerted by the state apparatus to develop or impose squeeze measures** | [1] Incremental resetting of existing structures or schemes (e.g. changes in tax rates/thresholds, alteration in qualifying periods or benefit levels), [2] straightforward and limited changes, e.g. in closing down discrete services, [3] fairly clear political priorities, [4] fairly high levels of public compliance | [1] Some non-incremental changes, e.g. non-trivial changes in fiscal rules/decision systems, crafting of some new (but not 'mainstay') taxes, [2] spending cuts that go beyond incremental changes and current organizational boundaries (e.g. quango culls), [3] some division over political priorities, [4] moderate levels of public compliance | [1] Wholly new decision procedures, major restructuring of 'mainstay' tax and/or benefit systems, introduction of quite new control regimes, [2] move to notably changed forms of working or policy delivery, production of long-term plans for change, [3] deep political splits over priorities, [4] high levels of public non-compliance (e.g. riots, strikes) |

example with a squeeze imposed at the end of a government's electoral term), when no ready-made scapegoats are available (such as when incumbents have been in office too long to plausibly blame their predecessors), and when the measures taken counter the views of orthodox economic experts. In between those two types come cases where experts are divided; when tax rises or spending cuts neither break nor fulfil pre-election promises, such that they can be defended in a 'terms and conditions' vein; where squeezes follow the electoral cycle, that is, with fiscal pain applied immediately after election victory and reversed before the following election; and where squeezes target swing and/or core voters to only a limited extent.

For the degree of effort exerted by the state apparatus to develop or impose squeeze measures, the lower levels identified in Table 1.2 consist of cases where the main effort required of the state machine involves incremental resetting of existing structures or schemes (in the same way as a fuel filling station might change the prices at the pumps when the cost of oil goes up or down), where the state machine works with relatively clear political priorities, and when changes in ways of working are limited and straightforward, such as in cancellation or delay of capital projects, or closure of discrete organizations. The higher levels come when fiscal decision procedures are completely restructured, when radically new methods of delivering public services have to be adopted under the pressure of fiscal stringency, when mainstay taxes or benefit structures have to be redesigned to deliver a squeeze, and when there are serious political conflicts within government over priorities. In between those two types come cases that involve some non-incremental change and some restructuring across existing organizational boundaries, and a moderate degree of division over priorities within government.

Such categorization is of course anything but an exact science. As we shall see, many tricky issues arise, including who exactly counts as an 'incumbent' in such analysis and whether we should focus on the planning or implementation of squeezes, or both. But nevertheless, some categorization along these lines is necessary for a qualitative comparative assessment of the intensity of fiscal squeezes and so, after giving qualitative accounts of the various squeezes in Chapters Three to Ten (exploring where they fit in terms of the square-bracketed items in Table 1.2), our final chapter classifies and compares the fiscal squeezes we observed in the UK over a century on these more qualitative measures as well.

## 1.4 Why a Single Country and Why the UK?

This book identifies every fiscal squeeze showing up in reported financial outcomes in the UK from 1900 to 2015. The first episode began in 1915, which saw the start of a tax squeeze to finance World War I that took the tax take-up to levels not seen since the Napoleonic Wars at the start of the nineteenth century (Daunton 2002: xiii). The last was not clearly concluded at the time of writing (though official deficit reduction targets had been abandoned), but is here explored up to 2015, which marked the end of a coalition government that set out to eliminate deficit and reduce debt arising from the 2008 international financial crash and the subsequent recession.

Of course massive changes occurred over that century, including two world wars, big demographic changes including greatly increased longevity and mass immigration, the secession of most of Ireland in 1922 to form what is now the Irish Republic, the entry of both states into the European Union fifty years after that, and marked changes in social attitudes and behaviour. Other obvious changes over that period included the dominant technology moving from the steam age to the digital age, the move from an economy based on primary and secondary industry (such as mining and manufacturing) to one based on tertiary industry in the form of services, concomitant changes in the educational levels of the population, and the country becoming a significant oil producer between the 1980s and the 2010s. The cumulative effect of economic growth meant that average earnings grew more than fourfold (in constant prices) over the period.

Nevertheless, throughout the period some important political factors remained sufficiently constant for over-time comparisons to be meaningful. The UK remained a leading, large, and developed parliamentary democracy, with parties competing for office at central government level in a single-member-constituency first-past-the-post electoral system that tended to penalize small parties unless their votes were regionally concentrated (as with the Irish and later Scottish nationalist parties), with a weak, non-elected second chamber and a powerful Treasury operating as a central coordinating agency in government. Over the period, as we show in the next chapter, the various fiscal squeezes were handled by governments of different types (mostly single-party, including two minority governments, but also with four coalitions, including one emergency 'National Government') and political stripes, comprising both left-of-centre and right-of-centre parties.

Those continuities allow us to explore how broadly the same political system operated and reacted to fiscal squeezes of various types over a century. This book therefore complements the various studies that have compared fiscal squeeze efforts across countries with different political systems and economic structures. In addition, this method of looking at a single country over time differs sharply from much of the econometric work that examines average effects of past financial crises using cross-country regressions—an approach that misses the variations across episodes, as pointed out by Christina Romer (2015), who argues that the aftermath of financial crises is far more varied than an average-effects analysis brings out. What we do here is to compare across various cases within that country and focus not so much on average effects as on meaningful similarities and differences across the various episodes, taking into account the political settings.

## 1.5 The Analytic Approach: Plan of the Book

We combine quantitative and qualitative comparison of the UK's various fiscal squeeze episodes over a hundred years. We look at historical statistics to see what they tell us about how steep spending cuts or revenue increases were, where and on whom the greatest pain seems to have been imposed according to the administrative categories under which spending and taxes were recorded, what the voting outcomes were in subsequent elections, and what if any other longer-term consequences seem to have flowed from fiscal squeeze.

But we also look at softer materials (mainly earlier published studies, documents, and some interviews), to help us go behind the officially reported numbers to the sort of qualitative issues identified in Table 1.2, notably how squeezes were presented and packaged, how outcomes compared to plans, how the decision-making process worked, and what the politically awkward or difficult issues were.

Accordingly, the next chapter (Chapter Two) examines a hundred years of fiscal squeeze on the basis of reported aggregate financial outcomes. That analysis shows up both variety and changes over time for two of the three aspects of fiscal squeeze we discussed earlier—tax versus spending, depth versus length, direct control versus blame avoidance. Tax hikes seem to have played rather less of a part in fiscal squeezes in the last thirty years of the period considered here than they did before, and likewise, in those final decades, there were three episodes of relatively long-drawn-out spending restraint compared to earlier squeezes.

The following eight chapters look qualitatively at the politics of successive fiscal squeezes in different political and economic settings. Those settings range from global financial crises and the conduct and aftermath of total wars, to less extreme conditions, and they include governments of a variety of types and ideological orientations. They also vary in terms of what other forms of austerity (or the reverse) accompanied fiscal squeeze, notably in terms of monetary restraint or expansionism, physical rationing or market supply, and wage controls or free labour markets.

These more qualitative accounts of the various squeezes highlight the difference between:

- the world war squeezes, when military spending soared, funded substantially by debt (particularly in World War I) but accompanied by steep revenue increases in the form of special war taxes, while spending on non-military civilian services was cut;

- the deflationary squeezes of the 1920s and 1930s (both undertaken during recession and accompanied by tight money policy in the 1920s but not the 1930s);

- the multiple-austerity squeezes of the late 1940s and early 1950s (when taxes remained at near-confiscatory wartime levels, external bailouts were important, and public spending restraint was accompanied, indeed overshadowed, by rationing and physical shortages);

- the 'stagflation' squeezes of the 1970s and early 1980s (when 'cash limits' and partial or non-indexing of benefits and tax thresholds were the central mechanisms of squeeze, and wage control policies added another element of restraint); and

- the shifting-relativities squeezes of the later 1980s, the later 1990s, and the early-to-mid-2010s, when steady periods of economic growth with lowish inflation allowed public spending to be cut relative to rising GDP without significant cuts in overall expenditure in real terms, mostly with fairly expansionary monetary policies and no other forms of non-fiscal restraint. Such revenue squeezes as there were over that period tended to rest on indirect or 'stealth' taxes of one kind or another rather than special war taxes or increases in the main rates of income and profits taxes.

Each of those types of squeeze is distinctive, with few episodes sharing exactly the same features. The eight chapters describing those episodes aim to look behind the reported financial outcome numbers as set out in Chapter Two, but while they aim to ask the same questions, the sources available are not uniform. For the earlier periods, only documentary and official archival materials are available, there were no public opinion polls until the 1940s, and for the most recent period there are no official archival materials and few political memoirs, so more reliance has necessarily to be placed on media, parliamentary speeches, and some interviews.

The final chapter concludes our analysis in three main ways. First, it compares the intensity of the fiscal squeezes described in Chapters Three to Ten according to the criteria identified in Table 1.2 earlier, and shows a fairly close correspondence between our first qualitative indicator (of imposed losses) and our quantitative measure of 'hardness' of squeezes on the revenue or spending side, but less correspondence between the other two qualitative measures of squeeze intensity and reported financial outcomes.

Second, it returns to the three issues raised earlier (tax versus spending, length versus depth, blame avoidance versus control), and explores particularly how blame-avoidance strategies changed over the century. What it shows is that outsourcing responsibility for proposing spending cutbacks and/or tax rises was rare (even though the outsourcing approach was applied both to economic forecasting and interest rate setting in the later part of the period). For a process often claimed to be so electorally toxic, that outcome raises some important questions for the 'blame avoidance' interpretation of fiscal squeeze.

Third, examining the electoral consequences of fiscal squeezes, it explores the association between electoral defeat by incumbents and fiscal squeezes, and finds a markedly higher incidence of loss of office by incumbents after fiscal squeezes when those squeezes were 'hard' on the revenue or spending side—a result that challenges the view that there is no clear association between 'austerity' and electoral defeat of incumbents.

Accordingly, we reflect in this final chapter on what future fiscal squeezes can be expected to be like if those past trends continue—that is, relatively long, 'soft', mostly spending-focused and unaccompanied by other forms of 'austerity'. But we also reflect on whether some of the older approaches to fiscal squeeze are necessarily gone for good, and if not, what might be different about future fiscal squeezes in the UK and elsewhere.

# 2

# UK Fiscal Squeezes over a Century

## A Summary Comparison

Working mainly from historical financial outcome statistics, this short chapter aims to do two main things. First, it reports and compares the main episodes of fiscal squeeze—in terms of major revenue increases, spending cuts, or both—identifiable from such statistics in the UK between 1900 and the mid-2010s. It then compares periods of 'austerity' when measured by our fiscal squeeze approach as against measures of fiscal consolidation in terms of deficit reduction. The aim is to show how many squeezes we can identify over that period from those statistics, how sensitive episodes of squeeze are to the metrics or statistical source employed, how deep or long the squeezes were, what mix of spending cuts and tax rises they involved, and what changes we can see over time.

Second, the chapter looks briefly at what conditions preceded or accompanied those squeezes, what kinds of spending were cut and what extra taxes imposed—and again, what changes over time we can identify.

Answers to some of those questions are indeterminate or contestable and inevitably there are limitations as well as possibilities in what we can learn about fiscal squeezes from reported historical statistics. But as explained in Chapter One, we aim to compensate for some of those limitations in the qualitative chapters that follow.

## 2.1 Fiscal Squeezes Identified and Compared

As explained in Chapter One, we conceive of fiscal squeeze as concerted effort by politicians and governments to impose losses on some individuals or groups by cuts in public spending and/or increases in state revenue to correct the public finances. In that chapter we distinguished that approach to 'austerity' from the more conventional focus on episodes when public debt or deficits were significantly reduced, given that our conception of fiscal squeeze represents effort rather than outcome in terms of fiscal correction. And we outlined two ways of identifying fiscal squeeze in that sense. One is to look at historical statistics for episodes of absolute or relative reductions in public spending or increases in revenue, distinguishing revenue from spending squeezes and 'hard' from 'soft' squeezes ('hard' squeezes meaning spending falling and/or revenue increasing both in absolute terms and relative to GDP). The other way of identifying fiscal squeeze is to look more qualitatively at the record of events (using items such as budget speeches, published histories, archival records, or interviews) to assess how much loss or deprivation is imposed on the population; the extent to which incumbent politicians have to expend their political capital or risk their reputations as they try to sell, broker, or fix fiscal squeeze policies with political parties, interest groups, or voters at large; and the degree of effort put in by the state apparatus in contriving ways to raise more revenue or reduce spending.

We turn to that latter approach in the following eight chapters and the conclusion. But this chapter uses historical statistics to identify episodes of spending reductions and tax increases as a proxy for the effort put into fiscal squeeze.

Any such venture immediately brings us to three unavoidable complications. First, 'the historical record' is often far from simple or unambiguous, not least because alternative statistical sources using different definitions of items such as 'public spending' may and frequently do show different results. As Richard Rose (1980: 205) puts it, 'Whether public spending is said to be rising or falling is a *matter of definition, not fact*' [emphasis in original]. Nor are many statistical series fully consistent over more than a short time period, so we have to take into account changing definitions and conventions to make valid long-term comparisons. Further, statistical series are commonly altered retrospectively and new definitions emerge of key items such as 'deficit'. So (as, for example, in 1931) the picture of an episode that we get from retrospectively compiled numbers may diverge sharply from what decision-makers faced at the time. Even where that does not happen, reported numbers reflect the point at which spending restraint or revenue increases were implemented, not the point at which such changes were announced, and yet the politics of fiscal squeeze often centres as much on the latter as the former. That lag can matter, as we shall see later in the book.

Second, as we have already seen, squeezes may differ according to whether the pain is inflicted on the revenue side or on the spending side or both, and according to whether spending goes down or taxes up relative to GDP and/or in absolute (constant price) price terms. Is 'squeeze' more meaningful, difficult, or painful when it involves relative or absolute change? We think that could be argued either way *a priori*, and much seems to depend on whether GDP is growing, stable, or falling.

Third, following our discussion in the previous chapter about the need to differentiate fiscal squeeze from ordinary budgetary politics and to avoid making distinctions that are not meaningful given likely measurement error (for example, between a period when taxes rise by 0.001 per cent of GDP and another when they fall by a similarly infinitesimal amount), we need to specify thresholds for what is to be counted as a squeeze.

We deal with the first complication by comparing different data sources to see how much the timing, existence, or extent of fiscal squeezes varies between different sources. We deal with the second complication by analysing changes in revenue and expenditure both relative to GDP (the ratio method) and in constant prices (the 'levels' method). As already explained, we define a squeeze as 'hard' if spending falls or revenue rises on both of those measures; and 'soft' if spending falls or revenue rises on only one of them.[1] And we deal with the third complication by setting a threshold of significance. We defined a squeeze on the ratio method as a fall in spending or rise in revenue, or both, recorded in historical statistics which was sustained for at least two years with an average annual change (fall for spending, rise for revenue) of not less than one percentage point of GDP. We defined a squeeze on the levels measure (that is, changes in spending and revenue in constant-price terms) as a fall in spending or rise in revenue of not less than 1 per cent for a single year or at least 1 per cent on average for two or more consecutive years.[2]

Any such threshold of course involves some 'rule-of-thumb', but for the ratio measure at least it broadly follows the conventional literature on fiscal consolidation, and reflects a view once said to have been commonly held by the IMF, that a reduction of public spending by about 1 percentage point of GDP per year was the normal limit of politically feasible spending squeeze in most countries (Hood, Heald, and Himaz (2014): 11–12 and 29).

Within those analytic settings, we identify numerous periods of fiscal squeeze (of the sixteen types identified in Table 1.1 of Chapter One) over the century in the UK, and the Appendix to the book provides summary tables and graphs comparing those episodes. Tables A1 and A2 in the Appendix

---

[1] A cut in public spending on the levels measure normally seems to involve more effort than a cut in such spending on the ratio measure (unless GDP is falling), and conversely a rise in revenue on the ratio measure normally seems to involve more effort than an increase on the levels measure, particularly when GDP is growing. Further, a spending fall on the levels measure might be argued to be more painful when GDP is falling than in other circumstances (though we have no case of that kind in the UK data considered in this book). But we avoid making those more refined distinctions here.

[2] Another way of putting it would be as negative growth in real spending or positive growth in real revenue above these thresholds.

show that the instances of revenue and spending squeeze identified from financial outcome statistics are not highly sensitive to which particular historical data source is chosen, in that those squeezes show up, albeit with slight variations in depth, duration, and timing, in most of the available statistical sources. As for differences between the 'ratio' method and the 'levels' method of measuring squeeze (as discussed earlier), the episodes are roughly the same for spending squeezes following either method, as Table A1 in the Appendix shows, while Table A2 shows that the same does not apply on the revenue side.[3]

Having established that, the analysis of squeeze episodes in the rest of this chapter is based on two separate sources of UK financial data, namely the well-known dataset compiled by Brian Mitchell (1988) for the period up to 1949 and data from the UK Office of National Statistics (ONS) (ONS 2014 and IFS 2014) for the post-1949 period.[4] Similarly, having explored episodes using both the ratio and levels method, as shown in the Appendix, we base the timings of the various squeezes on the ratio method in the rest of this chapter.

Most of the episodes defined using the ratio method comprised expenditure and revenue changes well above the thresholds we specified earlier. Two cases were marginal. One is a fiscal squeeze under the post-World War II Labour Government, starting in the late 1940s, that straddles the two different historical datasets we used. If we combine those two different data sources (ONS (2014) and Mitchell (1988)) that squeeze ends in 1949/50, but if we use another data source (Middleton (1996)) it extends to 1951/52. We follow the combination approach here, but the point at which that squeeze ended is undeniably ambiguous and Chapter Five looks carefully at qualitative accounts of the Labour Government's efforts at fiscal restraint over this period. The other case, a spending fall in the late 1960s (involving major defence cuts) under Harold Wilson's Labour Government, falls right on the margin. We chose to include it here and discuss it in Chapter Six, but that is another of those line-ball categorization decisions.

Accordingly, Table 2.1 summarizes the fiscal squeezes (as defined above) that can be identified between 1900 and 2015. If we include all the times (derived from the ratio method) when there was a spending squeeze, revenue squeeze, or both (column 2) we can identify eighteen episodes in total.[5]

---

[3] Table A2, columns 2 and 3 in the Appendix, reveals three revenue squeezes in the later part of the period (1993–2001, 2003–07, and 2010–12) that show up using the levels method but not the ratio method, and for those revenue squeeze episodes that can be identified using both methods, the episodes are generally longer under the levels method than the ratio method.

[4] Most of the quantitative data used in this chapter and in the rest of the book has been archived with the UK data service (see Himaz (2015)).

[5] It would be nineteen if we included the one episode of soft revenue squeeze (using the levels method), namely 2003–07, that does not also show up as a spending squeeze episode on the ratio method.

**Table 2.1.** UK fiscal squeeze episodes 1900–2015

| Overall episode (ratio method)[a] | Sub-episode (ratio method) | Spending (average) | | Revenue (average) | | Significant reduction in budget deficit[d] | Type of Overall Squeeze[e] H=Hard, S=Soft, R=Revenue, E=Spending |
|---|---|---|---|---|---|---|---|
| | | % point fall of EXP/GDP[b] | % fall in constant prices[c] | % point rise of REV/GDP[b] | % rise in constant prices[c] | | |
| 1916–18 War Finance | 1916–18 | | | 1.2 | 9.3 | No | HR |
| 1919–25 Post-war politics | 1919–21 | 6.8 | 21.8 | 6.7 | 18.7 | Yes | HR/HE |
| | 1923–25 | 3.0 | 5.6 | | | No | HE |
| 1931–35 Financial crisis | 1931–32 | | | 1.8 | 4 | No | HR |
| | 1933–35 | 1.3 | 1.0 | | | No | HE |
| 1941–45 War Finance | 1941–45 | | | 3.5 | 11.7 | | HR |
| 1946–49 Post-war politics | 1946–49 | 8.3 | 13.5 | | 1.9 | Yes | HE/SR |
| 1953–55 | 1953–55 | 1.4 | | 1.1 | 1.6 | Partly (1954–55) | SR/SE |
| 1960–61 | 1960–61 | | | 1.2 | 4.4 | No | HR |
| 1964–69 | 1964–67 | | | 1.5 | 6.2 | No | HR |
| | 1968–69 | 1.0 | | 1.6 | 7.4 | Yes | HR/SE |
| 1973–78 Stagflation | 1973–75 | | | | 5.2 | No | HR |
| | 1976 | 1.1 | 1.0 | | 2.1 | Yes | HE/SR |
| | 1977–78 | 1.7 | 1.3 | | | Partly (1977) | HE |
| 1980–88 Thatcherism | 1980–81 | | | 2.2 | 2.9 | No | HR |
| | 1983–88 | 1.6 | | | 1.9 | Partly (1985–88) | SR/SE |
| 1993–00 | 1993–00 | 1.0 | | | 4.4 | Yes | SR/SE |
| 2010–15 Post-2008 crisis | 2010–15 | 1.1 | | | 3.1 | Yes | SR/SE |

[a] The ratio method refers to defining episodes by looking at percentage point changes to spending/GDP and revenue/GDP. The years refer to financial years. e.g., 1916–18 refers to 1916/17–1918/19. [b] Total percentage point change during episode divided by the number of years the episode lasted. [c] Total percentage change during episode in constant prices divided by the number of years the episode lasted. [d] Coded yes or partly if deficit/GDP improved on average by more than 1 percentage point; No otherwise. [e] As explained in the text, identified by changes in spending and revenue as proportions of GDP and in constant price terms over each squeeze episode.

*Source:* Spending: See Table A1 note a; Revenue: See Table A2 note a. There is a break in the data at 1949, due to differences in sources.

However, as indicated in column 1 of that table, some of those periods can more meaningfully be grouped together, as representing continuing effort by the same government (as with the Thatcher squeezes from 1979 to the late 1980s), or as responses to the same problem or policy initiative by more than one government (as with the implementation of the 'Geddes Axe' in the early 1920s or the responses to the deep financial crisis of the early 1930s). Grouping the episodes in that way produces twelve episodes over a century— slightly more than one a decade.

As Table 2.1 shows, those fiscal squeezes varied in length, depth, and type, raising the question of what accounts for that variation. It also raises the question of what makes governments put the stress on spending cuts or on increasing revenue, and why 'double hard' squeezes were apparently so rare over this period.

What Table 2.1 also shows (in the seventh column) is a marked difference between episodes of fiscal squeeze as identified from revenue increases or spending reductions and episodes of 'fiscal consolidation' as identified by significant reductions in deficit. In the previous chapter we underlined the difference between looking at 'austerity' in terms of deficit or debt reduction outcomes as against efforts to increase revenue and/or cut public spending. As can be seen from Table 2.1, while there were no episodes of significant deficit reduction that did not involve fiscal squeeze as defined earlier, by no means all episodes of fiscal squeeze in that sense involved deficit reduction. Indeed, as that table shows, if we define 'austerity' episodes as those involving 'substantial' deficit reduction (here taken to mean a reduction of not less than 1 percentage point of GDP), half of the eighteen fiscal squeeze episodes in Table 2.1 would disappear from view.

Moreover, as Table 2.2 shows, if we use deficit reductions as the criterion for identifying squeezes, the start and end times of the episodes as well as their length is markedly different, and in general the duration of those episodes is shorter. So it really does matter which approach we take to identifying episodes of austerity, and as we show in Chapter Eleven, conclusions about the electoral effects of austerity efforts can turn on whether we define such efforts in terms of substantial deficit reduction or of changes in revenue and spending.[6]

In the following subsections we pick up two of the three analytic themes that Chapter One introduced and comment on apparent changes over time (we leave the third theme, on management of blame, to be considered in Chapter Eleven following our narrative chapters). One is the overall mix of expenditure cuts and revenue increases in fiscal squeeze, together with an apparent diminution of 'hard tax squeezes' towards the end of our period.

---

[6] Guajardo et al. (2014) discuss other problems with using deficit reduction to identify episodes of austerity.

**Table 2.2.** Episodes of deficit reductions using various definitions and data sources 1900–2015

| Public sector primary deficit[a] | Current budget deficit[b] | Primary budget deficit[b] | Primary budget deficit (cyclically adjusted)[b] |
|---|---|---|---|
| 1917–1920 (7.7) | n.a. | n.a. | n.a. |
| 1922–23 (2.0) | n.a. | n.a. | n.a. |
| 1932 (1.9) | n.a. | n.a. | n.a. |
| 1942–49 (2.9) | n.a. | n.a. | n.a. |
| 1954–55 (1.7) | 1955 (1.1) | 1954–55 (1.1) | n.a. |
|  | 1961–65 (0.6) |  | n.a. |
| 1968–69 (2.3) | 1968–69 (2.1) | 1968–69 (2.7) | n.a. |
| 1976–77 (1.5) | 1977–78 (0.7) | 1976–77 (1.4) | 1975–77 (1.8) |
| 1979–82 (0.7) | 1981–82 (1.6) | 1979–81 (1.0) | 1979–81 (2.0) |
| 1985–88 (0.8) | 1985–86 (0.9) | 1984–88 (0.8) | 1985 (0.6), 1988 (0.9) |
| 1995–00 (1.2) | 1994–00 (1.1) | 1994–00 (1.2) | 1994–00 (0.9) |
| 2010–13 (0.9) | 2010–15 (0.8) | 2010–15 (1.1) | 2010–13 (1.1) |

*Note:* Numbers in brackets refer to the average percentage point in deficit relative to GDP over the episode.

*Source:* [a] Derived from Hills, Thomas, and Dimsdale (2015), calendar years, [b] ONS public sector finances aggregates databank April 2015. See http://budgetresponsibility.org.uk/data/#databank.

The other is the length and depth of squeezes, with an apparent shift from 'short and sharp' spending squeezes to longer and shallower ones over the period.

### 2.1.1 *The Varying Spending/Taxation Composition of Fiscal Squeezes*

Table 2.1 shows the different mixture of revenue and spending that went into the squeezes we have identified. Of the eighteen cases shown in column 2, ten were 'single' squeezes—seven revenue-only squeezes, three expenditure-only squeezes (the two interwar cases, plus the late-1970s Labour squeezes)—while the remaining eight were a mixture of the two. As can be seen, governments quite frequently carried out hard revenue squeezes over much of the earlier part of the century (we comment on the later period shortly). Single hard expenditure squeezes were rare over the century as a whole and seemed to come only in particularly dire economic circumstances.

The table also shows variations in the relative part played by expenditure and revenue in those nine squeezes which involved a mixture of the two. 'Double hard' squeezes (that is, spending decreases and tax increases in both constant prices and as a proportion of GDP) were so rare over the period as a whole that only one of the nine cases (that taking place immediately after World War I) comprised such a squeeze. More generally, fiscal squeezes were rarely symmetrical, in the sense of equal pressure being applied on spending and revenue (at least on these financial outcome measures). In some episodes, spending was squeezed so that taxes could be cut (as happened in the early 1920s, in response to electoral pressures for tax cuts), while in others revenue was increased so that spending could be increased (as in most of the revenue-only squeezes shown in Table 2.1). Two of the hybrid squeezes were 'hard' on spending and 'soft' on revenue (those occurring in the aftermath of World War II and the Labour squeeze associated with the IMF loan of 1976), while one was 'soft' on spending side and 'hard' on revenue (the 1968–69 Labour squeeze). The remaining squeezes were all 'double soft', and that mixture seems to be associated with more recent episodes.

Third, of the periods shown in Table 2.1, two (1916–18 and 1941–46) were instances of war finance under wartime coalition governments, and show up here as 'single hard revenue' squeezes, in that taxes were sharply raised while overall government spending and borrowing shot up. But as we note in the chapters that follow, it can be argued that those periods were effectively cases of 'hybrid' or double squeeze, at least as far as civilians were concerned, since most non-military expenditure was cut back while defence spending soared.

## 2.1.2 The Disappearing 'Hard Revenue Squeeze'?

As noted above, it is striking from Table 2.1 that up to the early 1980s, 'hard' revenue squeezes were quite common and indeed on five occasions (the early 1920s, early 1930s, mid-late 1940s, mid-1970s, and 1980–81) such squeezes show up in the financial outcome records as coming before spending squeezes.

But that type of single revenue squeeze seems to have diminished if not vanished in the last thirty years of our period. There were individual years of 'hard' revenue squeeze on two occasions in the 1990s (sandwiched between longer periods of soft squeeze) but no revenue squeeze preceding a subsequent spending squeeze.[7] How can we account for the apparent absence for such a long period of this once quite common type of squeeze?

There is no received explanation of this observation, as far as we know. Did tax become more politically sensitive towards the end of our period for some reason? Does this apparent disappearance of the hard revenue squeeze simply reflect the fact that the three fiscal squeezes over that period, with the exception of the 'New Labour' period for two years after 1997, were all initiated by Conservative or Conservative-led Governments which may have been more politically predisposed to squeeze by cutting spending rather than raising taxes? Or again, might the answer be more administrative and economic? Might there have been more constraints on managing tax revenues associated with a move to a more open economy and the constraints imposed by

---

[7] As already mentioned, one soft revenue squeeze observable from the 'levels' method does not appear in Table 2.1 but is shown in Table A2 in the Appendix, namely 2003–07, which did precede the episode of double soft squeeze beginning in 2010.

membership of the European Union in the later decades? Might so-called 'Laffer curve' effects (Wanniski 1978; Laffer 2004)—in which increased tax rates do not produce commensurately increased overall revenue—have become more marked in the later part of the period for some reason? Or could this outcome be explained by long-term changes in tax structure (with relatively more reliance on VAT, income tax, and compulsory social insurance contributions related to earnings) making tax revenues rise and fall more sharply as GDP changes?[8]

### 2.1.3 *Spending Squeezes: From Short and Sharp to Long and Shallow?*

A third general point suggested by Table 2.1 is that there seems to have been some shift towards longer and shallower spending squeezes in the last three decades of the period, and the final episode, beginning in 2010 and analysed up to 2015/16 in this book, also seems to fit that pattern. Spending squeezes appear to have lasted longer in those final three decades, with lower average annual falls, than applied to the earlier episodes. Indeed, the majority (five out of eight) of spending squeezes since the 1950s were 'soft' squeezes, compared with the pre-1950 period when all four spending squeezes were hard. And almost by definition, long episodes are less likely to take the form of 'hard' squeezes than short episodes generating the same fiscal consolidation.

How can we account for this apparent shift towards longer and shallower spending squeezes? Does it reflect a changing position relative to financial and currency markets over the period, for instance in the movement to floating instead of fixed exchange rates from the 1970s? Does it reflect longer business or financial cycles in the recent past, consistent with the observation of long periods of positive and relatively stable growth since World War II (Hills, Thomas, and Dimsdale 2010)? Or might the explanation be more political, for example, as a result of Conservative electoral tactics in the 1990s and 2010s, discussed in later chapters, of challenging the Labour opposition to pledge to match plans for spending restraint in the future, or face election-campaign accusations of planning a 'tax bombshell'? Or is there something about the way modern state spending is constituted (for example, through long-term contracts with private suppliers, or through a changing mix of welfare and other spending) that makes it harder than it might have been previously to put the brakes on quickly?

---

[8] Such a change in the elasticity of revenues relative to GDP would augment so-called 'automatic stabilizer' effects in hard economic times (Hood, Heald, and Himaz (2014): 6), causing revenues to fall further in such conditions.

## 2.2 Triggers, Accompanying Conditions, and Composition of Fiscal Squeezes

The second set of questions raised at the outset of this chapter concerns what we can say from reported economic and financial statistics about what triggered fiscal squeezes or what the accompanying conditions were, and what categories of spending or taxation were most affected by those squeezes. The fiscal squeezes shown in Table 2.1 occurred in varying economic and financial conditions (for example, at different levels of debt and deficit and in periods of boom and bust in the world economy), and Tables A3 and A4 in the Appendix give more details about such variations.

Table 2.3 shows that those squeezes were applied by governments of different types and political stripes (coalition, minority, and single-party governments and by both left- and right-of-centre governments). More squeezes occurred under single-party government than under coalition or minority governments, and right-of-centre governments initiated roughly twice as many squeezes as left-of-centre governments (but that approximately reflects the preponderance of single-party and right-of-centre government in the UK over the period).

But while Table 2.3 shows fiscal squeeze was not an exclusive preserve of either the right or the left in politics over this period, some party-political differences are observable from the right-hand columns reporting the composition of spending cuts or tax rises. For instance, while defence and education were substantially cut in spending squeezes by both right- and left-of-centre governments, social security only appears in the 'most cut' category of spending under right-of-centre governments.

Table 2.3 also indicates two noticeable changes over time that we briefly discuss in the following subsections. One relates to major changes in the composition of government spending over time—in particular long-term change in capital spending—and its implications for what spending can be squeezed. A second, picking up on points made in the previous section about the disappearance of hard revenue squeezes, relates to the notable absence of income tax rate rises in the later part of our period.

### 2.2.1 *The Implications of a Changing Public Spending Profile for Fiscal Squeeze*

One noticeable variation over time in spending squeezes is reflected in the sixth column of Table 2.3, which shows an appreciable fall in the proportion of spending cuts accounted for by reductions in public sector investment in spending squeezes since the 1970s (when such spending cuts accounted for between one-third and all of the total spending squeeze).

**Table 2.3.** UK fiscal squeeze episodes 1900–2015: Decision-making features and composition of squeezes

| Overall episode | Sub-episode | Govt. orientation | Form of government | Composition of spending | | Composition of revenue | Income, profit, & capital tax (% of rev. rise)[d] |
|---|---|---|---|---|---|---|---|
| | | | | Most cut categories[a] | Gross Inv. fall as a % of total fall[b] | % changes to Lower (L), standard (S), & highest (H) tax rate[c] | |
| 1916–18 | 1916–18 | Mixed | War coalition | Def. | –6.6 | L 70, S 100, H 80 | 61.6 |
| 1919–25 | 1919–21 | Right | Con–Lib coalition | So. Sec., Edn, Def | 23.2 | | |
| | 1923–25 | Right | Mixed & volatile | | | | |
| 1931–35 | 1931–32 | Mixed | Min. Lab & emerg. coalit. | Edn, So. Sec. | 35.9 | L 30, S 10, H 10 | 53.2 |
| | 1933–35 | Right | National Govt. coalition | | | | |
| 1941–45 | 1941–45 | Mixed | War coalition | | | L 30, S 20, H 10 | 78.8 |
| | 1946–49 | Left | Majority Labour | Def. | –21.9 | S –10, H –10 | |
| 1953–55 | 1953–55 | Right | Maj Con | So. Sec. | 33.3 | L –25, S –11, H –5 | 46.3 |
| 1960–61 | 1960–61 | Right | Maj Con | | | No change | 39.5 |
| 1964–69 | 1964–67 | Mostly left | Maj Con & Lab | | | S 10, H 3 | |
| | 1968–69 | Left | Maj. Lab | Def. | 57.1 | L 50 | |
| 1973–78 | 1973–5 | Right, Left | Maj Con & Lab | | | S –10, H –6 | 54.6 |
| | 1976 | Left | Min Lab | — | 109.1 | No change | |
| | 1977–78 | Left | Min Lab | Edn | 57.1 | No change | |
| 1980–88 | 1980–81 | Right | Maj Con | | | No change | |
| | 1983–88 | Right | Maj Con | So. Sec, Def. | 28.7 | S –17, H –33 | 33.3 |
| 1993–99 | 1993–99 | Right, Left | Maj Con, Min Con, & Lab | So. Sec, Def. | 26.1 | L –50, S –12 | |
| 2010–15 | 2010–15 | Right | Con–Lib coalition | Edn, Pub. order | 31.6 | H –25, VAT 33 | |

*Notes:* [a] Current spending categories recording the biggest fall as a proportion of GDP. So.Sec = social security, Edn. = education, Def. = Defence, Pub. Order = public order. Figures for 2010–15 episode use data up to 2013/14. [b] Government investment on new infrastructure projects including Public Finance Initiative payments from the 1990s. [c] L = Lower rate (reduced rate to 1969/70), S = Standard rate (basic rate from 1973/4), H = top tax rate on earned income, VAT = value added tax at standard rates. [d] Increase in income, wealth, and taxes on profits relative to GDP as a proportion of overall percentage point increase in revenue/GDP.

*Sources:* Spending derived from Table A5. Revenue derived from Table A6 and data used in Figure A1.

On the face of it, this change might appear to reflect a move away from sacrificing capital or 'seed-corn' spending, so often highlighted in the past by critics of spending cuts (Dunsire and Hood 1989: 37 and 47–8). But it also reflects some long-term changes in the organization of capital spending over the later part of our period. Gross capital spending in the sense recorded in Table 2.2 declined as a category of reported public spending after the mid-1970s, at first because of transfer of large amounts of local authority public housing to private ownership and the decline in the building of new social housing by local authorities, then because of wholesale privatization of former nationalized industries in the 1980s, and further in the 1990s as a result of a major reduction in central government investment at that time (Crawford, Emmerson, and Tetlow 2009: 37).

That fall in the proportion of spending cuts accounted for by reductions in gross investment spending might be also be explained by a new way of financing capital expenditure (such as new schools, hospitals and public buildings) that developed in the 1990s. It took the form of long-term contracts with private firms which both raised the necessary capital on the financial markets and built and operated the relevant facilities. That arrangement contrasted with an older pattern in which government raised the funds and then organized and managed the construction and operation of the facilities. That meant older accounting distinctions between 'capital' and 'current' expenditure became harder to draw: in principle the ONS data from which the column in Table 2.3 is taken corrects for such effects, but the changing accounting conventions surrounding the treatment of capital spending over the period makes the consistency of such time-series data quite problematic. As we shall see in later chapters, capital spending did not disappear as a target in expenditure squeezes, but the change in the organization of such spending meant that would-be spending squeezers in the later period found themselves locked into long-term construction and supply contracts that would need to be renegotiated or abrogated for costs to be cut, in contrast to traditional ways of cutting costs in public organizations (including such familiar standbys as no-replacement hiring policies, pay freezes, or cuts in maintenance and repair budgets).

The other long-term change in the composition of public spending affecting spending squeezes is the changing distribution of public spending across different policy domains, as indicated in Figure 2.1. The steep decline in defence spending relative to GDP and the marked proportional increase in social security spending means that the kind of spending cuts applied after the two world wars, in which huge sums were taken from defence (involving mobile people, some below voting age, and a classic 'public good' in economic terms) were much less of an option for governments by the end of our period.

It is true that absolute sums spent on defence remained significant and defence continued to figure in some later spending squeezes, but by that

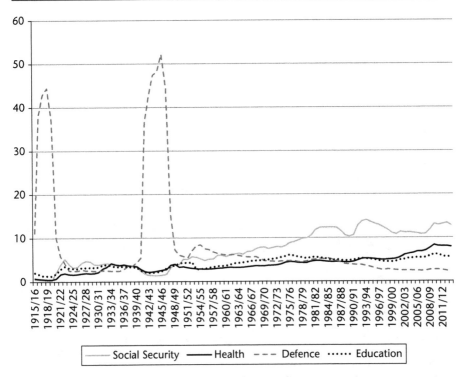

**Figure 2.1.** Trends in selected disaggregated expenditure categories as a percentage of GDP

*Sources*: Health (1900–79) Social Security (1900–49) Education, Defence (1900–52) derived from Mitchell (1988), Chapter XI, Tables 4, 12, 13, 15, and 16. Health (1980–2013); Social Security (1950–2013), Education, Defence (1953–2013) compiled from IFS (2014). Defence costs after 1998 include non-cash costs.

time really substantial spending cuts could only be achieved by cuts in 'welfare state' spending of one kind or another, for which one of the biggest beneficiary groups, the over-sixty-fives, was both growing in numbers and highly electorally significant because of relatively high turnout rates.

Both of these changes in the composition of public spending over time might help to explain and predict why there might be longer periods of shallower spending cuts than in earlier decades, as discussed in the previous section, though they do not obviously explain the apparent demise of the revenue-only squeeze.

### 2.2.2 Changing Profiles of Revenue Squeezes

In the previous section we commented on the apparent disappearance of the 'hard' revenue-only squeeze in the later part of our period. As with spending, the composition of taxation changed substantially over the century, as shown

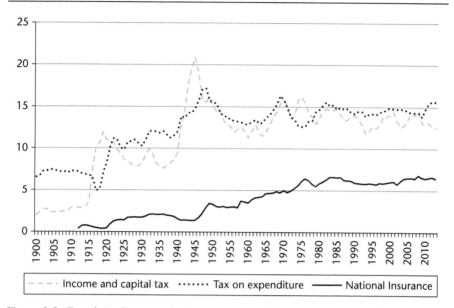

**Figure 2.2.** Trends in disaggregated revenue categories as a percentage of GDP

*Source*: 1900–49: Middleton (1996) Appendix 1; 1949–2014: ONS (2014) Public Sector Finances supplementary tables, includes local and central government revenue but excludes public corporations. Post Office treated as a Public Corporation after 1961. There is a break in the data in 1949 due to differences in sources.

in Figure 2.2, and that alteration may explain the change in revenue squeezes. Figure 2.2 shows three components of taxation, namely: taxes on income, wealth, and profits; taxes on expenditure (customs, excise, and other sales taxes); and compulsory contributions for health and welfare benefits, in effect a second income tax for employees combined with a payroll tax on employers and roughly equivalent to social security taxes in other countries but called 'National Insurance contributions' in UK parlance. Those contributions were originally (and ostensibly remain) an 'insurance' levy, and traditionally were not fully graduated relative to income, so they fell proportionately harder on middle and lower earners than on the topmost earners. As can be seen, this second income tax rose from 0.1 per cent or so of GDP in the early 1910s to 6 or 7 per cent a hundred years later, and that change needs to be considered when considering what happened to the total taxation of income over the period.

As can also be seen from Figure 2.2, revenue from taxes on expenditure and consumption was exceeded by that from taxes on income, wealth, and profits as a share of GDP in the two twentieth-century world wars (when rates of income and wealth taxation were raised vertiginously) and a short period in the early 1970s. But for the remaining part of the century the revenue from expenditure taxes was slightly higher (and rather less volatile) as a proportion of GDP than taxes on income, wealth, and profits.

The relative proportions of the three categories of taxation shown in Figure 2.2 varied considerably among the seven revenue squeezes (calculated on the ratio method) over the century). We might expect left-leaning governments to put more emphasis during revenue squeezes on income and wealth taxation relative to expenditure taxes and/or social security contributions, with right-leaning governments doing the opposite. But only one of the seven ratio-method revenue squeeze episodes over our period (the tax increases imposed by the minority Labour Government in 1931/32) clearly fits such expectations.

Indeed, along with the apparent decline of hard revenue squeezes from the early 1980s, as noted earlier, there seems to have been a change in the type of taxes used in fiscal squeezes in the later part of our period. For example, as the seventh column of Table 2.3 shows, the pre-1980 revenue squeezes all involved rises in income tax rates (with the exception of the 1940s and 1950s) whereas since 1980, when there was only one hard revenue squeeze, the revenue squeezes involved marked falls in income tax rates.[9]

## 2.3 Conclusion

This chapter has identified, analysed, and compared eighteen episodes of fiscal squeeze in the UK over a century, defining fiscal squeeze in terms of spending reductions or revenue increases and taking reported fiscal outcomes as the point of departure. It shows that episodes of fiscal squeeze so defined are not the same as episodes of 'fiscal consolidation' as identified from significant reductions in deficit. There was no episode of 'fiscal consolidation' without an accompanying fiscal squeeze episode (though as we have shown, the timings tend to vary), but about half the fiscal squeeze episodes were not associated with fiscal consolidation.

This chapter has also shown that fiscal squeeze was far from uncommon over the period (there was a fiscal squeeze of one kind or another approximately every decade, with the exception of the 1900s and 2000s). But it has also shown that there was only one unambiguous instance in the entire century of what we called 'double hard squeeze'—that is, when revenue rose and spending fell by more than 1 per cent in constant prices and relative to GDP, occurring in very unusual circumstances immediately after World War I.

Further, this chapter has brought out what variations in spending and revenue squeezes can be discerned from reported numbers. While the categories used for those administrative numbers are too coarse to bring out some important analytic distinctions (for example, in the types of welfare spending cut),

---

[9] Figure A1 in the Appendix shows the change graphically.

such an analysis can show what broad spending domains get hit hardest during spending squeezes and what types of taxation dominate revenue squeezes.

Finally, this analysis shows that the short, sharp, hard revenue squeeze, once a staple of fiscal squeeze in the decades after World War II, became less prominent over the last three decades or so of the period considered here. That might seem surprising, given political pressures on governments to raise taxes to mitigate or avoid spending cuts. It may reflect a world in which globalization and related developments somehow make revenue harder for governments to control than spending, but there might be some electoral explanation as well—issues to which we return in the concluding chapter. At the same time, the changing composition of public spending over the century, discussed earlier, has meant that spending squeezes through slowing or cutting capital expenditure—also once a staple of fiscal squeeze—may have become more difficult as a result of privatization or radical reduction of government spending in the domains that once figured large in this type of squeeze.

We return to these issues in the concluding chapter. But first, in the eight chapters that follow, we explore the political story behind the numbers presented here for each of the squeeze episodes, to give us the basis for rating the intensity of the squeeze episodes on the three dimensions we identified in Chapter One.

# Part II
# Selected Periods of Fiscal Squeeze over a Century

# 3

# World War I and the 1920s

## From Tax Squeeze through Double Squeeze to Spending Squeeze

### 3.1 Background: The Period in Perspective

The period from 1916 to 1925 has at least four notable features as a time of fiscal squeeze. First, it includes the only episode of 'double hard' squeeze in the whole century (that is, significant spending falls and tax rises both relative to GDP and in constant-price terms). Second, it includes both an episode of very hard revenue squeeze (with sharply increased direct tax rates, later to be maintained at their wartime levels for some years after World War I) and sudden and deep cuts in public spending in the 'surgery without anaesthetics' style.

Third, this decade witnessed a succession of three types of squeeze, running from a hard wartime revenue squeeze (while military spending ballooned but civil spending was held back), to a double hard squeeze immediately after the war, followed by an abrupt switch to a deep spending-only hard squeeze. That latter shift, with deep spending cuts applied to a budget already in balance without sudden pressure from financial markets (albeit at very high levels of debt to GDP), reflected a remarkable political U-turn by the government of the day, for which there is no exact parallel in the period covered by this book. And fourth, that final hard spending squeeze, initiated by a coalition government, extended over the lifetime of the subsequent two short-lived governments (Conservative and Labour), during a period of messy and volatile electoral politics.

### 3.2 The Wartime Revenue Squeeze

World War I began under a minority Liberal Government elected in 1910 and dependent on Irish nationalists for parliamentary support. At first that government expected the war to be short and its costs limited, with the UK using its navy to blockade Germany but the land war waged mainly by France and Russia. Further, fearing that tax increases might provoke popular resistance, the government decided to fund the war from borrowing to a much greater extent than in the Napoleonic or Crimean Wars in the previous century—a policy that continued even after it became clear that those initial expectations of a short, cheap war were utterly mistaken (Daunton (2002): 38).

As the war continued, electoral competition was effectively suspended and replaced by two successive war coalition governments. The first comprised Liberals and Conservatives led by the Liberal Prime Minister Herbert Asquith from May 1915 to December 1916. The second, after the Conservatives withdrew their support for Asquith as war leader, was led by the Liberal David Lloyd George from 1916 to the end of the war and included Conservative, Labour, and some Liberal MPs (the remaining Liberals formed the Opposition under the former leader Herbert Asquith). Those three wartime governments imposed exchange controls that weakened the Gold Standard fixed-exchange rate system for the currency (without formally suspending it) and probably contributed to inflation during the war, and they imposed conscription as well as other deprivations, so there was certainly some non-fiscal austerity accompanying fiscal squeeze in this case. Although overall public spending rocketed during the war, as we saw in the previous chapter, that increase was concentrated on military activity, not civilian public services, so in effect there was a squeeze on civilian spending that accompanied the hard revenue squeeze imposed during the war.

But that revenue squeeze did not comprise extra taxes on the bulk of the population through higher indirect taxes and taxes on lower incomes (despite calls from John Maynard Keynes and others for such taxes), because, as already mentioned, the governing politicians seem to have feared such taxes might fuel industrial unrest or even Bolshevik-type revolution (Daunton (2002): 42–3). Instead, extra taxes were levied almost exclusively on middle and higher incomes, business profits, and inheritance, and war spending was funded mostly by borrowing, creating a huge debt overhang after the war. The wartime revenue squeeze included a fourfold increase in the standard rate of income tax between 1913 and 1919 (to 30 per cent), together with a reduction in tax thresholds that targeted middle and upper middle earners. Taxes on profits were also sharply raised during the war, with an Excess Profits Duty (EPD, a form of corporate tax based on the extra profits earned by each enterprise above their pre-war levels) levied at a rate that rose from 13 to 26 per cent between 1916 and 1918. Two successive wartime Chancellors of the Exchequer declared EPD to be an 'emergency tax' that would apply only during the war.[1]

---

[1] The Liberal Chancellor Reginald McKenna declared in 1915 (House of Commons debates, Hansard [hereafter 'HC Deb'] 13 November 2015, c.1397) 'This is . . . only a temporary tax, during

## 3.3 Post-War Politics: Double Hard Squeeze

After the war a coalition consisting mainly of Conservatives and Liberals headed by the wartime Liberal Prime Minister David Lloyd George, campaigned together on a joint manifesto for post-war reconstruction (stressing policies to improve and expand social housing and expand educational opportunities, a process that had been stalled by the squeeze on civilian public spending during the war, while avoiding extra taxes on food or industrial raw materials). That coalition decisively won the so-called 'coupon' general election held shortly after the November 1918 armistice which ended the war with Germany.

The post-war government and its successors operated in a financial and economic environment that was far from benign, as a result of serious disruptions to international trade by the war, associated developments (such as the 1917 Russian Revolution and the formation of the Soviet Union) and lack of currency convertibility following the exchange controls and abandonment of the Gold Standard by several European countries. In the UK, a brief, unexpected post-war inflationary boom was swiftly and equally unexpectedly followed by a deflationary slump and mass unemployment. That in turn led to political turbulence in the form of electoral volatility and strikes against pay cuts, such as a three-month miners' strike and a general strike at the docks in 1921. That turbulence was compounded by rebellion in and the later secession from the UK of what is now the Irish Republic, and the associated partition of Ireland in 1922.

That was the background to the 'double hard squeeze' we identified in Chapter Two, in the two years after the war. The squeeze on spending at that time consisted entirely of deep cuts in defence expenditure arising from demobilization, while tax revenue increased because of the coalition government's policy of keeping income and profits tax rates high after the war, combined with the short post-war inflationary boom. Indeed, the government increased some tax rates above their wartime levels, while resisting demands from the left for a capital levy or wealth tax to pay down the war debt.

There seem to have been several reasons for this revenue squeeze. One was to correct a massive budget deficit; a second was to finance the huge cost of servicing the public debt incurred as a result of the war; and a third was to finance the enhanced social programmes associated with the coalition government's 1918 election promises of post-war reconstruction, notably in housing and education.

the war', and two years later McKenna's Conservative successor Andrew Bonar Law said, 'Excess Profits Duty is only to continue during the War' (HC Deb 16 July 1917, c.106).

The post-war government's first Chancellor (the Conservative Austen Chamberlain, who became leader of his party in 1921) described his political dilemma in his first budget speech in 1919:

> I am called upon at one and the same time to remit or to repeal the taxation which was imposed [during the war]...and, not merely to resume the civil expenditure which was interrupted under the stress of war, but to provide the means for creating...a new heaven and a new earth; and the same people...expect me at the same time to accomplish vast reductions in expenditure...[2]

As already mentioned, the work of cutting spending during this period was concentrated on defence (as demobilization led to big cuts in expenditure on the armed forces and the ministries of Munitions and Supply), not on cuts in civil spending. So although the estimates for FY 1919/20 comprised a reduction of nearly 60 per cent of the equivalent spending for FY 1918/19, and the estimates for 1920/21 represented a further reduction of some 35 per cent on those of 1919/20,[3] none of that pain was felt in civilian services, meaning that the political cost of those spending cuts for the incumbents was relatively low, while the fiscal squeeze on the tax side was arguably more visible to citizens and voters and thus represented greater political costs. In his first budget in 1919, Chamberlain disappointed expectations of post-war cuts in income tax and supertax (the tax on the highest earnings) by retaining those taxes at the high wartime levels, and increased taxes on beer and spirits. As mentioned earlier, he broke the pledges of his wartime predecessors to abolish Excess Profits Duty after the war by retaining that tax for a further year, albeit at a reduced rate. While disappointing those on the left who were calling for a general wealth tax, he also sharply raised inheritance tax rates as an alternative approach to taxing wealth.

The government continued the fiscal squeeze in the following year's budget (1920). The budget deficit was reported as having fallen from £1.6bn for FY 1918/19 to £0.3bn for FY 1919–20, but taxes were raised again. The Excess Profits Duty was not only retained for a further year, but the rate went back up again to 60 per cent. On top of that, Chamberlain introduced a new Corporation Profits Tax of 5 per cent for all limited companies (intended to be the successor of EPD, which by that time was encouraging ways of artificially limiting profits). At the same time the rate of 'supertax' was increased and the standard rate of income tax kept at its wartime level of 33 per cent, along with more graduation of income tax. Further, Chamberlain raised postal charges, levied extra taxes on motoring (which was becoming more prevalent as more middle-income people acquired cars), doubled stamp taxes and increased taxes on tea, beer, wine, and spirits, arguing that these unpopular

---

[2] HC Deb 30 April 1919, c.175–6.    [3] HC Deb 19 April 1920, c.78.

tax changes were needed for fiscal consolidation and to improve the UK's credit standing.[4]

## 3.4 Tax Revolt and the Shift to Expenditure Squeeze, 1921

However, those 1920 tax increases took effect just as the economy went into a sudden, deep, and unexpected trade slump after the post-war boom. Having been only 2 per cent in 1920, unemployment suddenly doubled in three months between December 1920 and March 1921 and rose to over two million in June 1921, reaching 11.3 per cent in that year—one of the highest rates recorded over the whole century considered here.

The government's first reaction was to stick to its policy of keeping tax rates high. Sir Robert Horne, a Unionist who succeeded Chamberlain as Chancellor (after Chamberlain became Conservative leader), finally scrapped the Excess Profits Tax in 1921, but even though the previous large budget deficit had turned into a reported surplus (of £0.2bn or 3 per cent of GDP) for FY 1920/21, Horne kept other direct taxes at their previous levels, including the Corporation Profits Tax that had been introduced alongside the Excess Profits Tax in 1920.

However, within months of Horne's 1921 budget, the government abruptly shifted from double hard squeeze to a severe expenditure-only squeeze. And this shift to a hard spending squeeze, which did not apply to military spending alone but also to the policies of improved housing and education on which Lloyd George's coalition had swept to electoral victory in 1918, seems to have been triggered mainly by sudden domestic electoral pressure to cut taxes.

It is true that there were at least three other closely interlinked pressures for that policy shift. One was a widespread belief that public spending cuts to finance tax reductions (not fiscal expansion through borrowing, Keynesian-style) were the key to economic recovery through revived trade and employment. At that time the Treasury followed a modified balanced-budget rule, the so-called 'McKenna Rule', which required non-defence expenditure to be met by revenue year-by-year (Daunton (2002); Nason and Vahey (2007)). More broadly, the prime minister and many other politicians saw 'public economy' as a way to reduce unemployment (Jones (1969): 124).

Interlinked with that view was the challenge of financing existing levels of public spending at a time when tax revenues were falling in a slump, and of re-financing government debt amounting to some 150 per cent of GDP in 1921.

---

[4] HC Deb 19 April 1920, c.100.

At that time, the UK government not only had a large 'floating debt' (that is, continuously refinanced short-term debt), but nearly 14 per cent of its other internal debt was due to mature within the next three years, and repayments on large debts to the USA incurred during World War I were due to start in 1922/3 (McDonald (1989): 654–5). To refinance the debt, interest rates had to be kept high, meaning debt interest accounted for some £300m—a third or more of total public spending. With little immediate prospect of debt redemption, it is perhaps not surprising that the Treasury saw little headroom for even more borrowing to compensate for falling tax revenues.

A third element in the pressure for spending cuts was the view that the slump and associated unemployment could only be effectively tackled by restoring pre-war international trade, which in turn required a return to currency convertibility through restoration of the pre-war gold standard, abandoned by many countries during World War I. And, much as occurred with the 'Maastricht rules' for the euro in the late 1990s, balanced budgets were seen as the route to restoring the gold standard. Senior Treasury officials were keen to see a return to the pre-war gold standard, and Prime Minister David Lloyd George declared in 1922: 'before trade can be fully restored you must be able to establish everywhere the convertibility of currency into gold or its equivalent . . . to achieve that, one of the first considerations is to induce the nations to balance their budgets.'[5]

However, the immediate trigger for major spending cuts in 1921 seems to have been political, in the form of a middle-class electoral backlash against the high tax rates which had been carried over from the war. It began at the start of the year, when a leading press magnate, Lord Rothermere, sponsored a movement called the 'Anti-Waste League', which attacked the coalition government's policy of maintaining high taxes for post-war reconstruction and campaigned for cuts in 'wasteful' public spending to allow taxes to be reduced. The Anti-Waste League successfully challenged the incumbent parties in by-elections by appealing to financially hard-pressed southern English middle-class voters on whom the coalition government (and particularly the Conservatives) depended for re-election. And given that income tax rates had risen four-fold since before the war (as noted earlier), there was a constituency for the League to appeal to—particularly from those living on fixed incomes from investments, who had experienced a fall of approximately two-thirds in the real value of their income since 1914, as well as a fall in the value of their assets of about 30 per cent.

The Anti-Waste League made a major political splash by winning three by-elections against Coalition Conservative candidates in southern England in

---

[5] HC Deb 3 April 1922, c.1885–996.

1921 and induced Liberal and Conservative candidates in other elections to re-brand themselves as 'anti-waste'. The League's first by-election victory in January saw a Conservative coalition candidate defeated by a large majority in a previously Conservative-held seat. In June 1921 the League won two other by-elections against Conservative Unionist candidates, and in August and September, it threatened two Conservative candidates in what were considered to be safe seats for the Party, with those candidates only narrowly scraping home in both cases.

It was those by-election losses and the associated threat to their Southern English electoral base that dismayed the Conservatives, the biggest party in the Coalition, and panicked David Lloyd George, the Liberal prime minister, into an abrupt switch from the expansionary policy of post-war reconstruction to spending cuts and tax reductions designed to outflank the Anti-Waste League electorally and keep the Conservatives in the coalition.

The institutional arrangement used by Lloyd George for this policy switch was a five-person semi-autonomous 'Committee on National Expenditure', comprising a group of prominent businessmen, headed by the retiring Minister of Transport, Sir Eric Geddes.[6] The prime minister announced the Committee's formation in August 1921 (following Conservative by-election losses to the Anti-Waste League in July). It worked in stages, delivering reports to the government every month from December 1921 to February 1922.

There was no pretence of party, let alone gender, balance on the Committee, which was controversial both in its composition (as a group of wealthy businessmen) and in its form, as an external body imposed into the normal process of bilateral bargaining between the Treasury and spending departments (Jones 1969: 166). Its chair, Sir Eric Geddes (1875–1937), was one of Lloyd George's close political confidantes, having worked with Lloyd George since his days as Minister for Munitions in World War I, first as a special civil servant (one of the 'men of push and go' Lloyd George recruited from business) and later as a political colleague in the cabinet (Stevenson 1971: 225). Though its appointment had been announced by the prime minister, the Committee's brief was to make recommendations to the Chancellor of the Exchequer 'for effecting forthwith all possible reductions in the National Expenditure on Supply Services, having regard especially to the present and prospective position of the revenue'. But the Committee's formal power was only to recommend: proposals for changes of 'policy' had to be approved by cabinet committees and its three reports were considered by such committees before they were published in February 1922.

---

[6] The others were Lord Inchcape, Lord Faringdon, Sir Joseph (later Lord) MacLay, and Sir Guy Granet—all senior business figures closely connected to government and politics.

Sir Robert Horne, the Chancellor of the Exchequer, set the Committee the target of finding £100m of savings from total supply expenditure for FY 1922/23 on top of £75m of reductions already agreed between the Treasury and spending departments following a call by the Treasury in May 1921 (shortly before the Anti-Waste League's by-election victories over the Conservatives in June) for proposals for cutting back 1922/23 spending by about 15 per cent compared to 1921/22.

Much of this £75m in 'savings' offered by departments—closer to 10 than the requested 15 per cent—comprised decidedly 'low-hanging fruit', in that they included special war-related spending that was due to end anyway, or simply reflected falling prices as a consequence of the recession (Committee on National Expenditure (1921): 3). The Geddes Committee's task was therefore to find higher-hanging fruit in the form of over 15 per cent of additional cutbacks from total spending, such that government spending would fall by over 27 per cent between 1921/22 and 1922/23.

The Committee apparently worked virtually full-time from its appointment in summer of 1921 to February 1922. In the event, it fell slightly short of its target of £100m of extra cutback proposals, recommending reductions of £87m, of which £52m were finally accepted by the cabinet. Even so, those are remarkable reductions in historical perspective, amounting to about 20 per cent of central government spending, when the 'Geddes' cuts are put together with those agreed earlier between Departments and the Treasury.

The Committee approached its task in a way followed by many subsequent cutback exercises. Its first interim report analysed what could practically be cut and what was beyond the reach of 'economy', at least in the short run. In the latter category it put debt charges, payments that could only be unwound by legislative changes (such as road-building grants), pension obligations, and various politically sensitive financial commitments to war veterans and the bereaved (notably war graves and grants to veterans). The Committee therefore concluded that most of the cuts had to be concentrated on three main classes of spending, namely defence, operations in the Middle East arising from World War 1 (mainly Palestine and Iraq, which had become British mandates under the League of Nations after the fall of the Ottoman Empire), and other items of civilian expenditure that were not statutory obligations that it would take primary legislation to overturn (Committee on National Expenditure 1921: 164–8).

The Geddes cuts came on top of the deep post-war reductions in defence spending, and the axe again fell sharply on defence, reflecting a cabinet resolution that no major war was to be expected within ten years. Over half (nearly £53m) of the £87m of extra cuts recommended by the Committee fell on defence and war pensions. But what was different about the Geddes cuts was that they also fell heavily on civil spending, striking hard at the coalition government's expansionary plans for post-war reconstruction. Almost a quarter of the Geddes Committee's proposed reductions (£18m) were aimed at education spending, and the remaining quarter of proposed cuts was distributed in smaller packages among other items of civilian spending. The Committee declared that the remaining £13½m of its original £100m target could easily be achieved as a result of naval disarmament agreements that would cut naval shipbuilding, further reductions in other military spending, and by the effect of a greater than anticipated fall in prices (Committee on National Expenditure (1922): 165–70).

In the event, the planned cuts agreed by the cabinet in early 1922 amounted to some £127m in total, comprising the £75m 'low-hanging fruit' cutbacks agreed before the Geddes Committee was appointed, plus £52m out of the £87m suggested by the Geddes Report. Cabinet committees watered down the Geddes proposals in most policy domains (for example, accepting £28.5m of Geddes' proposals for cuts of £46m in military spending, and £11.7m out of the proposals for £22.7m cuts in 'social services' spending, which included £18m of proposed cuts in education (Higgs 1922: 257)).

The main resistance to the extra proposed cuts seems to have come from the education departments and the Admiralty (Grigg (1948): 77), the latter probably encouraged by Winston Churchill (then Colonial Secretary), who chaired the cabinet committee considering the proposed defence cuts. In education, the Geddes proposals included suspension of some key provisions for expanding tertiary education in the Education Acts of 1918—a high political cost proposal given that the principal architect of those Acts, the Liberal Herbert A. L. Fisher, was a senior cabinet minister as President of the Board of Education for England and Wales. £10m out of Geddes' £18m package of proposed education cuts was targeted at elementary education (replacing matching grants to local education authorities with cash limits, raising the school entry age, closing small schools, increasing class sizes, cutting teachers' pay and administration spending), while £8m of the proposed cuts was directed at higher levels of education (Committee on National Expenditure (1922): 103–23). Those latter proposed cuts comprised substantial increases in tuition fees, a cap of 25 per cent on free places for lower-income students, a 20 per cent reduction in grants to universities and in particular suspending plans for developing Technical Schools that were a key part of the extension of compulsory part-time education in the 1918 Education Act.

Unsurprisingly, these proposals were strongly resisted by the Board of Education, which initially offered only £2½ million out of the £18m proposed cutbacks (Jones 1969: 191–2). The prime minister had to back down over the Geddes proposals for cuts in teachers' pay after teachers protested that they were being singled out for harsher treatment than other public service workers, and to promise Fisher that the suspended parts of his cherished 1918 Education Act would be reintroduced in better economic conditions. George Peden (2000: 169) argues that less than one-third of the Geddes proposals for cuts in the education budget were realized, but an analysis based on Brian Mitchell's (1988) historical data indicates that the overall cuts realized in education spending amounted to substantially more than that, and that in constant-price terms the total cuts effected between 1922 and 1923 were some £176m—almost exactly the target the Geddes Committee was set in 1921.

Such a conclusion is remarkable, indicating that (in contrast to many plans for cutting public spending) the Geddes proposals were more than implemented: actual spending cuts in 1922/23 exceeded the £127m the cabinet had agreed and even the £162m that the Geddes Reports had recommended. The Geddes cuts certainly amounted to a substantial spending squeeze, but the extent of the fall in spending differs as between different data sources,[7] and the fact that prices were falling at the time meant some kinds of spending reduction in nominal terms cut less deeply than would have been the case if prices had been stable or rising.

In any event, the cuts sufficed to deliver the tax reductions needed to outflank the Anti-Waste League electorally. In his 1922 budget the Chancellor, Sir Robert Horne, duly announced a cut of income tax rates by approximately 1/6th (to take effect in 1923), cuts of about one-third in some politically salient indirect taxes (notably those on tea, coffee, cocoa, and chicory) and cuts in postal and telephone charges. And those tax cuts seem to have taken enough electoral pressure off the Conservatives for the coalition government to survive for another few months until October 1922. The break-up came after a by-election victory by an Independent Conservative (indicating that the Conservatives could win power on their own) and over a different issue (the Chanak crisis[8] over the conduct of foreign policy) when Conservative MPs led by Stanley Baldwin voted to pull out of the coalition, rejecting the views of their leader, Austen Chamberlain.

## 3.5 After Geddes: Expenditure Squeeze after the Fall of the Lloyd George Coalition

A further striking feature of the Geddes Committee is that the sharp spending reductions it helped to set in train survived the government and prime

---

[7] See Table A1 in the Appendix. Using Mitchell's (1988) data, the Geddes cuts amount to about 3 percentage points of GDP a year, amounting to the deepest spending cuts over the whole century (if post-war cuts concentrated entirely on military demobilization are excluded). But on Middleton's (1996) data the fall in total public expenditure was about 1.3 percentage points of GDP a year, while another set of data (White and Chapman (1987)) indicates a fall in total public expenditure of about 1.9 percentage points of GNP (rather than GDP) a year.

[8] When Lloyd George (in the absence of the Conservative Foreign Secretary, Lord Curzon) threatened to declare war on Turkey as Turkish troops advanced on the Dardanelles neutral zone then guarded by British and French troops.

minister that had set up the committee. Public spending continued to fall under the three governments that succeeded the post-war Lloyd George coalition after it fell in November 1922, namely the majority Conservative Government that ruled for a year until a new leader (Stanley Baldwin) called an early general election over protectionist trade policy in December 1923 and was replaced by an equally short-lived minority Labour Government propped up by the Liberals until it in turn was replaced by another majority Conservative Government in the October 1924 general election.

That continuing fiscal squeeze applied only to expenditure, since revenue fell by more than spending between 1923 and 1925. And when we look at the spending that was cut over that period, the sharpest fall was in social security expenditure (nearly 2 percentage points lower than the 1922/23 levels, reflecting cuts in some of the social, welfare, and pension provision introduced in the previous decade), followed by a drop of 1.7 percentage points in defence and 0.5 percentage points in education.

Most of these spending cuts (7 out of the 9 percentage points by which public spending fell relative to GDP) applied to central government, especially spending on defence and social security. Local government spending fell by just over 2 of those 9 percentage points. Central government transfers to local government (then amounting to 6–10 per cent of central government spending, as compared with roughly 20 per cent today, and about 2 per cent of GDP, compared to about 9 per cent today) fell by 0.5 per cent as a proportion of GDP over 1923–25. So (in contrast to other cases where central governments pass the pain of spending cuts down to lower levels through 'unfunded mandates') these cuts apparently did not fall more heavily on local than central expenditure. The strategy of targeting spending that could be cut without heavy-duty legislative changes meant the axe initially fell onto capital as well as current spending, but capital spending was restored relatively quickly, no doubt reflecting pressures to stimulate economic growth to counter mass unemployment.

At local government level, the biggest reduction was in housing expenditure—those much-vaunted 'homes for heroes' (arising from Lloyd George's 1918 pledge 'to make Britain a fit country for heroes to live in') and the 'comprehensive' approach to social housing promised by the coalition government in its 1918 manifesto (Swenarton 1981). Civil service cuts reduced the number of civil servants by a third between 1920 and 1931, largely by dismissing temporary staff (most of them women) who had been taken on during World War I. Excluding debt charges, total spending fell by about 9 per cent of GDP over this period, and national debt fell from 180 to 175 per cent of GDP between 1923 and 1925.[9]

---

[9] Such that the fiscal adjustment was 'successful' according to Alesina and Perotti's (1997) criterion.

So why did the spending cutbacks initiated by the Geddes Committee continue under three successive governments, including one Labour Government? Part of the reason may be that for three years running (1922, 1923, 1924) there was a change of government following a general election held late in the financial year (November, December, and October respectively), such that there was little time for newly appointed Chancellors and cabinets to make dramatic changes to financial plans already in train or—at least for the first two governments—to follow up in a subsequent budget.[10] But that outcome is also explicable by the fact that two of the three governments were Conservative Governments and that the 1923–24 Labour Government was a minority government dependent on other parties (notably the Liberals) for support.

After the Conservative Party led by Andrew Bonar Law won the November 1922 general election with a comfortable overall majority, the new Chancellor, Stanley Baldwin, broadly followed the fiscal course set by his party colleague Sir Robert Horne in the coalition government the previous year. Indeed in his 1923 budget speech, Baldwin praised his predecessor's efforts, expressed satisfaction at spending reductions that had considerably exceeded those planned and approved as a result of the Geddes Committee, and proceeded to announce further tax reductions, notably another small reduction in the standard rate of income tax, a halving of the Corporation Profits Tax, reductions in taxes on tea, coffee, and cocoa and in charges for postage and telephone services.[11]

As noted earlier, despite its secure majority, the Conservative Government elected in 1922 lasted only a year. The prime minister, Andrew Bonar Law, fell ill and resigned just six months into his premiership, and his successor, the former Chancellor Stanley Baldwin, called and lost a general election only a year into the government's tenure over a policy of protectionism that was unsuccessfully pitched to the voters as a route to cutting unemployment. The minority Labour Government led by Ramsay MacDonald that took office in December 1923, lasted ten months before it lost a vote of confidence, precipitating a third general election in less than three years (October 1924).

The Labour Government's single budget, introduced by Chancellor Philip Snowden in 1924, envisaged (and delivered) a budget surplus based on a continuation of reductions in spending, matched by cuts in several indirect taxes. No new taxes were introduced and no tax rates were increased. Snowden, who had no previous ministerial experience, portrayed this budget—the very opposite of the 'tax-and-spend' stereotype of the way left-of-centre governments approach fiscal policy—as a result of the fact that he had only been in office for a few months and that budget preparation had been at a late stage

[10] As noted by Winston Churchill in his 1925 Financial Statement (HC Deb 28 April 1925, c.58–9).
[11] HC Deb 16 April 1923, c.1721–41.

within the Treasury when he became Chancellor. But the design of the 1924 budget could be interpreted not just as a matter of late-stage inheritance, but also of political calculation based on the constraints of the parliamentary arithmetic, in the sense of the need for substantial support from other parties for the budget to pass.

## 3.6 Conclusion

Returning to the themes raised in Chapter One, we conclude by trying to place the squeezes of the eventful decade described earlier in terms of the three types of squeeze choices we identified in Chapter One; of the loss, cost, and effort involved in the various squeezes described here; and of the apparent consequences of those squeezes, electoral and other.

### 3.6.1 *Tax and Spending, Depth and Duration, Blame and Control*

As noted at the start of this chapter, the near-decade of squeezes described here comprises several of the types we introduced in Chapter One, running from a hard wartime revenue squeeze, through the only case of double hard squeeze in the century considered by this book, to a substantial spending-only squeeze initiated by the Lloyd George coalition and extending over the (mostly short) lives of the three following governments. But none of the squeezes explored in this chapter was of the 'slow-burn' variety that we discussed in Chapter One.

However, when we delved a little further into those various squeezes in this chapter, we noted that the wartime tax squeeze mainly hit those on middle and higher incomes and that the soaring public expenditure that accompanied it consisted wholly of defence spending, while spending on civilian services was severely squeezed, falling by nearly 10 per cent in constant-price terms between FY 1916/17 and FY 1918/19. Similarly, the apparently draconian 'double hard' post-war squeeze between FY 1919/20 and 1921/22 counts as a spending squeeze only because of steep falls in defence spending accompanying demobilization: civilian spending was not squeezed at all over this period. Such observations highlight the importance of going beyond global aggregated numbers to pick up some of the important particularities of each of those squeezes.

When it comes to choices over blame and control, we also noticed variety in the episodes explored in this chapter. One distinctive feature was the suspension of electoral competition among the main political parties accompanied by coalition governments during World War I—a pattern repeated in World War II but not in any of the other episodes that we discuss in this book. Another was the use of business leaders chaired by an ex-minister to look over the whole range of public spending and identify targets for expenditure cuts in the 'Geddes Axe' episode—a pattern only followed in one other episode during the century covered by this book.

### 3.6.2 Loss, Cost, and Effort Involved in these Episodes

In Chapter One (Table 1.2), we sketched out a way of qualitatively assessing the intensity of fiscal squeezes on three dimensions, namely the extent of loss imposed on citizens and voters, the extent of reputational cost and stress incurred by governing politicians, and the degree of effort required from the state machine, for example, in devising new taxes or expenditure cuts requiring radical changes in organization or modes of service delivery.

Our grading of the various episodes discussed in this chapter is shown in Table 3.1, and the numbers given in square brackets relate back to the categories we introduced in the opening chapter in Table 1.2. For example, the degree of loss imposed on citizens and voters by the World War I revenue squeeze (plus the non-fiscal austerity that accompanied it) appears to have been high,

**Table 3.1.** A qualitative classification of imposed loss, political cost, and state effort associated with World War 1 and 1920s fiscal squeezes

| | Low | Moderate | High | Overall classification |
|---|---|---|---|---|
| **1916–18. Squeeze type: Hard Revenue; Wartime Coalition government** | | | | |
| Loss | | | [1] | High |
| Cost | [2], [3], [4] | | | Low |
| Effort | | | [1],[2],[3] | High |
| **1919–21. Squeeze type: Hard Revenue/Hard Spending; Coalition 12/1918–11/1922** | | | | |
| Loss | [1] | [1] | | Low/Mod |
| Cost | | [2], [3] | [1] | Moderate |
| Effort | [1], [2] | | | Low |
| **1923–25. Squeeze type: Hard Expenditure** | | | | |
| Coalition 12/1918–11/1922 (incumbents who announced and enacted the squeeze) | | | | |
| Loss | | | [1], [2], [3] | High |
| Cost | [2],[5] | [1] | [2],[3] | Moderate |
| Effort | | [3] | | Moderate |
| Conservative 11/1922–12/1923 | | | | |
| Loss | [1] | | [1], [2], [3] | High |
| Cost | [4] | | | Low |
| Effort | [1] | | [4] | Moderate |
| Minority Labour 12/1923–10/1924 | | | | |
| Loss | | [3] | | Moderate |
| Cost | [1], [4] | | | Low |
| Effort | | [1] | | Moderate |
| Conservative 10/1924 onwards | | | | |
| Loss | [1] | | | Low |
| Cost | [1] | | | Low |
| Effort | [1] | | | Low |

*Note*: Numbers in square brackets refer to categories in Table 1.2, Chapter One.

and the state machine had to exert significant effort in managing the war finances and developing taxes such as the Excess Profits Duty, but the political costs of the fiscal measures experienced by governing politicians was significantly muted by the combination of coalition government and the absence of electoral competition during the war.

Similarly, the post-war 'double hard squeeze' arguably involved a lower degree of loss to voters and citizens (since the spending cuts applied exclusively to defence, and all other major categories of spending saw increases), and governing politicians ran rather more reputational risk, for example, as they broke promises to abolish Excess Profits Duty after the war and as electoral competition resumed.

For the various governments involved in the 'Geddes Axe' squeezes, the losses imposed on voters certainly seem to have been significant (especially at first), but the effort required of the state machine could only be counted as the top of the scale if we include items such as handling strikes or insurgency in Ireland that arguably were not directly related to fiscal policy. As for the political losses incurred by governing politicians, there is unavoidable ambiguity over who is to count as 'incumbents' for that episode, in several ways. The squeeze begun by the 'Geddes Axe' shows up in the financial outcome numbers we set out in Chapter Two as starting in 1923, by which time the Liberal–Conservative coalition had collapsed. But that squeeze was clearly announced and enacted by the coalition government well before it fell, with spending cuts under way by November 1922, so we have analysed the political costs to the coalition as incumbents for that case in Table 3.1. The coalition parties had campaigned on a joint platform in the 1918 'Khaki' election, so we do not count the costs of the various parties in the coalition separately in this analysis (though as it happened, the Liberals seem to have incurred stronger voter punishment than the Conservatives, consistent with the 'asymmetrical punishment' idea considered in Chapter Two).

Of course such a scoring exercise is necessarily limited, and some of these judgement calls are debatable. But it underlines the value of combining qualitative analysis with the sort of quantitative analysis we pursued in Chapter Two, because it shows how squeezes that look severe from aggregate analysis can be judged differently on other criteria (for instance, if we strip out military spending, or take account of grand coalitions or suspension of party competition). We will show in the concluding chapter how those distinctions can matter when it comes to analysing the consequences of fiscal squeeze.

### 3.6.3 *Electoral and Other Consequences*

Finally, what did these various squeezes leave behind them? As far as electoral effects are concerned, there was no opinion polling at the time or even detailed write-ups of election campaigns, so election results are the only data available for assessing the electoral punishment or credit accruing to incumbents, in line with the retrospective voting ideas discussed in Chapter One. And such an assessment is tricky for several other reasons.

One is the 'noise' problem, the difficulty of isolating the impact of efforts to raise revenue and/or cut spending from all the other issues in play in a general election campaign. For example, in the snap election called by Stanley Baldwin in 1923, the Conservative Government's proposals for new protectionist and Imperial preference policies (presented as a way of reducing mass unemployment and arguably a key case of 'heresthetic', as discussed in Chapter One) were a key issue in the campaign, and it is not clear how far continuing spending cutbacks weighed relative to protectionism with the voters. Similarly, the 1924 election (caused by a vote of no confidence over the Labour Government's decision to drop the prosecution of a communist editor for publishing an open letter calling on soldiers not to use force against workers) included much discussion in the last four days of the campaign of the so-called Zinoviev letter. This letter, purporting to originate from a high official in the Communist International and published in a Conservative newspaper, said that more settled relations between the USSR and the UK (brought about by the Labour Government's diplomatic recognition of the USSR and conclusion of a trade deal with the new state in 1924, opposed by the Conservatives) would facilitate Communist agitation in Britain. The effect of this famous, almost certainly forged, document on the election outcome is still disputed.

Further, there is the question of whether it is really plausible to assume that voters would be heavily influenced by retrospection rather than consideration of future policy promises in circumstances such as those of 1918, at the end of a catastrophic war. Even if voters had chosen to behave in that way, the fact that all three major parties (Liberal, Labour, and Conservative) had been part of the wartime government at one stage or another would have made it difficult to differentiate blame among them for the substantial tax increases imposed during the war.

Third, the problem of identifying 'incumbents' (discussed in Chapter One and in section 3.6.2) is particularly tricky for the 1923–25 hard spending squeeze episode, constituting as it did a package of spending cuts planned, approved, and announced by a coalition of two main parties, that broadly continued under three successor governments, partly because all of them happened to be elected late in the budgetary cycle. That messy party-political pattern linked with policy inheritance also seems to have made blame attribution by the voters more difficult than it would have been in a world of two-party politics without policy inheritance.

Fourth, as we have shown, given that the period considered in this chapter includes one case of a spending-only hard squeeze accompanied by tax cuts, retrospectively minded voters in that case faced the choice of whether to punish incumbents for spending cuts or to reward them for tax cuts, and it is plausible to argue, as we suggested in Chapter One, that punishment for spending cuts or reward for tax cuts might apply asymmetrically to right-of-centre versus left-of-centre parties.

In the light of these considerations, the 1918 and 1929 general elections do not really seem to present a convincing test of electoral punishment for fiscal squeeze through retrospective voting. The 1923 and 1924 general elections provide at best a weak test of how far blame and credit attaches to governments continuing a package of spending squeeze and tax cuts that they inherit from their predecessors. So it is by-elections from 1919 to 1922 and the 1922 general election that seem to present the most direct test, with the former accompanying the double hard squeeze and the early stages of the spending-only squeeze and the latter coming six months or so after the government had set in train dramatic spending cuts and announced future tax cuts.

Both of these electoral tests show outcomes consistent with the 'asymmetric credit and blame' hypothesis we discussed in Chapter One, namely that left-of-centre parties may tend to be punished more for spending cuts and rewarded less for tax cuts, while right-wing parties may tend to be punished more for tax increases and rewarded less for spending increases. In the by-elections, the party that seems to have suffered most from the voters from the double hard squeeze of 1919–21 was the Conservatives (as shown by the 1921 electoral appeal of the 'Anti-Waste League' in the south of England). And as we have shown in other work (Hood and Himaz (2014): 91) in the 1922 general election it was the National Liberals, that part of the Liberal Party that had been in the coalition government under David Lloyd George, that suffered the greatest electoral punishment, with the prime minister himself losing his seat, while the part of the Liberal Party that had not been in the government did not, and the Conservatives appear to have been rewarded.[12]

When it comes to other possible consequences of these squeezes, given that the period discussed here includes the only 'double hard' fiscal squeeze over the whole century, and one of the more severe spending squeezes outside the two post-world-war military demobilizations, there is a surprising absence of constitutional and major institutional effects directly attributable to these squeeze episodes. The institutional expedient of the Geddes Committee, as an outside body to recommend drastic spending cuts, served as a model for the

---

[12] After the election most of the Liberals re-formed into a single party under a different leader and fared better in the next election. But the Party then suffered a catastrophic decline in its vote after precipitating the fall of the first Labour Government in 1924, and was out of government at central level (other than as a minor partner in the 1931 emergency National Government and the World War II coalition) until 2010.

formation of a committee with an identical remit ten years later, albeit with some significant modifications, as we shall see in Chapter Four. Deep changes to the structure of the state or the delivery of public services are also hard to attribute to the squeezes over this period. It is true that the Geddes Committee came up with some radical restructuring proposals, such as the creation of a unified Ministry of Defence to replace the three ministries (Air, War Office, Admiralty) then responsible for separate fighting services, the dismantling of national public sector pay agreements in favour of local or regional variations, and radical alteration in the then national health insurance system by pushing most of the funding onto private or independent insurers. But none of these proposals survived the political process in 1921–22, and some have never been implemented up to the time of writing, despite regularly featuring in subsequent proposals for restructuring public services.

Other economic and social effects that might have flowed from the squeeze episodes discussed in this chapter include military rundown, arrested development of technical further education, and higher unemployment. But all of these are debatable too.

As for military rundown, both of the post-World War I squeeze episodes involved deep cuts in military spending, on the assumption that there would be no major war for ten years. Some (such as Wheeler-Bennett 1948 and Barnett 1970) have claimed that restraint on defence spending by successive governments in the interwar years left the UK militarily unprepared for war with a rearmed Nazi Germany in 1939, with a lack of up to date equipment and materiel that contributed to military failures in the early years of World War II and the UK's very narrow escape from defeat and invasion. But it seems more likely to have been continuing restraint on military spending after 1933, by which time Germany was spending three times as much as the UK on rearmament (Peden 1979: 7), that contributed most to this outcome. The unpreparedness problem seems less plausibly related to the military cuts in the immediate post-World War I years than to the failure to reverse those cuts in the early 1930s.

A second possible longer-term social effect of fiscal squeeze over this period is the 'Geddes Axe' suspension of plans for extending 14–18 technical education and the curbs imposed on other educational spending (a highly contested decision, as we saw earlier). Might the arrested development of technical and further education have exacerbated a long-term weakness in UK economic competitiveness relative to Germany and other competitor countries? Perhaps, but it is debatable whether it was spending cuts alone that had such an outcome (Barnard (1947): 274) as against deep-seated cultural and institutional factors that hampered such development, such as resistance by employers, parents' attitudes, and the lack of trained teachers (Curtis (1948): 246 and 251–7). Such cultural barriers are said to have still existed after the development of technical education formally resumed after the 1944 Education Act and indeed are often said to produce a bias towards 'academic' education to this day.

Finally, there is the common charge that at least the hard spending squeeze of 1922–25 and the last year or so of the double hard squeeze of 1919–21 could have exacerbated interwar mass unemployment. After all, both squeezes involved cutting spending and/or raising taxes in a recession—the precise opposite of the conventional Keynesian remedy for counter-cyclical fiscal policy, albeit championed again by advocates of monetary restraint in the 1980s and of 'expansionary contraction' in the 2010s.

As we saw earlier, there were practical difficulties in increasing borrowing at that time, given the very high level of post-war debt (whose servicing took up some 30 per cent or so of public spending) and high interest rates (in sharp contrast with the 2010s). It does seem likely that Austen Chamberlain's 1920 budget unintentionally served to increase unemployment, since it raised taxes and cut spending just as the economy plunged into deep recession. But things are more complicated when it comes to the 1922–25 episode of spending cuts accompanied by tax cuts, for two reasons. One is that it is difficult to separate the effects of cutting spending at that time from that of the currency exchange rate those spending cuts helped to prop up, and it has been argued (for instance by Temin (1976) and Eichengreen (2015)) that it was an overvalued exchange rate, rather than spending cuts as such, that most accounts for the UK's poor economic performance in the 1920s. The other is that it is debatable whether the strategy of cutting spending to cut taxes in 1922 went too far or not far enough. As we saw, there were reductions in income tax rates in 1922 to please middle-class voters, but there were no commensurate reductions in profits taxes which had risen so sharply in the World War I revenue squeeze, and Nason and Vahey (2007) argue that those high profits taxes are likely to have held back economic performance and employment during the interwar period, implying that taxes may have been cut too little rather than too much at that time.

Altogether, this qualitative analysis suggests there was both more and less to some of the apparently dramatic squeezes during this period than might appear at first sight, and that their consequences are remarkably hard to assess, even a century or so later.

Even the electoral effects are hard to show. But this analysis also shows the power of electoral politics in shaping fiscal squeeze policy, notably in the role of the Anti-Waste League in pushing the Lloyd George government from a double hard squeeze to a single hard expenditure squeeze.

# 4

# The 1930s Squeeze

## From Revenue Squeeze to Spending Squeeze via Political Crisis

### 4.1 Background: The Period in Perspective

Financial market upheavals played some part in most of the fiscal squeezes explored in this book. But (along with the mid-1970s and the period after 2008), the early 1930s stand out as a time when such upheavals were particularly dramatic and politicized. This squeeze episode occurred during a once-in-a-century world slump together with a global financial crisis that was arguably not equalled until 2008. And the market processes were politicized in that a narrative of an international 'bankers' ramp', forcing a weak, beleaguered Labour Government to abandon its socialist ambitions by cutting spending on welfare in a vain attempt to protect the currency, became the dominant account of this episode on the left of British politics for decades. And that dominant narrative arguably explains why the first enterprise to be nationalized by the 1945 Labour Government was the Bank of England (Williamson 1984: 770).

As Chapter Two showed, an analysis of reported financial outcomes reveals two different fiscal squeeze episodes in the 1930s. The first was a revenue squeeze originating in the 1930 budget, announced by the Labour Chancellor Philip Snowden and aimed at correcting what was seen at the time as a serious budget deficit. The second, originating in an emergency budget of September 1931, also announced by Philip Snowden as Chancellor, but by then operating within a three-party 'National Government', took the form of a squeeze on both spending and revenue, although not a 'double hard squeeze' on the criteria used in this book.

Britain's second Labour Government—like the first, a minority government and led by Ramsay MacDonald—took office in 1929. Only a few months later, a stock market crash in London preceded the biggest international market collapse in a century. Then, instead of a hoped-for quick recovery, a world depression ensued, with unemployment rising everywhere and prices falling. And in May 1931 Austria's largest bank collapsed, starting a European financial crisis in some ways redolent of what happened after 2008.

In contrast to the 'Geddes Axe' episode discussed in Chapter Three, when spending cuts were made on a budget already in balance, the UK government was running a deficit in 1931 (estimated at the time at about £170m,[1] or roughly 4 per cent of GDP, a figure that included a £70m deficit in its unemployment insurance fund as a result of mass unemployment). It also faced continuing severe pressures on the currency (which had been returned to the gold standard at the pre-World War I rate by the previous Conservative Government in 1925), with foreign investors withdrawing some £2.5m in gold per day at one point. That is why the often-overused term 'crisis', rather than merely 'stress', seems justified as a descriptor of the background to the squeeze in 1931.

Further, this period of fiscal squeeze seems to have produced more turmoil than any of our other specimens, producing political twists and turns redolent of some of the more dramatic eurozone fiscal squeezes of the 2010s, even though, as Chapter Two showed, it was by no means the deepest or longest over a century in the level of spending cutbacks or revenue increases achieved. Indeed, it is the only unambiguous case in this book where a government suddenly collapsed as a result of inability to agree on fiscal squeeze measures. Ramsay MacDonald's Labour cabinet agreed to substantial spending cuts and tax rises in August 1931, but collapsed after failing to finalize the package. What followed was the hasty formation (without an election) of an emergency coalition 'National Government' under the same Prime Minister and Chancellor, which proceeded to implement the fiscal squeeze measures the previous Labour cabinet had agreed on plus extra spending cuts that cabinet had been divided over. The emergency government then called a general election, which the coalition parties won by a landslide after asking the voters to grant them a 'Doctor's Mandate' to do whatever was needed to deal with the financial crisis.

As well as that remarkable electoral outcome, this episode produced a serious and long-lasting split in the Labour Party that had political significance for at least a generation, a constitutional crisis in which the political neutrality (or at least judgement) of the monarch was called into question, and

---

[1] According to retrospective data, the budget deficit was more moderate—some 1.6 per cent of GDP in 1932—and the public sector primary deficit was not in deficit but showed a surplus of some 7.6 per cent of GDP.

a mutiny in the armed forces over pay cuts leading to a financial market reaction that forced the currency off the gold standard.

## 4.2 What Triggered These Fiscal Squeezes

Like the succession of squeezes described in Chapter Three, the period covered here comprises a revenue squeeze later turning into a spending squeeze. But in contrast to the early 1920s, the switch to a spending squeeze in 1931 seems to have been triggered not so much by a tax revolt as by financial market pressures on government to balance its budget in a severe recession and maintain the exchange rate of its currency.

The minority Labour Government that presided over the first squeeze episode during this period came to office in 1929 after a general election, fought against the background of rising unemployment and bitter memories of a General Strike in 1926, had swept out the previous Conservative Government and led to a hung parliament. The Liberal Party, by then again led by David Lloyd George, held the balance of power in the House of Commons, but did not govern in formal coalition with Labour.

As well as depending on the Liberals for survival, the Labour Government was itself divided. Like some of their counterparts in the eurozone some eight decades later, several leading figures in the Labour cabinet, notably the prime minister and the Chancellor, Philip Snowden, believed the only feasible route to economic recovery and stability was through fiscal and monetary orthodoxy (that is, balanced budgets for all public spending other than defence, and the maintenance of fixed currency exchange rates through the gold standard to facilitate international trade). But others thought employment should be protected by spending funded by borrowing and/or by protectionist tariffs. Such divisions, coupled with dependence on the Liberals for the government's survival both meant that what might otherwise have been the 'normal' propensity of a left-of-centre government to increase public spending was muted and that when financial market pressure hit, pressure from other parties (particularly the Liberals) circumscribed the options available to the government.

When we look at the politics qualitatively and go beyond the reported financial outcomes we analysed in Chapter Two, we find three distinct phases of this fiscal squeeze period, namely (a) decisions made by the minority Labour Government up to the point when it split in August 1931 and was replaced without an election by a National Government under the same prime minister and Chancellor; (b) decisions about an emergency package of spending cuts and tax increases made by that National Government from its formation in late August up to a general election two months later; (c) the decisions made by the National Government subsequent to its landslide victory in the October 1931 election and prior to its re-election with a large though reduced majority four years later in 1935.

### 4.2.1 *Fiscal Squeeze and The Labour Government, 1931*

Labour's 1929 election manifesto[2] blamed the Conservatives for inaction in the face of recession and rising unemployment. It offered an 'unqualified pledge to deal immediately and practically' with unemployment, to improve unemployment benefits and pensions, extend social housing, abolish taxes on food and instead fund its programmes from higher taxes on the better-off, such as estate duties, extra taxes on higher incomes, and taxes on land values. The latter was a long-cherished policy aspiration of the left, which Snowden had tried to pursue during his brief Chancellorship in 1923–24 (Williamson (1992): 237).

But the Party's ability to deliver on these ambitious goals was limited both by its lack of a parliamentary majority, and by the economic crisis that accompanied the 1929 stock crash. The government's first budget statement in 1930 showed that the budget surplus for FY1929/30 envisaged by the previous Conservative Chancellor (Winston Churchill) had unexpectedly turned into a deficit of some £14m as a result of a collapse in tax revenues along with higher welfare spending. In response, the Chancellor retained the food taxes the 1929 Labour manifesto had pledged to remove, while increasing Beer Duty, raising the rate and progressivity of Estate Duty, increasing income tax on the highest incomes (formerly called 'supertax', now 'surtax') and putting up the standard rate of income tax while raising the threshold for that tax in a way designed to extract extra tax from only 25 per cent of taxpayers.[3] These post-election tax rises were intended to deliver a budget surplus in FY1930/31 and Snowden indicated that taxes would not be increased the following year.

But the government's finances remained precarious, and in February 1931 a currency crisis, combined with pressure from other parties, pushed the government into appointing a Committee on National Expenditure, redolent of the Geddes Committee of ten years earlier, and indeed with exactly the same formal terms of reference, but with at least two significant political differences, namely that it was not a response to an electoral threat posed by an anti-tax movement and that its membership consisted of two representatives of each of the three main political parties. The committee, which was chaired by Sir George (later Baron) May, a prominent business leader with experience in

---

[2] 1929 Labour Party manifesto, http://labourmanifesto.com/1929/1929-labour-manifesto.shtml.
[3] Financial Statement, HC Deb 14 April 1930, *c*.2676.

government during World War I,[4] started work almost at once and reported at the end of July, having split on party lines.

The Labour Government used the fact that the May Committee was at work on proposals for fiscal correction to justify a do-nothing stance in its April 1931 budget. The Chancellor offered a relatively optimistic view of the likely deficit in FY 1931/32 and neither cut spending nor raised taxes, apart from an increase in the tax on petrol (gasoline) and the announcement of another plan for a land values tax. But three months later, the May Committee majority report (disowned by the two Labour representatives on the committee) painted a dark picture of the fiscal situation and recommended swingeing public spending cuts to balance the budget, with about half of the savings coming from cuts in unemployment benefit and increased social security contributions (a tax increase in all but name).

The Labour Government set up an 'economy committee' of cabinet ministers to respond to these politically challenging proposals and that committee was due to meet on 25 August. But that timetable was overtaken by another currency crisis, itself partly caused by what critics saw as the excessively bleak account of the government's financial position that the May Committee's majority report had given to make the case for urgent and drastic corrective action. So instead of a cabinet committee, debate over what to do about May's proposals took place in prolonged meetings of the whole cabinet for five successive days in August. On 24 August the cabinet split 9–11 after a deadlock over proposed cuts in unemployment benefit as part of the spending cuts package, after which the prime minister, Ramsay MacDonald, offered his resignation to King George V.

Precisely what package of spending cuts and tax rises the Labour cabinet had agreed to before 24 August became heavily disputed in the 'blame game' that followed the fall of that government. Although the Trades Union Congress had opposed all cuts to public sector pay as well as welfare benefits, the Labour cabinet was said to have agreed to public sector salary cuts, including staged cuts in the then civil service 'bonus'.[5] Indeed, after the fall of the Labour Government, both Ramsay MacDonald and Arthur Henderson (the new leader of the Labour Party, now leader of the Opposition) said the Labour cabinet had agreed to a package of spending cuts of about £56m (as against the £70m proposed by the National Government just over a fortnight later).[6]

---

[4] Sir George May (1871–1946) was Secretary of the Prudential Assurance Company up to retirement in 1931 and had been Manager of the American Dollars Security Committee during World War I. In 1932 the National Government appointed him chair of the Import Duties Advisory Committee, overseeing the introduction of general tariffs.

[5] *Memorandum on the Measures Proposed by His Majesty's Government to Secure Reductions in National Expenditure*, Cmd 3952 1931, London, HMSO: 3.

[6] HC Deb 8 September 1931, *c*.32 and 256.

MacDonald also claimed that the Labour Government had contemplated a tax squeeze package greater than the £80m later proposed by the National Government, though a senior Labour figure, George Lansbury (who had been a minister and later became leader of the Party), denied that the Cabinet had agreed to extra taxes on tea and sugar.[7]

### 4.2.2 The National Government 'Emergency' Period, August to October 1931

The second phase of this fiscal squeeze period began after the Labour Government was replaced without an election by an all-party National Government. That emergency government, comprising a cabinet of just ten members, was headed by Ramsay MacDonald, the former Labour prime minister, who had been importunately called by King George V to form a new government to deal with the financial crisis. That government, drawn from the three major parties but dominated by the Conservatives under Stanley Baldwin, included Philip Snowden, the former Labour Chancellor of the Exchequer, who remained at the Treasury. The formation of the emergency National Government exposed the King to political criticism from the left, who argued that (in contrast to other cases where the monarch merely ratifies decisions already agreed among political parties) the monarch had in this case exercised choice and influence in an unavoidably party-political move which seriously split the Labour Party (see, for example, Moodie (1957); Marshall and Moodie (1964): 64–6; Bassett (1958); Williamson (1984); Bogdanor (1991)).

Once appointed, the new National Government presented itself as acting in 'emergency mode' to deal with the crisis. It rapidly issued a White Paper proposing some £80m of extra taxes and £70m of spending cuts to correct the budget deficit.[8] And—far from following the 'Geddes' policy mentioned in Chapter Three, of concentrating on cuts that could be implemented without legislation—it introduced an omnibus 'National Economy Bill' to put spending cuts rapidly into effect, by in effect overriding the normal legislative process. That Bill provided for Orders-in-Council (edicts of the Privy Council, a relic of monarchical government and normally used as a method of secondary legislation in exercising detailed powers under statute or bringing provisions of statutes into effect) to change existing legislation, those Orders having the effect of an Act of Parliament and only able to be changed by further legislation. The new government justified this draconian approach as a necessary response to severe financial emergency, enabling changes such as

---

[7] Debate on the Second Reading of the National Economy Bill, HC Deb 11 September 1931, cc.424–5.
[8] *Memorandum on the Measures Proposed by His Majesty's Government to Secure Reductions in National Expenditure*, Cmd 3952 1931, London: HMSO.

pay cuts in the public services to be made quickly and equitably across multiple policy domains. But the use of Orders-in-Council to supersede Acts of Parliament was of course contested by the Labour opposition as unwarrantably overriding normal parliamentary procedure.

These measures were introduced in a political atmosphere seething with bitterness and rancour. The bulk of the Labour Party stayed out of the National Government under a new leader (Arthur Henderson), and the Party expelled MacDonald immediately on the formation of the National Government. MacDonald and his Labour colleagues who supported the National Government came to be denounced as 'traitors' to the Labour cause by their erstwhile party companions, and MacDonald's accounts of decisions made under the previous Labour Government were fiercely contested.

On top of the spending cuts agreed by the Labour cabinet in August 1931, the National Government proceeded to implement the most politically contentious measure that had split that cabinet, namely a cut in unemployment benefits at a time of mass unemployment. But one of the main justifications given for crossing that political Rubicon and making those cuts—to maintain the exchange rate of the currency—was superseded within weeks. On 21 September the pound was forced off the gold standard as a result of the National Government's handling of a naval mutiny in protest against public sector pay cuts, which occurred in the warships stationed at Invergordon in Scotland. On the second day of that mutiny, the National Government announced that pay cuts for the lower ranks of the armed services (along with teachers and police) would be limited to no more than 10 per cent. That announcement spooked the financial markets to the point that the pound was forced off the gold standard and began to 'float', enabling devaluation to take place.

### 4.2.3 The National Government after the General Election of October 1931

The National Government formed in August 1931 had been presented as an emergency administration, aiming to balance the budget and restore confidence in the financial markets before dissolving itself and calling a general election. But that coalition split over the issue of whether to go into that election asking for a mandate for introducing protective tariffs to raise revenue and support domestic industry (a measure opposed by many of the Liberals in the coalition). The parties in the coalition could only agree to go into the October 1931 general election by asking for a so-called 'Doctor's Mandate' to do what was necessary, with each of the parties campaigning under its own manifesto.

Of the parties opposing the National Government in that post-squeeze election, the Labour Party campaigned on a manifesto that endorsed balanced budgets and free trade, but opposed cuts in unemployment benefit and called for nationalization of banks, energy, transport, and iron and steel as part of a programme of 'socialist reconstruction'.[9] The non-coalition Liberals split into two parties, because they were divided both over protectionism and over support or opposition to the National Government.

That general election produced a seismic electoral change. Far from being retrospectively punished by voters for the major expenditure and revenue squeeze measures it had announced the previous month or for its failure to maintain the gold standard that the squeeze was supposedly designed to secure, the National Government secured the greatest landslide in any UK general election to date. The coalition parties together won 556 seats in the House of Commons, against forty-six won by the section of the Labour Party that had stayed out of the National Government and thirty-five by the two different sections of the Liberal Party that opposed the coalition. That result was a disaster for the main group of the Labour Party, which lost 231 seats compared to those the Party had won in 1929, and the overwhelming gainers were the Conservatives, who won over two hundred extra seats. With both of the left-of-centre parties (Liberal and Labour) split over support or opposition to the National Government, the 'National Labour' group led by Ramsay MacDonald, the prime minister, won a mere thirteen seats, while the 'National Liberal' group (the group of Liberals willing to accept protective tariffs) led by Sir John Simon won thirty-five.

Even though the Conservatives after the election comprised by far the largest party in the National Government, Ramsay MacDonald remained prime minister for the rest of this fiscal squeeze episode, continuing in office until 1935 when he was replaced by Stanley Baldwin, the Conservative leader, six months before the general election of that year. By contrast, the Labour Chancellor of the Exchequer, Philip Snowden, who had remained in place under the National Government at its formation in August 1931 and introduced the dramatic budget that implemented the cuts in September 1931, did not contest his parliamentary seat in the general election of the following month—making this fiscal squeeze episode the most prominent case in the book of a political career-ending event for a Chancellor. Snowden was succeeded as Chancellor by the Conservative leader Stanley Baldwin, and thereafter played a marginal role in the government as Lord Privy Seal before resigning in protest over the introduction of tariffs.

Having put together its emergency fiscal squeeze package before the election, the National Government proceeded to implement it over the next two years, which included a second stage of public sector pay cuts, but two years

---

[9] 1931 Labour Party Manifesto, 'Labour's Call to Action: the Nation's Opportunity', http://labourmanifesto.com/1931/1931-labour-manifesto.shtml.

later, in July 1934, half of those pay cuts were reversed and the remainder of those pay cuts were reversed the following July, a few months ahead of the 1935 general election.[10]

## 4.3 Blame Politics and Blame Avoidance

The 'blame politics' and blame avoidance strategies adopted during the time of this fiscal squeeze episode were complex, and it is necessary to distinguish between the short-term assignment of blame and the longer-term 'narrative' surrounding this episode. As noted at the outset, some of the key figures from the period of the minority Labour Government blamed this episode on a 'bankers' ramp', in the form of deliberate pressure by the Bank of England and other financiers for the reversal of hard-won welfare measures. For example, echoing numerous other similar claims by Labour MPs in the September 1931 Economy Bill debate, the Labour MP Fenner Brockway asserted, 'it is not a National Government. It is in reality a bankers' Government and it is merely carrying out the interests of the financial classes.'[11] Some Labour politicians blamed the other parties on which the Labour Government depended for survival for demanding unnecessary cuts, some blamed the civil service for proposing politically unpalatable spending cuts, and others blamed the King for his actions after MacDonald resigned in August 1931, in replacing the Labour Government with a National Government under the same prime minister without an election. As we have already noted, MacDonald and his 'National Labour' group were blamed by trade union leaders and the Labour ministers who did not join the National Government as 'class traitors' who had betrayed the Labour movement by siding with right-wing parties to cut working-class living standards. Others blamed those leaders for pursuing misguided policies of financial orthodoxy that were ineffective or even counterproductive in relation to the economic benefits they were intended to secure (not even succeeding in maintaining the gold standard).

On the other side, MacDonald and his National Government colleagues blamed the previous Labour Government for dithering in a crisis, failing to take the decisive measures needed to stabilize the public finances in an emergency, and then passing the buck for making unpopular choices to others. And as already noted, key blame issues also turned on precisely what had been decided by the Labour Government before it left office on 23 August 1931 and what was decided after that date by the National Government. A case in point was that of wage cuts for War Department industrial (blue-collar) civil servants,

[10] HC Deb 2 May 1934, c.313; also T160 566 'Estimates 1933 and 1934 etc.'.
[11] HC Deb 11 September 1931, c.460.

for which the May Committee had recommended the abolition of a preferential bonus scheme, on the grounds that the scheme gave more than the 'fair wages' principle demanded (that pay and conditions for such employees should not be inferior to those operating in the most comparable industry (Committee on National Expenditure (1931), para 91)). In 1934 a leading Labour politician associated with the National Union of General and Municipal Workers, John Richard Clynes (who had been Home Secretary in the minority Labour Government and who Ramsay MacDonald had defeated for the Labour leadership in 1921) claimed these pay cuts were an act of the National Government, while MacDonald asserted that the decision to withdraw the bonus had been approved by the Labour cabinet of which Clynes had himself been a member.[12]

In the short-run, the massive defeat of the bulk of the Labour Party in the 1931 general election suggests that at the time of the crisis many voters were more convinced by the second set of blame arguments than the first. But over time, as many commentators (such as Wrigley 2013) have observed, the first set of blame arguments became strongly entrenched in the Labour Party as a dominant narrative, and indeed in this case it could be said that the history was more written by the losers than by the winners of the struggles of August and September 1931.

Institutionally, the blame politics of this episode looks at first sight similar to that of the 1923–25 Geddes Axe period, in that the job of evaluating and proposing fiscal squeeze and other measures to deal with the crisis was passed out to a committee of 'experts', though in this case two such committees with overlapping briefs figured in the process. One was a committee composed mainly of economists (the Macmillan Committee), formed in 1929 when the financial crisis first broke, and commissioned to explore measures to deal with the economic depression. The other (the May Committee) was a Committee on National Expenditure formed by the Labour Government in early 1931, as already mentioned. But in contrast to the Geddes Committee, both of these committees split, the second seriously.

The May Committee, as noted earlier, was effectively forced on the minority Labour Government in February 1931 by motions put down in the House of Commons by Liberals and Conservatives calling on the government immediately to appoint a 'small and independent committee to make recommendations to the Chancellor of the Exchequer for effecting forthwith all practicable and legitimate reductions in the national expenditure consistent with the efficiency of the services.' The Committee was given a brief identical to that

---

[12] Memo '60/Factories/1553' dated 12.2.1934 in WO 32/3404 Factories: Royal Ordnance (Code 49 (A)): Wage cuts as the result of the recommendations of the Committee on National Expenditure 1931.

of the Geddes Committee ten years before,[13] and like the Geddes Committee it was an all-male group composed largely of individuals with a business background (accountants, bankers, actuaries) and experience of service in government (plus one trade union leader). But its political composition was very different. The three main party leaders agreed on who should be asked to chair the committee (Sir George May) and each party then nominated two people from outside the House of Commons to serve on the committee, making the Committee both larger and more overtly partisan than the Geddes Committee had been.[14]

The political outcome of the May Committee's work was also different from that of the Geddes Committee in at least two ways. While the Geddes Committee seems to have helped to prop up the Lloyd George coalition over some politically difficult months in 1921–22, the May Committee arguably hastened the demise of the Labour Government because its predictions of the scale of the budget deficit (said by its critics to have been exaggerated for dramatic effect to underpin its recommendations of cuts in social security spending, and thereby to deter the Labour cabinet from watering down its proposals) had the effect of alarming the financial markets to such an extent that the cabinet was forced to respond quickly to its proposals in the middle of a financial crisis. Second, while the Geddes Committee produced an agreed report, the May Committee split on party lines. The committee (perhaps surprisingly) agreed on its gloomy estimate of the size of the budget deficit; where it disagreed was on how to reduce that deficit. The Committee's majority report advocated widespread spending cuts, but a minority report largely reflecting the views of the TUC and written by the two Labour appointees on the Committee (Charles Latham, a London Labour councillor and Arthur Pugh, leader of the steelworkers' trade union) took a different tack. That minority report accepted the need for some spending cuts, but (arguably outside the committee's brief to recommend spending cuts) called for more emphasis on a revenue squeeze directed at the better off, particularly through higher taxes on holders of fixed-interest securities who had benefited from deflation.

As well as the way the politics of the national expenditure committee played out, there are other notable differences in the way blame for fiscal squeeze was handled in this episode as against the squeezes of the 1920s. First, as we have seen, after the collapse of the Labour Government in August 1931, the subsequent episode of mixed revenue and spending squeeze was carried through by a coalition formed explicitly for the purpose of dealing with the national finances, originally on an emergency basis to be followed by a swift general

---

[13] T160/398 Committee on National Expenditure 1931.
[14] The seven members were Sir George May (Chairman), Ashley Cooper, Sir Mark Webster Jenkinson, Charles Latham, Lord Plender, Arthur Pugh, and Sir Thomas Royden.

election. Second, the squeeze package that the National Government produced in its budget of September 1931 was presented as a temporary, time-limited emergency response, not a permanent policy shift.

Third, much more emphasis than in the 1920s was laid on a rhetorical theme of 'equal sacrifice' across the country, with all citizens represented as 'in it together' in facing tax rises and spending cuts. 'Equality of sacrifice' was the central theme in a parliamentary statement by Ramsay MacDonald in September 1931, and the term became a catchphrase in political debate. Even the Civil List (the allowance made to the monarch) and the costs of running the then Royal Yacht, *Victoria and Albert*, were pointedly cut to demonstrate 'equality of sacrifice'. This ponderous vessel had a crew of no less than 380 and cost some £75,000 a year to run, despite the King's 'notorious dislike of going abroad', and it was agreed to cut the costs by £5000 a year by taking six of the ship's eighteen boilers out of service (thus cutting its speed) and reducing the crew by roughly 10 per cent by not filling vacancies.[15]

## 4.4 Winners and Losers: What Was Spared and What Was Sacrificed

As we have seen, the period covered by this chapter began with a hard revenue squeeze initiated by the minority Labour Government's 1930 budget. In that budget, the Labour Government chose to lay aside (or postpone) its manifesto pledges of the previous year by retaining the food taxes it had promised to abolish, while steeply raising direct taxes. After the Labour Government had fallen in August 1931, the National Government's emergency budget introduced the following month comprised further significant increases both in direct and indirect taxes. The standard rate of income tax was raised by another 6d in the £ (meaning it had risen by some 20 per cent in total between April 1930 and September 1931), while tax allowances were cut,[16] and at the same time indirect taxes were increased on a range of items, including not only beer, tobacco, and petrol but also tea and sugar—staples of those who were in 'food poverty' at that time and which the Labour Party had promised to cut.

On the spending side, the planned cuts announced in a White Paper by the National Government in September 1931[17] amounted to some £70m, rather less than the May Committee had recommended. Half of that sum comprised

---

[15] See T161 538 May Committee 1931.

[16] Finance Bill 1931 Clause 6 (Increase in standard rate of income tax for 1931–32), HC Deb 30 September 1931, c.423–30.

[17] *Memorandum on the Measures Proposed by His Majesty's Government to Secure Reductions in National Expenditure*, Cmd 3952 1931, London: HMSO.

cuts in spending on unemployment benefits and increases in compulsory National Insurance contributions from employers and workers. Of the remainder, the biggest single cut was in spending on education (over £10m), reflected in relatively deep cuts in teachers' pay (15 per cent, as against the 20 per cent the May Committee had recommended) and reductions in grant funding for all levels of education, with spending reductions for England and Wales automatically triggering a reduction of 11/80th of the grants made for Scotland under the territorial funding formula that applied at that time. After education, a major reduction in spending on roads accounted for over 10 per cent of the total cuts package, and that was followed by a series of smaller savings across the whole range of public services, including some £4.5m from reductions in pay of government ministers, MPs, judges, civil servants, and members of the defence forces.

That spending cuts package was distinctive in at least two ways. One is that, apart from cuts in pay of the armed services (which provoked the Invergordon naval mutiny and was said to have broken a tradition that the pay of service personnel should not be reduced during the period of their service), only 10 per cent or so of the package came from defence cuts, in contrast to what happened in the 1920s or the 1940s. A senior Treasury civil servant observed, 'The fact is that the [May] Economy Committee were hard put to it to discover any outstanding economies in the Fighting Services.'[18] So these cuts fell largely on civilian expenditure and the welfare state.

Second, in contrast to all the other episodes considered in this book, both public sector wages (including police and industrial civil servants such as those working in the Ordnance factories) and welfare benefits were cut in absolute terms for a period of years, as an emergency measure. Rates of welfare benefit for the unemployed were cut by 10 per cent (the issue that broke the minority Labour Government, though that government had evidently been prepared to consider extended means-testing and changes in qualifying periods for benefit), while rates of contributions to the Unemployment Fund from employers, employees, and government were steeply raised. In addition, unemployment benefit from the (contributions based) Insurance Fund was limited to six months in any 'benefit year', with claimants thereafter having to prove continued unemployment and undergo a 'needs test' assessed by the

[18] 'Remarks of the Services Departments etc. on the Recommendations of the Committee on National Expenditure', memo to Sir Richard Hopkins dated 12 August 1931 from A.P. Waterfield, Treasury; T161/494 Finance accounts general: May Committee on Economy 1931; Fighting Departments Economies. The May Committee had floated the idea of a contributory pension fund for the armed forces, rather than funding pensions out of general taxation. But that proposal was easy for the Service departments to resist, since a Royal Commission had recently recommended against establishing a contributory pension scheme for the civil service.

Public Assistance Authority before further benefits could be paid from general tax funds.

As for public sector wages, the National Government decided to cut all public service salaries from October 1931, but with proportionately higher cuts applying to those earning higher salaries. Government Ministers' salaries were accordingly cut by between 10 and 20 per cent (according to their individual salary level). Something similar applied to officers in the armed services and to civil servants, with cuts of 10 per cent in the highest salaries but proportionately less for those earning less (in the case of the civil service, the 10 per cent cut applied to salaries of over £1000 a year, 5 per cent on salaries between £200 and £1000, and less than 5 per cent on salaries of less than £200). These public sector wage cuts, which were imposed in two stages in most cases, were presented as 'emergency reductions' and indeed half of those temporary pay cuts were restored less than three years later, in July 1934.[19]

For local government services, cuts were made to pay for those local officers of services financed by percentage grants from central government, and to the pay of doctors and pharmacists operating under the then National Health Insurance scheme (the precursor of the National Health Service). Apart from that, no explicit targets for pay reduction were set by central government: there were general exhortations to other local government officers 'to make their contribution in the present emergency' and to each local authority to review and rein in their spending 'till better times'.[20]

Despite the lofty 'equality of sacrifice' rhetoric, many argued that the sacrifices made were anything but equal in practice, and that equal percentage cuts in salaries and benefits did not necessarily represent 'equality' in other important senses. Indeed, the archival record is full of wrangling about the small print of who was to sacrifice what, and the detailed implementation of the pay cuts across the public services evidently did not always square with those 'equal sacrifice' pledges. There were inevitably complexities arising from prior agreements, pension entitlements, and other elements of reward. For example, police pensions, pension entitlement, and pensionable pay were not actually cut at all, despite serious concerns expressed by the May Committee about the financial consequences of what they saw as a dangerous pension 'time-bomb' building up in the police force.[21] And there were numerous hard cases, particularly relating to more powerful groups in the public service, such

[19] T160 566 (Estimates 1933 and 1934).

[20] Ministry of Health circular 1222 to local authorities, 11 September 1931, HO 185 76, Reduction of Expenditure in State Management districts.

[21] The May Committee proposed to reduce the pensionable salaries of all constables and sergeants, and called for the right of voluntary early retirement on 2/3rds pay after twenty-five years of service (thirty in Scotland) to be withdrawn from existing police officers over a period, with retirement no longer permitted before the age of fifty.

as munitions factory workers. For example, there was a mighty battle between the Treasury and the Home Office over the imposition of the second stage of a 10 per cent cut in police pay in 1932. The police were a sensitive case, given their importance in maintaining public order (after all, the General Strike of 1926 was still fresh in memory at that time, and there had been a major police strike only a decade or so before in 1919). The pay of serving police officers had been cut by 5 per cent in October 1931 as an initial response (that of new entrants had been cut considerably more), but during a parliamentary debate on the omnibus bill that gave effect to the cuts in 1931, the Home Secretary had suggested that 'administrative economies' in the police budget might be used to offset the need for further police pay cuts,[22] and accordingly the Home Office argued strongly the following year for setting of the second stage of the police pay cut against 'administrative economies'.[23] But despite the political sensitivity of imposing sacrifices on the police, this proposal was resisted, since ministers presiding over 10 per cent pay cuts in other departments (notably those in the Defence Departments, who were conscious of the Invergordon naval mutiny against pay cuts the previous year) were unwilling to agree special terms for the police.

## 4.5 Conclusions

As mentioned at the outset, this episode is the most dramatic of the fiscal squeezes considered in this book in terms of its political impact, and there is a sizeable literature on the politics and constitutional issues of the late summer of 1931. As with the previous chapter, we conclude by returning to the three sets of issues raised in the opening chapter about the politics of fiscal squeeze.

### 4.5.1 *Tax and Spending, Depth and Duration, Blame and Control*

The squeezes discussed in this chapter comprise a two-year hard revenue squeeze initiated by a minority left-of-centre government and a three-year hard spending squeeze partly initiated by that left-of-centre party but extended and implemented by a multiparty coalition dominated by a right-of-centre party.

As we have seen, the relative balance of tax increases and spending cuts to correct the perceived deficit was much debated in this episode, particularly

---

[22] Home Office memo to the Cabinet Sub-Committee on Police Economies [undated] MEPO 5 294, Reduction of Police Expenditures.
[23] Memorandum by Sir Warren Fisher, 5 September 1932, 'Police Pay Cut' in T162 287 on Police Pay Reductions following the May Committee report.

within the Labour Party. The debate also focused on what kind of taxes—and taxpayers—should be targeted for a revenue squeeze, with the left resisting increases in indirect taxes on staples and insurance contributions from employees and calling for higher taxes on upper-level incomes, 'unearned' income and inherited wealth. On the expenditure side, one of the things we noted earlier about this episode is the relatively small proportion of spending cuts that came from defence (but even that provoked a naval mutiny that forced the government to soften its position on public sector pay cuts) and the correspondingly large proportion of the cuts that came from social security and education. Another striking feature on the spending side was the fact that most of the spending cuts (especially on public sector pay and benefits) were explicitly presented as time-limited and applying for a limited period, rather than (as in some episodes we will discuss later in the book) part of a longer-term project to shrink the state or at least check the long-term growth of state spending.

When it comes to choices over blame and control, minority and coalition governments dominated this episode, making blame attribution harder than under majority government. And as we saw, there was both a short-term blame game over who had agreed to what spending cuts at what precise time in August and September 1931 and a longer-term narrative battle over the merits of the September 1931 measures enacted by the emergency National Government. And as in the previous episode, an 'expert committee' (indeed, two in this case) figured in the blame politics of the process, having been handed the poisoned chalice of identifying a spending cuts package, but with composition and outcomes different from those observed in Chapter Three, in that the committee was formed and split on party lines and seems to have become part of the problem it was intended to solve by the effects of its estimate of the size of the deficit on the financial markets.

### 4.5.2 Loss, Cost, and Effort Involved in These Episodes

Following our analysis in the previous chapter, Table 4.1 sketches out our assessment of the extent of loss imposed on citizens and voters, the extent of reputational cost and stress incurred by governing politicians, and the degree of effort exerted from the state machine in handling fiscal squeeze.

The 1931/32 to 1932/33 episode is notable for the high political cost incurred by the governing politicians in the minority Labour Government, as they coped with serious party splits and faced the abandonment of cherished policy goals and election promises. Arguably, those high political costs continued for those Labour politicians (such as Philip Snowden) who joined the National Government in August 1931, and that is why we show political costs separately for different parties in that coalition in Table 4.1. The losses

**Table 4.1.** A qualitative classification of imposed loss, political cost, and state effort associated with 1930s fiscal squeezes

| | Low | Moderate | High | Overall classification |
|---|---|---|---|---|
| **1931–32. Squeeze type: Hard Revenue** | | | | |
| Labour 5/1929–8/1931 | | | | |
| Loss | | [3] | [1] | High |
| Cost | | | [1] | High |
| Effort | | | [1], [4] | High |
| National government (non-elected) 8/1931–10/1931 | | | | |
| Loss | | | [1] | High |
| Cost (Cons and Lib) | | [1], [3] | | Moderate |
| Cost (Labour rump) | | | [1] | High |
| Effort | | [1], [2], [3] | | Moderate |
| National government 10/1931– end of episode | | | | |
| Loss | | | [1], [2], [3] | High |
| Cost | [1], [2], [4] | | | Low |
| Effort | | | [1] | High |
| **1933–35 Squeeze Type: Hard Expenditure** | | | | |
| National government (elected 10/1931) | | | | |
| Loss | [3] | [2] | [1] | Mod/High |
| Cost | [1], [2], [4] | | | Low |
| Effort | [1], [2], [3] | | | Low |

*Note*: Numbers in square brackets refer to categories in Table 1.2, Chapter One.

imposed in the tax squeeze were relatively high too, but much of the extra burden fell on the top 25 per cent of income earners, as we saw. The state machine was exposed both to high effort from managing the financial crisis and preparing new policy machinery (for example, for Snowden's plans for a land values tax) and indeed over the role of the monarch in helping to engineer a change of government without a general election (seriously splitting the Labour Party in the process), which exposed the state machine to constitutional crisis and not just administrative effort.

For the 1933/34 to 1935/36 spending squeeze episode, losses imposed on citizens and voters seem to have been relatively high as well on the criteria set out in Table 1.2 in Chapter One, for example, with the cut in unemployment benefits, pay cuts across the public sector, and the heavy cuts in education spending. And there was certainly non-fiscal austerity in the form of mass unemployment. But as we have seen, the spending cuts were presented and planned as temporary emergency measures, and in contrast to the earlier 1930s episode, they were accompanied by relatively loose monetary policy that to some extent offset the fiscal austerity and has been argued by scholars such as Nicholas Crafts to have been very important in mitigating the effects of recession (see Crafts and Fearon (2010); Middleton (2010): 414–41). The political costs incurred by governing politicians over this period were variable (higher in the emergency period of the autumn of 1931 than after the general election, higher for the rump of ex-Labour ministers than for those from other parties), but for the period and the governing group as a whole seem to have been relatively low, in the sense that election promises did not have to be broken and there was a ready-made political scapegoat in the blame game. Nor does this episode seem to have produced notable effort on the part of the state machine, a point on which we comment in section 4.5.3.

### 4.5.3 Electoral and Other Consequences: Turkeys Voting for Christmas?

This squeeze period seems to be a critical case for the electoral politics of fiscal squeeze. As we have seen, it helped to produce the greatest ever general election landslide in modern British electoral politics in October 1931, even though the Conservatives and the other parties in the National Government had just announced major cuts to welfare benefits, public servants' pay, and other key items of public spending that would impact significantly on a large mass of voters. Far from being punished by those voters for those measures which were fresh in memory, as the standard version of 'retrospective voting' theory might suggest, the Conservative Party won some 55 per cent of the popular vote and gained over two hundred seats, while the Labour Party was punished rather than rewarded for not applying a painful fiscal squeeze, losing over two hundred seats.

That outcome has to be qualified in two ways. First, we can only say that fiscal squeeze 'helped to produce' this outcome, because fiscal squeeze, although undeniably a key element, was not the only major issue in play in this watershed election. Indeed, an element of 'heresthetic', discussed in Chapter One, clearly applied here, because cutting across the fiscal squeeze versus expansionism issue, was the Conservatives' campaign for the introduction of tariffs to protect British industry and employment, which seems to have been a factor in that party's electoral victory. But given that there is no opinion poll data from that period we cannot assess the relative effect of the fiscal squeeze and tariff issues on the voters' choices.

Second, it might be argued that the key test of retrospective voting might lie in the general election after the squeezes had been *applied* rather than the one immediately after they had been *announced* and begun to take effect. And indeed, if we take that post-squeeze general election, which was held in November 1935, we do see a clear swing (just over 7 per cent) from the Conservatives to Labour (with the former losing some eighty-three seats and the latter gaining 103), while MacDonald's National Labour group was reduced to a mere eight and MacDonald lost his own seat. That result is more compatible with the orthodox 'punishment' view. But even so, the Conservatives were comfortably re-elected, with a majority of 161 over all other parties in the legislature, even leaving aside their remaining forty-one

Labour and Liberal allies in the National Government. Accordingly, the biggest post-squeeze electoral punishment was suffered by MacDonald's own Labour group.

Going beyond electoral consequences, the policy impact of this squeeze has been much debated by historians, with a range of different 'narratives' and interpretations of the merits or otherwise of the tax rises and spending cuts adopted in this episode. Advocates of Keynesian economic policy, notably Robert (Lord) Skidelsky (1967), see fiscal squeeze in the 1930s as a classic case of misguided policy response to depression and financial crisis. But others have offered a more 'revisionist' position, notably Ross McKibbin (1975; 1990), who argues that a full-blown Keynesian approach was not a practicable policy option for the UK at that time, because the state did not have the necessary administrative capacity, such that the real options available to the minority Labour Government came down to 'drift' (the approach it followed in its do-nothing April 1931 budget) or 'deflation' (the approach taken by the emergency National Government in the September 1931 budget) and that by sticking too long to the 'drift' option the Labour Government brought about its own collapse.

Others have argued that the Treasury's position in resisting Keynesian-style ideas in favour of financial orthodoxy was more defensible in the circumstances of the time than the standard Keynesian critique had allowed for, and that given the scale and nature of unemployment at that time the loan-financed public works programmes then being advocated by Lloyd George and others would have been ineffective or even counterproductive if they had been implemented (Williamson (1992): 9–10; Middleton (1982); Booth and Glyn (1975)). In short, the 'battle of the narratives' among economic historians of this period has produced a far from clear-cut outcome.

Further, picking up a point mentioned in section 4.5.2, although this fiscal squeeze clearly combined high political drama with some very long-lasting party-political effects, it is much less clear that it produced any significant once-for-all reshaping of the state or of the way public services were delivered. As we have seen, the 'emergency cuts' focusing on reductions in unemployment benefits and public officials' salaries were reversed after a few years. Some cherished policy initiatives ground to a halt for some time, such as the provisions of the minority Labour Government's 1930 Housing Act that required local authorities to draw up plans for slum clearance (Mowat (1968): 340–2). But the relationship between central and local government and between business and the state did not fundamentally alter, and nor did the basic structure of the developing welfare state or the bureaucracy. For example, in contrast to the 2010s, no plans were announced for increasing the age of old-age pension entitlement or for widespread privatization or outsourcing.

It is true that in the archive records of discussions about economies, there are one or two references to automation and new technology in public services as a possible route to lowering costs, for example, by traffic lights to replace the earlier and costlier system of police officers on 'point duty' directing traffic by hand at busy road junctions[24] and a Treasury injunction to government departments to reduce costs by making more use of the infant office-automation technology of that era.[25] But if necessity is the mother of invention, not much invention, in the sense of dramatically new ways of delivering public services, seems to have ensued in this period.

In short, the clearest consequence of this squeeze episode seems to have been political, in the sense of a serious split in the Labour Party, with effects that lingered for decades, as we shall see in later chapters—for instance, in the choice of the Bank of England as the first institution to be nationalized by the first majority Labour Government in 1945 (following the 'bankers' ramp' narrative of the 1931 crisis developed by George Lansbury and others), in the battles over that Labour Government's fiscal squeeze in the late 1940s, and even over the handling of social security benefits in the fiscal squeeze applied by a later Labour Government in the 1970s.

---

[24] Minutes of a meeting of the Consultative Committee of the Police Council on Administrative Measures of Economy, held at the Home Office on 21 October 1931, item 6. 'Point Duty', MEPO 5 294, Reduction of Police Expenditures.

[25] Treasury Circular No 12/32, 15 July 1932, 'Administrative Costs'.

# 5

# World War II and Post-War Labour Austerity

## 5.1 Background: The Period in Perspective

This chapter explores a long period of fiscal squeeze stretching from the formation of the World War II Churchill coalition government in 1940 (comprising the three main parties, Labour, Liberal, and Conservative) to the final years of the Labour Government that won a landslide victory in the post-war 1945 general election. The World War II coalition government imposed a revenue squeeze not matched in any of our other episodes to pay for the war—including development of mass income taxation, a broad sales tax with variable rates on different goods, and confiscatory top tax rates. Along with those tax increases went a Soviet-style command economy and reduced spending on many civilian services such as road-building, together with vertiginous increases in defence spending.

Further, on top of that fiscal squeeze went a high degree of non-fiscal austerity. Conscription began for single men in their early twenties shortly before the war but extended by 1942 to include all men between eighteen and fifty-one and women between twenty and thirty who were unmarried or had no children. Government rationed scarce goods, beginning with petrol at the outset of war and by 1942 extending to almost all foods except vegetables and bread (Zweiniger-Bargielowska (2002)).

As in World War I, those exposed to these squeezes also temporarily lost the right to vote out the government in general elections, with no such elections during the war and electoral competition among the main political parties largely suspended.[1] But during the war the three main parties in the coalition all committed themselves to several 'jam tomorrow' promises to the voters that implied steep rises in post-war spending on civilian public services.

---

[1] Under electoral law a general election was due by 1940 but general elections were suspended by legislation each year from 1940 to 1944, with almost no dissent expressed in Parliament.

The fiscal squeeze imposed by the post-war majority Labour Government included continuation of very high levels of direct and indirect taxation together with massive cuts in defence spending. As a result, the gigantic wartime budget deficit turned into a surplus by 1947, and remained in surplus for the rest of that government's life (Cairncross (1985): 421, Table 15.2). But the government still had to manage a huge debt overhang accumulated from the two world wars and depended for its survival on overseas borrowing after the war. It also faced pressures for checking the growth of spending on civilian public services as a result, not of budgetary deficits but of persistent balance of payments deficits, associated currency-management issues, pressures to cut taxes, and later by a big spike in defence spending associated with the outbreak of the Korean War in 1950.

The Attlee Government was therefore caught politically between resistance within its own ranks to efforts to restrain the growth of welfare state spending and electoral challenge from the Opposition Conservatives' (who first overtook Labour in the opinion polls in 1947) calls for spending cuts to fund lower taxes. That electoral challenge all but wiped out Labour's huge 1945 majority less than five years later in the 1950 general election and resulted in a narrow defeat for Labour in the 1951 general election.

## 5.2 The World War II Revenue Squeeze

World War II saw a perhaps unprecedented (and certainly unrepeated) revenue squeeze, greatly exceeding that of World War I, with both tax rates and tax coverage dramatically increased. Martin Daunton (2002: 176–7) points out that whereas the main features of what he calls the 'fiscal constitution' survived in World War I—that is dependence on progressive direct taxation and rejection of both a general sales tax and regular taxes on business profits—and that war had been funded largely by borrowing rather than by tax increases, the relative share of loans and taxes was reversed in World War II. The share of indirect taxation started to rise in 1942 for the first time in a century, with higher rates on existing indirect taxes and a broader sales tax (Purchase Tax, collected from wholesalers) with rates ranging from zero per cent on some goods to 100 per cent on others. But those tax increases were partly offset— particularly for those on lower incomes—by food subsidies introduced at the start of the war.

The numbers paying income or surtax rose from ten to fourteen million between 1939 and 1945, the standard rate of income tax rose from 29 to 50 per cent, and surtax rose from 41 per cent on incomes over £50,000 to 48 per cent on incomes over £20,000, amounting to nominally confiscatory rates of taxation (98 per cent) for top earners. As in World War I, an Excess Profits

Tax on companies was introduced early in the war (before the formation of the Churchill coalition in 1940), levied on the difference between wartime profits and pre-war or 'standard' profits, but at even higher rates than those imposed in World War I (the tax was initially levied at 60 per cent and later at 100 per cent). In addition, a completely new administrative system, 'Pay as You Earn' (PAYE) was introduced in 1944 for collecting income tax from millions of employees by obliging their employers to deduct tax at source from each wage payment through a coding system updated through the year instead of the previous system of annual or twice yearly lump sum payments from each income tax payer. Many have described this system as the major tax invention of World War II and see it as having enabled governments long after the war to tax earnings more heavily than would otherwise have been possible (for example, Houghton (1979): 97).

Along with that extreme revenue squeeze during World War II went a squeeze on civil expenditure that is concealed in the aggregate numbers shown in Chapter Two. Those aggregate numbers for total government spending reflect a huge spike in defence expenditure partly funded by borrowing (including the wartime 'Lend-Lease' scheme begun in 1941, under which the United States supplied the UK, along with other Allied countries, with food, oil and military materiel in exchange for use of military bases) and producing massive, off-the-scale budgetary deficits. Little or no investment took place throughout the war in domestic public services (such as schools, hospitals, roads, housing), and in many cases staffing in these services was severely run down as well, for example through the conscription of many doctors of military age into the armed forces, creating a major shortage of doctors for the civilian population.

These huge tax hikes and the accompanying squeeze on civilian spending took place at a time when, as noted earlier, mainstream party competition for votes was effectively suspended, under a wartime coalition government. All the political parties in that coalition consequently shared the blame for the wartime fiscal squeeze and the non-fiscal austerity that accompanied it. But the three parties also combined to make big promises to the voters for 'jam tomorrow' after the war. One such promise comprised 'post-war credits' for both income and corporate taxes. These credits (a unique policy innovation, not having applied to World War I) were in effect post-dated cheques in the form of a promise to repay that part of the extra tax paid as a result of the reduction of personal tax allowances. But of course it was not specified precisely when after the war that repayment would occur.

A second was the famous 'Beveridge Plan' for expansion of the welfare state (incorporating new family allowances, an extension of social insurance, and plans for free public health care), which was agreed in principle by Parliament in 1943. As with post-war credits, this promise was not fully specified—the

Lord President of the Council (later to be Chancellor) said on behalf of the government in 1943 that there could be no final commitment to the Plan until after a comprehensive review of the financial situation.[2] A third major promise made in the following year was the1944 Butler Education Act which provided for free secondary education combined with a higher school leaving age (implying educational expansion of the kind that had been hit by the cuts of the 1920s). In all of these cases (and for other less expensive promises made during the war, for example, for the development of town and country planning), there was scope for delay and modification of details, but it would have been politically difficult for any of the three parties to have reneged completely on these promises.

An exchange of correspondence in 1944 between the Chancellor, Sir John Anderson, and the wartime prime minister Winston Churchill (who was alarmed about the likely cost of the coalition government's commitments to extra public spending after the war) shows what those promises were expected to cost at that time.[3] The extra costs of the National Health Service and family allowance scheme involved in the Beveridge Plan were then estimated at some £239m per year, with £147m of that amount being met through extra compulsory 'insurance' contributions from employees and employers (public and private), and the other £92m per year to be raised through higher taxes or extra borrowing. The cost of the plans for free secondary education up to the age of fifteen provided for in the 1944 Butler Education Act were estimated at £58m per year, and there was also another extra £90m per year of spending expected on post-war water supply, temporary housing, Town and Country Planning, new roads, and extra pensions. The Chancellor noted the power of delay (by using Treasury approval powers to slow down developments) as a way of checking these costs, and there seems to have been some disagreement within the cabinet about the speed with which to press ahead with developing bureaucracies to plan the implementation of the Beveridge Plan, and thus over whether any post-war government would hit the ground running or crawling on the issue.[4]

Each of the parties in the coalition government developed its own 'spin' and image during the course of the war, with the Labour Party in particular successfully producing a 'narrative' that discredited the Conservative-led governments of the 1930s as years of policy failure and wasted opportunities. But there were no national general elections for a whole decade between 1935 and 1945 and no regular local government elections were held during the war

---

[2] Letter from the Chancellor to the Prime Minister, 27 June 1944, T160/1408 (Treasury file, National Archives).
[3] Letter from the Chancellor to the Prime Minister, 27 June 1944, T160/1408.
[4] Note from the Prime Minister to the Chancellor, 25 June 1944, T160/1408.

either. Further, as in World War I, the three parties within the wartime coalition government operated a 'truce' or cartel, in the form of an agreement not to contest by-elections when vacancies arose in the seats held by other parties. So the possibilities of electoral punishment by voters for the revenue squeeze (or indeed any other aspect of policy) were greatly diminished, and many of the wartime by-elections resulted in candidates from the incumbent parties being returned unopposed with very low voting turnouts. But in a few cases radical independent or minor party candidates succeeded in defeating candidates of the coalition parties, such as the 'independent Labour' candidate Tom Driberg, who defeated the incumbent Conservatives in Maldon in 1942, and the Scottish National Party candidate Robert McIntyre, who defeated the incumbent Labour Party in Motherwell in 1945 (producing the SNP's first electoral victory, and echoing Éamon de Valera's victory for Sinn Féin in the North Clare by-election in World War I).

The post-war general election was therefore the first for ten years, and produced an unexpected landslide victory (with a 145-seat majority in Parliament) for the Labour Party under Clement Attlee, while reducing the Liberals to a fringe party. The Labour Government therefore did not depend on the support of other parties for its survival as the two pre-war Labour Governments had done. But of course it also approached that task with memories—and the mythology—of the dramatic politics of the 1931 fiscal squeeze fourteen years earlier, as described in Chapter 4.

## 5.3 The Post-War Labour Squeezes

The six years of Labour Government after World War II were all a period of 'austerity' in a broad sense, and invariably described as such in general accounts of this period. Food, fuel, and consumer goods were rationed throughout the period, there was a huge backlog of construction and repair work on housing and infrastructure after years of bombing and neglect of public and private buildings, and the severe balance of payments challenges throughout the period meant continuing pressures to divert manufactured goods for export rather than domestic consumption. The six years can also be seen as a continuous period of fiscal squeeze in that taxes remained high by pre-war standards, and total government spending dropped dramatically after the war, as we showed in Chapter Two.

However, that aggregate picture needs to be qualified in two ways. First, as with the immediate post-World War I episode discussed in Chapter Three, the aggregate fall in government spending between 1946 and 1948 was entirely a product of deep reductions in defence spending associated with post-war demobilization, while every other major category of public spending showed an increase. And there were at least two (and arguably three) distinct sub-periods of squeeze over these six years, each with its own characteristics. The first was the transition period immediately after hostilities ended, when massive demobilization led to huge falls in military spending (albeit temporarily offset to some extent by payment of lump-sum gratuities and other benefits to those being discharged from the armed forces), but at the same time the welfare measures promised during the war (particularly the National Health Service) had not yet been put fully into effect.

The second sub-period began in the later period of the Attlee Labour Government, after the immediate post-war cuts in military spending had taken place and the new welfare state measures were beginning to come fully into effect. Dependent on the data source used (difficult in this case because there is a major data break in 1949, as we noted in Chapter Two) a noticeable dip shows up in non-defence spending both relative to GDP and in constant-price terms between FY1948/49 and FY 1949/50. Those numbers reflect the first attempts to rein in civil expenditure, and that squeeze in civilian spending reflected a combination of balance of payments deficits and the need for government to borrow heavily from overseas, particularly in connection with a substantial 30 per cent devaluation of the currency in 1949.

Further, there is the final year or so of the Labour Government, when pressures for steeply increased defence spending associated with the outbreak of the Korean War in mid-1950 combined with electoral threats to that government, with two general elections barely a year apart witnessing calls by the Opposition Conservatives for spending cuts to fund tax cuts. Such challenges led to a further push for cuts in civilian spending in the final year of the Attlee Government under its third Chancellor, Hugh Gaitskell, which are partly reflected in falls in civilian spending relative to GDP in FY 1952/53, while rises in defence spending pushed overall government spending up. That final Labour year is thus on the cusp of counting as an 'episode' according to the thresholds we specified in Chapter Two, but it is certainly important qualitatively because tussles over spending cuts at that time produced a left–right split in the Labour Government that had lasting significance within the Party.

### 5.3.1 *The Immediate Post-War Squeeze*

The Attlee Labour Government was elected in July 1945, two months after the end of the war in Europe. But the war with Japan did not end until the following month, demobilization of those who had been conscripted into the armed forces was not complete until 1947 (Allport 2009), and the UK remained on a 'war footing' as far as parliamentary control of public finance was concerned until 1946.[5] But the Treasury resumed its control of large parts of departmental spending (delegated to departments during the war) in mid-1945, meaning it could once again challenge and delay spending plans in many policy domains.

The challenge facing the government was to deliver on promises for post-war welfare state expansion while managing a transition from a wartime command economy to a peacetime mixed economy in the face of severe financial challenges. There were serious balance of payments problems arising from the dissolution or sale of UK overseas investments during the war and consequent loss of invisible earnings. And to cover the gap left by the abrupt ending of 'Lend-Lease' in 1945, 'soft' loans had to be negotiated in 1946 with the governments of the United States (some $3.75bn over a fifty-year period, conditional on sterling being made convertible from 1947) and Canada ($1.25bn). But even these amounts were soon exhausted.

The Labour Government's first Chancellor, the economist Hugh Dalton (who had hoped to be Foreign Secretary) cheerfully set about increasing welfare state spending as military spending fell. During the first eighteen months after the Labour Government was elected, some 4.3m service person-nel were demobilized, which involved extra short-term government spending on gratuity payments on discharge[6] and other benefits (considerably more generous than those issued after World War I), but meant that defence spending and staffing fell rapidly in the medium term.

Against that drop in military spending, Dalton increased spending on education and food subsidies (the latter intended to offset living costs and limit pressure for higher wages). He also brought a key (and costly) part of the Beveridge Plan into effect in mid-1946, namely universal family allowances to mothers with children. But severe physical shortages of building and other materials, partly imposed by shipping constraints, also limited the government's capacity to deliver on some kinds of expansionary policies, for example, for building houses, schools, and hospitals, for some years after the war, and those shortages helped to keep spending in check at first. Moreover, the National Health Service, the flagship and most costly part of the Beveridge Plan agreed by the wartime coalition in 1943, did not come into existence until mid-1948, such that its first full year of operation was FY 1949/50, and that also had the effect of postponing the associated spending increases.

---

[5] The 'Votes of Credit' system (the system for wartime financing through blocks of funding allocated without estimates) was replaced at the start of FY1947/47 by the pre-war system of estimates and appropriations, following what had been done at the end of World War I (T160/1313 (1945 estimates), file 11904, p. 45).

[6] *The Spectator*, 'War Gratuities', 9 February 1945, p. 2: Total demobilization costs were estimated at about £7bn at then current prices.

On the tax side, wartime Treasury archives record discussions among officials (reflecting on what had happened two decades earlier after World War I) about how far it would be feasible and desirable to continue with high wartime tax levels after the war. For example, in mid-1941 Hubert Henderson (a leading academic economist working in the wartime Treasury) accurately predicted there would be inflation rather than deflation after the war, and advocated 'maintaining taxation at a high level' to restrain consumer purchasing power and pay for wartime government promises entailing expansion of the welfare state.[7] In similar vein, the Permanent Secretary of the Treasury, Sir Horace Wilson,[8] two years later argued for retaining war taxation after the war ended 'until we can see other means of keeping the situation in control' and to pay for extra social expenditure. Others were more sceptical about the political feasibility of continuing with high wartime tax rates during peacetime. For example, Sir Herbert Brittain, a career official who had been in the Treasury since 1919 and therefore lived through the post-World War I episodes described in Chapter Three (Booth 2004), wrote that 'onerous taxation readily endured in war becomes very irksome in peace. Public opinion will . . . expect large reductions in rates of taxation rather than the maintenance of wartime rates . . . of previously unexampled severity.'

Brittain's political judgement seems to have been partially correct. There was some easing of wartime taxation, and tax revenues fell relative to GDP over this period. The Excess Profits Tax was abolished in 1946, immediately after the war, in contrast to what happened after World War I, and contrary to Sir Horace Wilson's suggestions for prolonging the tax into peacetime. Chancellor Dalton also significantly narrowed the tax base by raising income tax thresholds to take some 2.5m of the 14m income taxpayers in 1945 out of the tax net. But at the same time, post-war credits (the system in which part of extra taxes were to be repaid after the war) were abolished, while high tax rates remained, particularly for higher earners, meaning that the fiscal squeeze on those taxpayers increased.

Even the lower earners taken out of income tax by higher tax thresholds in many cases faced increased compulsory National Insurance contributions (a social security tax, but administratively separate from income tax) to cover half of the cost of extra spending on the National Health Service and family allowances. Dalton also doubled tobacco duty at a stroke in the 1947 budget (coupled with a costly and elaborate scheme to limit political resistance to the

---

[7] Sir Hubert Henderson 'Notes on Post-War Economic Problems', June 1941 in T160/1407 'Economy in Public Expenditure'.

[8] Undated 1943 memo to the Chancellor from Sir Horace Wilson, in T160 1407, 'Economy in Public Expenditure'.

tax increase by allowing old-age pensioners who declared themselves to be habitual smokers to reclaim part of the duty).

Further, many taxpayers faced a long wait for repayment of post-war credits on their wartime income and tax payments. The Treasury's strategy for repaying these credits was to redeem the business tax credits quickly (to provide firms with working capital to enable them to move to peacetime operations), while delaying repayments to individual taxpayers for as long as possible until they had been eroded by inflation. Hence those credits were not released to individuals until they reached pension age (then sixty-five for men, sixty for women), no interest was paid until 1959, no adjustment for inflation was made on delayed payments, and no repayment was made even in cases of hardship.[9] Indeed, those credits were not fully repaid until the 1970s, almost thirty years later.[10]

The post-war combination of redistributive taxation and food subsidies linked to rationing seems to have hit middle-class voters harder than the lower paid or those on benefits. But at the same time, the Attlee Government followed the same course as its post-World War I predecessor in choosing not to impose a levy on wartime increases in wealth to pay down wartime debt. As was noted in Chapter Three, the left called for such a levy in World War I, arguing that if labour was conscripted for war service, the same should apply to capital. The idea re-emerged when the government that preceded the Churchill coalition introduced conscription just before the outbreak of World War II and promised that in the event of war there would be heavy taxation of the wealthy and an Excess Profits Tax. The then prime minister, Neville Chamberlain, had tentatively mooted the idea of a levy on wartime increases in wealth, and the first Chancellor of the Churchill coalition government (the Liberal Sir John Simon) even implied in his first budget that such a scheme was being prepared for possible introduction at the end of the war.

But, as in World War I, Treasury officials vigorously opposed the idea, on grounds of the cost and bureaucratic effort required to value all the country's capital assets at once, particularly during a time of unstable prices such as had occurred in the aftermath of World War I, as well as the possibly adverse effects on business confidence and entrepreneurship.[11] Instead, as also happened after World War I, Dalton raised rates of inheritance tax and surtax on higher incomes, which Treasury officials had argued to be a more practical and efficient alternative to a capital levy. Indeed, Martin Daunton (2002: 189)

---

[9] HC Deb 2 November 1948, cc.676–8.
[10] Sir Horace Wilson's 1943 memo said, 'the desirable course would be to pay out the E.P.T. [Excess Profits Tax] money very quickly and the Income Tax credits after as long an interval as possible' (T160/1407, 'Economy in Public Expenditure').
[11] Undated memo (probably 1943) by Sir Richard Hopkins on the question of a capital levy after the war, T160/1407 'Economy in Public Expenditure'.

argues that high levels of income tax at that time functioned as a form of capital levy, forcing the wealthy to live on their capital assets and all but confiscating high unearned incomes.

### 5.3.2 *Mid-Term Fiscal Squeeze Pressures, 1947–49*

1947 was the first full calendar year of peacetime finance, and it proved to be highly problematic for the Labour Government both in politics and public finance. Non-fiscal austerity continued and even increased for the civilian population, with potatoes rationed for the first time in that year, coming on top of the bread rationing that had been introduced in the summer of 1946. Despite the government's emphasis on expert planning, there was a severe shortage of coal—then the main fuel source for domestic heating and many industrial processes, as well as electric power generation—at the end of one of the two hardest winters of the century, followed by major floods and associated damage. A few months after that, there was a major balance of payments crisis in the summer of 1947, which led to suspension of the convertibility of the currency (required as a condition of the 1946 loan from the United States). That crisis underlined the fragility of the British economy at that time[12] and showed how dependent UK public finances would be on continuing overseas loans from the US and Canada, which needed to be negotiated at the highest political level in the face of sceptical questioning from those governments about the affordability of Labour's plans to expand welfare state services. Following the balance of payments crisis, a supplementary budget raised taxes further, on top of tax increases already imposed in the April 1947 budget, and the government decided to accelerate the run-down in the armed forces for financial reasons.

Those economic and financial difficulties in 1947 contributed to political unpopularity for the incumbents. The Conservatives pulled ahead of Labour in opinion polls in that year, and the political stresses also led to dissatisfaction with the prime minister's leadership among some of his leading cabinet colleagues, producing an unsuccessful move by party heavyweights Herbert Morrison and Stafford Cripps in 1947 to unseat Clement Attlee as prime minister and replace him with the Foreign Secretary, Ernest Bevin.

In the same year Stafford Cripps replaced Hugh Dalton as Chancellor (after Dalton resigned over a minor indiscretion in leaking budget details to a journalist) and came to personify 'austerity' in his personal image as well as his policy actions. Cripps raised taxes on alcohol, tobacco, and betting in the 1948 budget and imposed a special 10 per cent extra tax on investment

---

[12] See *Economic Survey* 1949, London HMSO, Cmd 7647.

income for those with annual incomes over £2000. Despite his austerity image, Cripps cut income tax for the lower paid and also cut beer duty in his 1949 budget ahead of a general election in 1950, but the continuing high tax levels on the better-off gave an opportunity to the Opposition Conservatives to campaign for tax cuts, to be paid for by reduction of 'waste' in government spending.

On the expenditure side, we have already seen that what happened in the early post-war years was a mirror image of wartime spending, with sharply increasing civil expenditure outweighed by a huge drop in military expenditure. Over those immediate post-war years those falls in defence spending outweighed the corresponding increases in civilian spending, and as has already been mentioned, more than half of the rises in social spending on family allowances and the National Health Service were offset by higher National Insurance contributions and the free national health care system did not begin until three years after the end of the war.

But if we look at the reported financial outcomes data we explored in Chapter Two and exclude defence spending, we see a 'hard' fall in civilian public service spending in both constant prices and relative to GDP in FY 1948/49. In 1949 the Treasury expressed anxiety about the outlook for financing government expenditure,[13] and Sir Bernard Gilbert wrote,

> There is no rapidly growing national income out of which a rapid growth of existing services and the undertaking of new services can be met...all the social estimates are...increasing rapidly and are likely to go on so increasing, and... there is little sign of...compensatory reductions in other ways...Even if there were such a margin our difficulties would still be considerable because we should merely have shown that we could finance our present programmes out of the produce of taxation at existing rates. But those rates are so high as to be bound to bring discouragement.[14]

Perhaps in line with this gloomy assessment, Cripps' 1949 budget marked a notable political turning point. His budget speech proposed a cap on food subsidy payments (which meant a rise in retail food prices), stated there was little scope for extra redistributive taxation to pay for expanded public services, and indicated that, with taxes already running at more than 40 per cent of GDP, it was necessary to slow welfare state expansion.[15] Only a few months after that, the emphasis went from slowing expansion to attempts at reversal, with an initiative to cut civilian spending by 5 per cent introduced by the

---

[13] Paper by Robert Hall dated 25 February 1949, T230/151, 'Forward Planning of Government Expenditure'.

[14] Memo by Sir Bernard Gilbert dated 10 March 1949, T230/151, 'Forward Planning of Government Expenditure'.

[15] HC Deb 6 April 1949, cc.2083–4.

prime minister in August. That initiative was part of an overall package that included a big devaluation of the currency by some 30 per cent from $4.03 to $2.80 linked with high-level negotiations with the International Monetary Fund (IMF) and the US and Canadian governments to secure further soft loans. Currency devaluation, which was scheduled for 18 September 1949 after those talks, represented an embarrassing political U-turn for the government, and particularly for the Chancellor, Stafford Cripps, who had repeatedly gone on the record saying currency devaluation was not the way to solve the country's economic difficulties. Part of the package, designed to convince the IMF and other lenders that further devaluation would not take place, was an attempt to show that vigorous measures were being taken to rein in government spending and halt the long-term growth of such spending.[16]

This squeeze initiative was led by the prime minister rather than the Chancellor, with Clement Attlee writing to all ministers in August 1949 to say the cabinet believed that 'the present economic circumstances make it necessary, not only to avoid new increases in expenditure, but to introduce measures of retrenchment—if only to offset the increases which must automatically follow from the expansion of policies already approved'.[17] Attlee's memo announced an intention to cut spending by about 5 per cent and asked departments to come up with proposals for spending cuts, under two heads. One was 'curtailment of services which are not essential to major Government policy', and the memo indicated there were many such services that could be delayed or cut out entirely. The other was 'more economical administration of policies which must be retained' (to which was added the observation 'I am confident that there is room for a... substantial reduction in the numbers of Government staffs'). Ministers of civil departments who could not achieve a 5 per cent reduction in their spending by those two means were asked to indicate what further action would have to be taken to cut spending by that amount.

A week after the prime minister's memo, the Permanent Secretary of the Treasury, Sir Edward Bridges, urged his fellow Permanent Secretaries to keep the 'economy drive' confidential for the time being (it was not to be mentioned to local authorities, presumably to limit the political backlash) and declared that 'what was really needed for submission to Ministers in September was a substantial collection of economy measures (involving in all a large sum of money) which Ministers might find difficulty in approving individually', but which, when presented as a group might secure collective

---

[16] 'Top Secret' draft brief for Ministerial Talks in Washington by E.H.W. Atkinson, 4 September 1949, T229/212 (Devaluation of the Pound, 1949).
[17] 'Government Expenditure', memorandum by the Prime Minister, CP (49) 170, 4 August 1949 in T233/276.

approval.[18] The plan was for the cabinet's Economic Policy Committee to consider the politically sensitive issue of economies in the social services and any cases for termination of particular policies or activities (one that was floated was the scrapping of the 'Festival of Britain', a feel-good public celebration project planned for 1951, the centenary of the 1851 'Great Exhibition'), while the administrative Treasury dealt with the individual departments which had made specific economy proposals.

That 1949 economy drive followed a pattern which was to be repeated in several subsequent economy drives over the next decade or so. What began as confidential discussions behind closed doors in Whitehall soon came to light through leaks to the press, in the form of stories in *The Manchester Guardian* and *The Yorkshire Post* on 25 August, apparently coming from the US Embassy, which had briefed the American press the previous day about a UK government initiative to cut spending ahead of the talks over further bailout loans that were scheduled to take place in Washington the following month.[19] But in a pattern also to be repeated in numerous cutback episodes in the following decades, the reductions in 'inessential services and administration' volunteered by departments in response to the prime minister's memo amounted to a grand total of £26m.

That was roughly one-eighth of the total required to secure the 5 per cent spending reduction target, and indicated that few if any departments would propose a 5 per cent spending cut without raising policy issues that could prove politically difficult or embarrassing to the government. Indeed in several cases, the departments included under 'proposals that would achieve the 5% cut but require a change of policy' a number of schemes certain to be deeply unpalatable to Labour ministers facing the prospect of fighting an election within a year or two. For example, the Ministry of Education mooted the introduction of fees in primary and secondary schools (saving £20m), the National Assistance Board raised the possibility of more stringent means testing for welfare payments and the Ministry of Pensions offered a cut in the basic state pension. At the end of September (also drawing conclusions that would apply to future spending cut exercises), a Treasury official concluded from the submissions offered by departments by that time:

'(1) Administrative economies and cutting out inessential services will only produce a fraction of the required reduction in the level of civil expenditure...

---

[18] Minute dated 12 August of a meeting between Sir Edward Bridges and nine selected Permanent Secretaries held on 10 August 1949, T233/276.
[19] 'Curb on Government Spending: Treasury Order to Departments', *Manchester Guardian*, 25 August 1949.

(2) The 5% objective can only be achieved by cuts in the Social Services.'[20]

As Treasury officials tried to handle what they could at official level, the Chancellor, Stafford Cripps, engaged his fellow ministers in bilateral discussions, and the cabinet's Economic Policy Committee collectively applied a political reality check to the various proposals for spending cuts in social services. In that winnowing-down process, the serious runners started to emerge and politically unfeasible options were laid aside (including reduction in the basic rate of war pensions, top-up fees for state schools at primary and/ or secondary level, alteration of the school entry or leaving age, an increase in the retirement age for schoolteachers, and the abolition of non-contributory old age pensions). The proposals that remained on the table included reductions in the government contribution to the National Insurance Fund (in effect breaking the intention that the fund should operate on an insurance basis), increasing National Insurance contributions to help pay for the NHS, add-on charges for hospital patients and for some NHS services that had previously been free at the point of delivery (such as supply of dentures or spectacles), rent increases for local authority housing, increases in school meal charges, and cuts in food subsidies.[21] Defence was not heavily hit, although a Treasury minute reported 'a strong feeling [among officials] that there was a lot of waste in Research Matters connected with Defence, but it was almost impossible for officials to attack this'.[22]

Following these deliberations, the Chancellor at the end of October announced a package of spending cuts that included reductions in foreign information services, extra charges for school meals above what was already in train, and reduced school transport facilities, a delay in de-requisitioning property that had been taken over by government in World War II, delay in the introduction of the Legal Aid scheme for support of litigants, a cut in the funding for the Festival of Britain planned for 1951, charges for NHS prescriptions, removal of subsidies for animal feedstuffs and fish, and reduction of some other food subsidies. Not included in those announcements, but still under discussion within government, was the possibility of cuts in the fire services, dropping the National Registration (identity card) scheme that had been introduced at the start of World War II, and postponing the census due to be conducted in 1951.

However, in the event, the cuts announced amounted to some £90m, less than half of the 5 per cent signalled by the prime minister in his August

---

[20] Memo by Mr Compton, 26 September 1949, T233/276, Review of Government Expenditure—Autumn 1949.
[21] 'Top secret' memo from Sir Bernard Gilbert, 29 September 1949, T233/276, Review of Government Expenditure—Autumn 1949.
[22] Record of a meeting between Sir Edward Bridges and eight other senior Treasury officials, 28 October 1949, T233/276, Review of Government Expenditure—Autumn 1949.

memorandum, and though the legislation needed for the introduction of NHS prescription charges was passed in 1949, it turned out to be another three years before such charges were introduced.

### 5.3.3 *The Final Labour Years 1950–51*

Shortly after the 1949 spending squeeze, a general election held in February 1950 returned Labour to office with the slimmest of majorities. In that election, the Conservatives had promised to cut 'wasteful' public spending to finance tax cuts, particularly on the main sales tax of that time.[23] That tax-cutting promise evidently had electoral traction: though the Conservatives did not win the election, Labour only squeaked back into office and saw its 1945 landslide 146-seat parliamentary majority reduced to a mere five, which imposed severe challenges for party management and made it unlikely that the government would survive another full electoral term.

Faced with that prospect, the Attlee Government in its remaining twenty months in office was caught between pressures to squeeze welfare state spending to fund the Korean War (which broke out in mid-1950), pressure to cut taxes to counter continuing Conservative tax-cutting election promises, and contrary pressures to maintain and extend welfare state spending to appeal to core Labour voters and meet the demands of the left within the Party, for example, over restoring 1950 cuts in the housebuilding programme.

This final period of Labour Government is ambiguous in our analysis of reported financial outcomes since (as already noted) the overall spending squeeze we identified in Chapter Two ends after FY 1949/50 on two out of three sources, and that applies both to total spending and to civilian spending excluding defence. Nevertheless the historical record points to considerable efforts to restrain the growth of public expenditure over this period under Labour's final Chancellor, the economist Hugh Gaitskell (who succeeded Stafford Cripps in October 1950 after Cripps had to resign due to of ill-health). In late 1950 Hugh Gaitskell asked all government departments for proposals for major cuts in civil spending for FY 1951/52 (Gaitskell was said to be privately aiming for a cut of 5 per cent, but chose not to name a figure). Gaitskell's letter referred to the rise in defence spending as a result of the Korean War and the consequent need for

> really big reductions in civil expenditure ... it must, I am afraid, be accepted from the start that we cannot confine ourselves to administrative economies, important

[23] Conservative Manifesto, 1950, 'This is the Road: The Conservative and Unionist Party's Policy', http://www.politicsresources.net/area/uk/man/con50.htm.

though these are. We must face the necessity for change in policy too if the reductions in expenditure are to be in the least adequate.[24]

Written to Accounting Officers (officials) in each department rather than ministers and not asking for replies with specific proposals for cuts, Gaitskell's letter was evidently intended as a softening-up exercise to indicate that some of the proposals rejected in the 1949 spending squeeze (such as fees for state schools and NHS charges) would be back on the agenda for FY 1951/52. But his letter produced a swift remonstrance from the Health Minister, Aneurin Bevan, who urged Gaitskell to reconsider his ideas and have a general discussion in cabinet (preferably in the absence of officials) before taking his proposals further.

> I was hoping that you would be searching...for new sources for augmenting revenue rather than adopting...the fixed Treasury habit of...cutting expenditure in the public sector...I notice particularly your sentence: 'We must face the necessity for changes in policy too if the reductions in expenditure are to be in the least adequate.' If that sentence has any meaning it must mean that in order to re-arm we intend to reverse the policies we have followed since 1945.[25]

That salvo was the beginning of a conflict that was to produce a serious split in the Labour Government over the 1950 budget. In that budget, Gaitskell retained the level of food subsidies, while increasing income tax, taxes on profits, petrol and entertainments, and raising Purchase Tax (the general sales tax introduced during World War II, as described earlier) from 33 to 66 per cent for items such as cars, TV sets, and domestic appliances. But the part of the budget package that proved most politically divisive within the Labour Party was the introduction of user charges for some NHS services that had been provided free for the previous three years (namely spectacles and dentures). Those charges—in a way that was partly echoed almost fifty years later when the Blair Labour Government introduced higher education fees—was seen on the left as breaching the principle of a free health service, and led to Nye Bevan's resignation from the government. Bevan was later joined by two other up-and-coming Labour ministers, Harold Wilson and John Freeman, and the split continued to resonate in the Party into the 1950s and 1960s.

While the Labour Party was split over such spending-squeeze measures, the government continued to be challenged to cut taxes by cutting 'wasteful' expenditure by the Conservative opposition and by Conservative-supporting newspapers. For example, in December 1950 *The Daily Express* carried a series

---

[24] Letter from the Chancellor to Departmental Accounting Officers, 24 November 1950, T233/547, Chancellor's Memorandum on Economies in Government Expenditure (November 1950).
[25] Letter from Aneurin Bevan to the Chancellor, 28 November 1950, T233/547. Chancellor's Memorandum on Economies in Government Expenditure (November 1950).

of fiery articles, partly drawn from a report by the parliamentary Public Accounts Committee, calling for cuts of some £250m a year in government spending, through measures that included mergers of departments and big cuts in civil service numbers, information services, new government offices, and particularly government cars and motoring.[26]

Similarly, in the budget debates in April 1951, Captain Waterhouse (Conservative MP for Leicester South East) attacked what he portrayed as unnecessary waste on 'frills' and 'administration'. As 'frills', Waterhouse cited the amounts being spent on the 126 professors who had been commissioned to write war histories, rising spending on universities and colleges (which had increased tenfold in nominal terms since before the war), and the growth in numbers, salaries, and travelling costs of civil servants in general and of those in the Treasury in particular.[27] Such attacks seem to have hit home and to have played a part (along with other factors, including a further balance of payments crisis in summer 1951) in the Attlee Government's eventual demise. When that government called a snap election in October 1951 in the hope of achieving a more workable parliamentary majority, Labour instead lost a further twenty seats, with the Conservatives and unionists achieving a seventeen-seat overall majority.

## 5.4 Conclusions

Although it involved a serious split within the Labour Party towards the end of the period, this period of squeeze is rather less politically dramatic than that described in Chapter Four, but it involves far higher levels of taxation and striking levels of non-fiscal austerity. As in earlier chapters, we conclude by discussing the three sets of issues raised in the opening chapter about the politics of fiscal squeeze.

### 5.4.1 *Tax and Spending, Depth and Duration, Blame and Control*

The ten-year period covered by this chapter involves the wartime tax squeeze applied by the three-party coalition which on our measures in Chapter Two rates as the second most severe tax squeeze over the whole century considered in this book. That tax squeeze was accompanied by steeply rising government spending overall, but when we take out defence spending we find it conceals a 'hard squeeze' on non-defence spending between FY 1937/38 and 1943/44.

---

[26] *Daily Express*, 4 December 1950, 'How to Save £250,000,000 a Year'.
[27] HC Deb 12 April 1951, *c.*1261.

Equally, as we have seen, the deep fall in aggregate spending in the first few years after the war conceals a big jump in all the major areas of civilian spending in FY 1946/47 and 1947/48. On the tax side, the post-war Labour Government kept taxes high by pre-war standards, but tried to alter the distribution of taxation to protect lower earners, and produced a 'soft' revenue squeeze with taxation rising in constant-price terms but not relative to GDP. Later in the government's life, civilian spending was squeezed in FY 1948/49 and 1949/50 (and beyond that on some data sources, as we noted in Chapter Two) as pressures built up to negotiate overseas loans and cut taxes in the face of Conservative electoral challenges.

The issue of tax versus spending in fiscal squeeze figured large toward the end of this period and Martin Daunton (2002: 221 and 224) argues that by 1950 there was a 'clear sense that the [Labour] government had reached the limits of its fiscal strategy' (of funding an expanded welfare state by high levels of redistributive taxation on the better-off) and that the Treasury itself and the government's economic advisers had come by that time to advocate a spending squeeze to finance tax cuts that would in turn stimulate private savings and investment.

On the issue of blame and control, the wartime revenue squeeze (and associated squeeze on civilian spending and non-fiscal austerity) resembled the World War I case discussed in Chapter Three in that it involved a 'grand coalition' of political parties such that it was hard for voters to attribute blame for particular measures among the partners in the coalition.

The later Labour revenue and spending squeezes, in contrast to the spending squeezes discussed in Chapters Three and Four, broadly involved normal political processes within government, though it is notable that one of them, the 1949 economy drive, was led by the prime minister rather than the Chancellor. There were elements of outside involvement in these spending squeezes in that the UK was dependent on soft loans from the USA and Canada at that time and the 1949 economy drive was part of a strategy for renewing those loans. But neither of those spending squeezes involved an outside committee of the type represented by the Geddes or May Committees, and that probably reflected sour memories of the May Committee fifteen years or so earlier among Labour leaders during this period.

### 5.4.2 *Loss, Cost, and Effort Involved in These Episodes*

As in previous chapters, Table 5.1 puts these episodes into the analytic perspective set out in Chapter One by sketching out our comparative assessment of the extent of loss imposed on citizens and voters, the extent of reputational cost and stress incurred by governing politicians, and the degree of effort exerted by the state machine in handling the squeeze.

**Table 5.1.** A qualitative classification of imposed loss, political cost, and state effort associated with 1940s fiscal squeezes

| | Low | Moderate | High | Overall classification |
|---|---|---|---|---|
| 1941–45 Squeeze Type: Hard Revenue Wartime Coalition: | | | | |
| Loss | | | [1], [2] | High |
| Cost | [2], [3], [4] | | | Low |
| Effort | | | [1], [2], [3] | High |
| 1946–49 Squeeze Type: Hard Spending/Soft Revenue, Labour 7/1945 onwards | | | | |
| Loss | [2], [3] | [1] | [2], [3] | Moderate |
| Cost | | [1] | | Moderate |
| Effort | [1] | [1], [3] | [1] | Moderate |

Note: Numbers in square brackets refer to categories in Table 1.2, Chapter One.

The wartime tax squeeze 'of unexampled severity', coupled with severe non-fiscal austerity and a hard squeeze on civilian spending, stands out as representing the highest level of loss imposed on citizens and voters over the century considered by this book. It was also an episode that represented a high degree of effort on the part of the state machine, involved as it was in devising and implementing completely new forms of tax collection (notably in the case of the PAYE system for extracting income tax at source from employers, and the development of a broad-ranging sales tax). But as in World War I, the reputation cost or political risks run by the governing politicians in respect of fiscal policy was limited by the existence of a grand coalition and the absence of electoral competition.

For the post-war Labour Government's fiscal squeeze, tax policy in part relied on 'inertia strategies' of continuing with wartime levels of taxation, while altering the distribution by higher taxes on inheritance and higher thresholds for lower earners. As we have seen, the spending squeeze for the first three years of the government's life fell exclusively on defence, only beginning to affect civilian services in FY1948/9, and although deprivations imposed on citizens through rationing and materials shortages were undoubtedly severe, there was no fiscal equivalent to the cuts in unemployment benefit in 1931, and the high taxes and materials shortages were accompanied by substantial food subsidies. Again, the state machine expended a high degree of effort in effecting these fiscal changes, for instance, in the massive task of demobilizing millions of service personnel. For the governing politicians (as Sir Herbert Brittain had warned), the effort to continue with high wartime tax levels (as with the Lloyd George reconstruction coalition after 1918) eventually produced electoral resistance and pressures to cut spending even though the budget was in surplus. But again, in contrast to the 1931 episode, the Labour Government was not driven into widespread abandonment of its election promises in this case, and therefore could not be said to have been exposed to more than a medium degree of reputational or political cost.

### 5.4.3 *Electoral and Other Consequences*

The electoral outcomes in the period covered by this chapter (Conservative defeat in 1945, narrow Labour survival in 1950 followed by defeat in 1951) is consistent with the hypothesis suggested in Chapter One that left-wing governments might be more liable to face electoral punishments for spending squeezes, while their right-wing counterparts might be more liable to face electoral punishment for revenue squeezes. After all, the general elections that all but removed the Labour Government's majority and later swept it out of office were held during the efforts at spending squeeze on civilian services that came during or after the 1949 devaluation and later continued under the pressures of the Korean War.

In the period of that post-war Labour Government, there was no 'Anti-Waste League' of the kind that challenged the Conservatives within the Lloyd George coalition in 1921, discussed in Chapter Three. But the Labour Government was exposed to similar attacks from the Conservatives, who as early as November 1945 demanded further cuts in 'wasteful' government spending to make tax cuts possible and continued to emphasize that theme.

When it comes to other consequences, in contrast to the episode discussed in Chapter Four, it is difficult to identify constitutional effects that can be traced to the fiscal squeezes over this period, separately from all the other changes that took place during six years of total war and the massive disruption that followed. One of the major political consequences of the post-war Labour Government squeeze (and the controversial charges on NHS spectacles and dentures that brought three ministerial resignations in the final months of the government) was a left–right split in the Party between 'Bevanites' and 'Gaitskellites' that continued to play out into the following decade but fell well short of the creation of a separate breakaway party such as occurred in 1931 and 1981. As for policy consequences, the permissive legislation introduced by the Labour Government before it drew back from imposing prescription charges for NHS medicines smoothed the way for the succeeding Conservative Government to implement such charges in 1952, as we will see in Chapter Six. But many of the options for spending cuts that the Labour Government considered and baulked at over this period (such as top-up fees for state primary and secondary schools and 'hotel charges' for NHS patients in hospital) remained 'off the table' for governments of different political persuasions in the succeeding decades, and indeed some remain so to the time of writing.

# 6

# The 'Stop-Go' Squeezes of the 1950s and 1960s

## 6.1 Background: The Period in Perspective

This chapter explores four 'stop-go' squeezes of the 1950s and 1960s under Conservative and Labour Governments. In Chapter Two we identified a double soft squeeze in the early to mid-1950s, a short-lived revenue squeeze in the early 1960s and two further squeezes (the first revenue-only, the second a hybrid of spending and revenue) in the middle and later 1960s. As Chapter Two showed, both the spending squeezes were modest compared to the episodes of the 1920s and 1940s and the revenue squeezes were all slightly more modest than that of 1931 in terms of revenue increase relative to GDP. Nevertheless, some of these squeezes (particularly the 'Butler' episode of the mid-1950s and the Labour squeeze after devaluation of the currency in 1967) represented real political effort, as we will show later.

All these squeezes occurred in conditions of low unemployment and during a time when a fixed exchange rate system for currencies established by international agreement in 1944 resulted in recurring balance of payments pressures on the UK in the face of low productivity growth, inflation, and weak export performance. So, as with the post-World War II Labour squeezes discussed in the previous chapter, fiscal policy at this time was heavily concerned with containing domestic demand and inflation and not just with financing government expenditure, such that the pressure for squeezes tended to come from balance of payments deficits as much as from budgetary deficits.[1]

---

[1] See Rollings and Middleton (2002); McCombie, Thirlwall, and Thompson (1994). There were surpluses on the primary balance during this period, though all four squeezes were preceded by budgetary deficits.

## 6.2 The 1950s Butler Squeeze

As mentioned in the previous chapter, a snap election called by the Labour Government in 1951 resulted in a narrow victory for the Conservatives, who then remained in office for thirteen years under four different leaders (and six Chancellors). The 'Butler squeeze' at the beginning of this period represents an effort to go beyond Labour's efforts to restrain civilian expenditure (described in Chapter Five) to deliver on tax-cutting election promises. As we shall see, efforts to achieve this outcome ran up against 'inertia pressures' and a spike in military spending associated with the Korean War and other military commitments.

In 1951 the Conservative party, led by the ageing World War II leader Winston Churchill, had campaigned on a 'set the people free' platform of cutting taxes and reducing state activity and spending. But as we saw in Chapter Five, it had also committed itself to the National Health Service and other welfare state measures promised by the coalition parties in World War II. The Chancellor, Richard ('Rab') Butler, was a 'centrist' figure in the Party who, as a minister in the World War II coalition, had championed legislation providing for an expansion of free secondary education and saw the education cuts of the 1920s (discussed in Chapter Three) as having resulted in a waste of human potential (Butler 1971: 91). In a 1951 campaign speech Butler promised that if they won government, the Conservatives would maintain the NHS, develop educational provision, and try to help old-age pensioners. The day after Butler's speech, another leading Conservative politician, Sir David Maxwell Fyfe, publicly promised, 'We shall not cut social services.'[2]

After the election, Butler (together with the Financial Secretary of the Treasury, John Boyd-Carpenter, who Margaret Thatcher later described as her political model[3]) faced the problem of how to reconcile 'setting the people free' with those campaign promises to maintain welfare state services. In his memoirs, he recalls beginning his work as Chancellor at a meeting with Sir Edward Bridges (Permanent Secretary of the Treasury) and William Armstrong (who was to be his Private Secretary): 'Their story was of blood draining from the system and a collapse greater than had been foretold in 1931' (Butler 1971: 157). He was pressed to cut spending in order to cut taxes both by some of his cabinet colleagues (and rivals) and some backbench MPs, notably Captain Waterhouse, whose attacks on 'government waste' under the previous Labour Government were mentioned in the previous chapter.

---

[2] Recorded in T233/928 (Economy Drive).
[3] See Lady Thatcher's speech at Lord Boyd-Carpenter's memorial service in London in 1988, http://www.margaretthatcher.org/document/109303 accessed March 2015.

The new government took office close to the end of FY 1951/52, but Butler announced plans for curbing FY 1952/53 expenditure less than a fortnight after the election. He told his cabinet colleagues that military commitments (due to the Korean War and other colonial military activities of that time) meant an increase in defence spending of about £300m, and that, since 'taxation is already at crippling levels . . . it is imperative that we should make a big reduction in civil expenditure', which was set to increase substantially in FY 1952/53 on current policies.[4] Butler did not propose targets for spending cuts, but urged ministers to impose or increase charges for services, reduce percentage grants to local authorities, cut capital spending plans, and freeze civil service staffing. Early in 1952 Butler also announced a plan to cut 10,000 civil service jobs in the first half of 1952 and more in the second half.[5] To restrain spending on the National Health Service, a particular concern, Butler proposed four measures: charges for NHS prescription medicines (a step that Hugh Gaitskell, his Labour predecessor, had planned for the 1951 budget, only for it to be dropped at the last moment); a big hike in National Insurance contributions, the social security tax, to help pay for the NHS; 'hotel' or 'amenity' charges for NHS hospital in-patients; and either charges for most NHS dental and ophthalmic services or the suspension of such services.

The response to such proposals by spending departments and ministers was unenthusiastic, and for two years Treasury ministers and officials struggled to restrain the growth of public expenditure. The outgoing Labour Government had bequeathed substantial increases in welfare benefits and public sector pay that its successor could not easily overturn, in the form of semi-automatic uprating of benefits or pay rises decided by independent tribunals (for example, over NHS doctors' pay in 1952), meaning the Treasury could only try to reduce the numbers being hired rather than rates of pay. In his 1952 budget, Butler was able to announce some increase in income tax thresholds and allowances, but he sharply raised road fuel tax and indeed (in a move reminiscent of Austen Chamberlain's post-World War I budgets) imposed a new Excess Profits Levy of 30 per cent on all firms, charged on profits in excess of their average profits in 1947–49. The budget also cut food subsidies by almost half (implying price rises in bread, flour, meat, tea, and other staple foods) while increasing welfare benefits. The extra charges for NHS dentistry and prescriptions that Butler had proposed were imposed, but there was only a modest increase in National Insurance contributions and the idea of suspending NHS dentistry and ophthalmic services was dropped.

---

[4] T233/925 Economy Exercise 1952/53, letter sent by Chancellor of the Exchequer on 12 November 1951 to all Ministers in Charge of Departments.
[5] Butler had talked of cutting civil service staffing by 20,000 or more, but in the event even the announced target of 10,000 job cuts was in deep trouble by April 1952. See Treasury memo by E.M. Abbott to Mr Johnston 4 April 1952, T233 925 Economy Exercise 1952/53.

Butler faced continuing political pressure to cut spending in 1952. The Conservatives suffered reverses in local elections, highlighting the electoral challenge they faced to keep or increase their slender parliamentary majority. Captain Waterhouse returned to the fray, chairing a Conservative backbench committee which reported before the 1952 party conference, identifying some £500–600m of spending that could be cut to enable the standard rate of income tax to be reduced by 10 per cent. Returning to a theme of Waterhouse's attacks on the previous Labour Government, the committee recommended that the Treasury should cut its own spending and staffing: '... since 1939 the staff in the Treasury has increased fourfold and its expenditure eightfold... an example in economy should be set here.' Waterhouse's committee proposed abolishing all food subsidies except for milk, abandoning 100 per cent central funding of any service provided by local authorities (especially school meals), cutting state funding of universities, reducing the funding of semi-state bodies, and financing more capital spending through borrowing rather than out of general taxation.[6] Sending this report to the Chancellor, Waterhouse declared, '... a drastic reduction in taxation should... be... the prime objective of national policy.'[7]

Within cabinet, too, Butler was pressed by colleagues who wanted more vigorous spending cuts, notably Peter Thorneycroft, then President of the Board of Trade and Lord Woolton, Lord President of the Council and wartime crony of Winston Churchill. Indeed, in mid-1952 Woolton launched a personal drive for cutting government spending via the cabinet's Home Affairs Committee, calling on ministers to send him reports on cuts they could make. This unilateral initiative (apparently taken after Woolton had turned the civil servants out of the cabinet committee and written to ministers himself) ruffled bureaucratic feathers and raised demarcation issues with the Treasury ('I can't have a Peer writing about expenditure to my colleagues', fumed Butler).[8] But in any case, departments' responses to Woolton were generally defensive and focused on staff cuts rather than cuts in programme spending, leading the Treasury to conclude that the limit of cutbacks achievable through simple admonition had been reached and a tougher line would be needed over spending bids for FY 1953/54.[9]

On the defensive at the Conservative Party conference in October 1952, in the face of the Waterhouse Committee report and vigorous calls at that

---

[6] T233/932. Report of the subcommittee of the Conservative Party's Finance, Trade and Industry Committee set up to Consider Taxation and Expenditure, and to make Recommendations, September 1952.
[7] Letter from Captain Waterhouse to the Chancellor, 16 September 1952, T233/932.
[8] Note from the Chancellor to Sir Edward Bridges dated 30 July 1952, T233 925 Economy Exercise 1952/53.
[9] T233/925 Economy Exercise 1952/53.

conference for further tax cuts funded by spending cuts, Butler said he was not satisfied with the level of public expenditure on domestic policies but defended his position as a 'centrist' Conservative:

> If you have got to have big economies, you can only get them by big changes of policy . . . I do not think, in view of the immense burden upon us at the present time and the things we have to carry out, particularly in the defence programme, in atomic research, in the civil defence and many other things, that this is going to be an easy year in which to make lush promises of favours to come.

Even so, his 1953 budget was the first budget since World War II that contained neither proposals for new taxes nor increases in existing ones. It announced, along with some relatively modest spending cuts, the ending of the Excess Profits Levy in 1954, a cut in rates of Purchase Tax, the main sales tax, and a small cut in the standard rate of income tax from 47.5 to 45 per cent.[10]

There is some parallel with the early 1920s, as described in Chapter Three, in these political pressures inside the Conservative Party for a squeeze on spending to enable cuts in taxes that had stayed high after the war, running up against election promises for post-war extensions of the welfare state. But there was no real equivalent of the 'Anti-Waste League' of 1921 and its by-election successes. And, like its Labour predecessor (and facing similar constraints, including rearmament associated with the Korean War from 1950 to 1953 and much the same menu of options for spending cuts presented by Treasury officials), the Churchill Conservative Government did not appoint an external Geddes- or May-type committee to propose spending cuts. Indeed Butler emphatically rejected such a possibility at the 1952 Conservative Party conference.[11] Further, and again in contrast with the 1920s, the prime minister, Winston Churchill, seems to have seen a radical change in defence strategy as the key to dealing with the government's fiscal difficulties, in the sense of adopting a policy of first use of nuclear weapons which he believed would enable defence spending to be cut substantially (Raya (1999): 77). But Churchill had a major stroke in 1953 (concealed from the public at the time), which put him out of action for some six months.

Even in the face of continuing pressures from within the Party, and a further assault within cabinet from Peter Thorneycroft in mid-November 1952 (calling for spending cuts of more than double what Butler was aiming for, to enable tax cuts to help UK firms compete in world markets), spending ministers did not offer Butler major reductions in spending for FY 1953/54. Butler's

---

[10] HC Deb 14 April 1953, cc.50–9.
[11] 'I am not in favour of a Geddes Axe and of asking an outside Committee to do the Government's job for it . . .' Speech by R.A. Butler to Conservative Annual Conference 9 Oct 1952, T233 926 Economy Exercise (1953–54 Estimates).

proposal for a big hike in compulsory National Insurance contributions to fund rising NHS spending was rejected by the Minister of National Insurance on the grounds that it would undermine the contributory basis of social security. A memo to the cabinet proposing a long-term plan to raise the age of entitlement to retirement pensions also seems to have got nowhere.[12] Butler commented, 'My...colleagues are not trying...I am now forced to revert to the idea of an Enquiry on the whole of Civil Expenditure. We shall not get any sense till Whitehall is frightened...'[13]

Indeed, as time went on between 1952 and 1954, Butler turned from his original 'soft' and 'collegial' strategy of appeals to party solidarity without specific spending-reduction targets, and moved to a possibly more 'frightening' process in which the drive for spending reductions was led by cabinet committees and explicit targets were set. In 1953 the Treasury pressed for the establishment of a special committee (the Guillebaud Committee) to review the National Health Service, but in the event that committee did not provide support for cutting NHS spending: instead it showed that NHS spending had fallen between 1948 and 1953 relative to GNP and that capital spending was well below pre-war levels. There was a separate defence review, and the Chancellor chaired a cabinet committee set up early in 1953 (late in the run-up to the 1953 budget) to review last-minute proposals for cutting government spending for FY 1953/54 and further reductions thereafter. Even so, in October 1953, a draft letter from the Chancellor to his ministerial colleagues said, 'I am most disturbed about the paucity of the economies which we have been able to make in the last two years. Expenditure has remained at a high level...few major economies have been achieved.'[14]

By 1954, there were only two years to go before the latest date at which another general election had to be held, the Conservatives were facing Labour charges that government spending was over £1bn year higher than under the Attlee Government, despite the Conservatives' 'set the people free' slogan in 1951,[15] and Butler faced his colleagues with the prospect of a substantial budget deficit for FY 1955/56 unless spending was cut. A draft briefing to the cabinet in March 1954 said,

> It is clearly impossible for us to contemplate a deficit of the order of £300 millions in what will be the fourth Budget during our stewardship...It is equally clear that we must at all costs avoid the need to impose fresh taxation, and particularly direct taxation...The only practicable way, therefore, of attacking the problem is by a

[12] T233 927 memo from J.G. Owen 13 December 1952 and memo from Sir James Crombie 5 January 1952 'Expenditure 1953–4'.

[13] Note from R.A. Butler to Sir E. Bridges, 16 November 1952, T233/926.

[14] Draft of Chancellor's letter, 3 Oct 1953, sent by Sir. James Crombie to Sir Bernard Gilbert, T233 1030 Economy for 1953–4 Estimates.

[15] Douglas Jay, questions to the Financial Secretary of the Treasury, HC Deb 4 May 1954, c.183.

substantial reduction of expenditure . . . Previous experience suggests that if we are to achieve positive results, each of the [Cabinet] Committees should be given a definite target for . . . reduction in expenditure . . .[16]

The result was a high-powered review of civil expenditure led by a cabinet committee chaired by the Commonwealth Secretary, Lord Swinton, a long-serving minister who had been one of the ten cabinet ministers in Ramsay MacDonald's National Government formed after the collapse of the Labour Government in 1931 (described in Chapter Four). Adopting a tactic repeated under the Thatcher Government some twenty-five years later, the Swinton Committee invited departmental ministers to say what would be needed to effect spending cuts of varying depth—in this case, making proposals about what would be necessary (a) to return forecast 1955/56 estimates to 1954/55 levels, (b) to cut spending by 5 per cent, and (c) to cut spending by 10 per cent.[17]

That review seems to have had some of the 'frightening' effect Butler wanted—for example, for good or ill it held up proposals for development of security and intelligence services for the Cold War (Adamthwaite 1992: 40–1)—but also seems to have prompted familiar strategic responses from departments. For instance, the Foreign Office produced no proposals for cutbacks, despite pointed Treasury calls for 'general reduction in Foreign Service standards of living abroad'. The Customs and Excise floated the idea of doing away with foreign exchange control and collection of trade statistics (knowing, presumably, that the Treasury would be bound to reject such cuts, as it duly did). Indeed, the Treasury resisted cuts in its own spending, on the grounds that such cuts would 'draw the teeth of the Exchequer watchdog.'[18] The idea of imposing 'hotel charges' on NHS hospital in-patients—something that had been on the Treasury's 'squeeze menu' ever since the advent of the NHS—was rejected by John Boyd-Carpenter, who said, 'I think it could have been politically possible as part of our measures to deal with the economic crisis which we found on assuming office', but that by 1954 the political moment had passed.[19]

As we saw in Chapter Two, the Butler squeeze of the 1950s produced a 'double soft' squeeze in that government spending fell relative to GDP but not in constant price terms, while revenue rose in constant price terms but not relative to GDP. Public spending was also checked by user charges, notably on school meals and on NHS prescription medicines (at which the previous

[16] T233 1048 Swinton Committee on Civil Expenditure, draft briefing 18 March 1954.
[17] T233 1053 Cabinet Committee on Civil Expenditure, letter to Ministers from the Rt. Hon Viscount Swinton 14 April 1954.
[18] T233 1053 Cabinet Committee on Civil Expenditure, note by A.J.D. Winnifreth 17 June 1954.
[19] T233 1053 Cabinet Committee on Civil Expenditure, note by John Boyd-Carpenter to the Chancellor 5 July 1954, 'Swinton Committee—Hotel Charges for Hospital In-Patients'.

Labour Government had finally baulked). At the same time, income tax thresholds were raised and rates were cut over the period, such that the Conservatives went into the 1955 general election having cut the standard rate of income tax by two percentage points (to 42.5 per cent) during their time in office and claiming to have taken large numbers out of income tax by raising tax thresholds. (Of course, a combination of inflation and rising real wages throughout the period would have tended to push more people into the income tax net if thresholds had remained unchanged).

On the spending side notable reductions over the period included: big cuts in food subsidies, made in several stages; cuts in civil defence and related spending on strategic stocks and facilities, for example on oil storage (in effect leaving the civilian population to shift for itself in the event of the kind of emergencies such spending was directed at); cuts in other 'hangovers' from World War II, for example the abolition of identity cards and the associated wartime National Registration system in 1952 (though that survives to the present day as the basis for NHS registration) and of many of the extensive agricultural and food controls that had developed during the war (there were some 800 civil servants in the Ministry of Food's Potato Division alone in 1952).[20] And at the end of the episode the 1953 armistice ending the Korean War (following threats by the USA to use nuclear weapons) created conditions for defence spending to fall relative to GDP after FY 1954/55, a fall that continued up to the 1980s.

What was *not* changed, despite repeated canvassing of these policy options within the Treasury, were items such as the age of pension entitlement (which had been lowered by Churchill as Chancellor in 1926), school entry and leaving ages, free 'hotel services' for all NHS hospital in-patients except retirement pensioners, and no top-up fees for state schools. In that sense, the 1953–55 spending cuts could be seen as winning a battle to check public spending growth by one-off measures reversing specific World War II programmes, but losing the war to bring down public spending in the longer run by leaving all the big long-term drivers of welfare state expansion untouched.

In the event, the Conservatives were electorally rewarded after presiding over this double soft squeeze. In the 1955 general election (held a month after Churchill's eventual retirement as prime minister, to be succeeded by a new leader, Sir Anthony Eden), the Party secured a modest overall vote swing in its favour which served to increase its parliamentary majority from the seventeen it obtained in 1951 to a more secure overall majority of sixty.

---

[20] T233/925 Economy Exercise 1952/53, Note of 20 June 1952 (unsigned) to Sir James Crombie on food and agriculture controls.

## 6.3 The Revenue Squeeze of the Early 1960s

Pressures for fiscal squeeze of one kind or another continued for the remaining nine years of Conservative Government up to 1964, though most of the squeezes fell below the threshold we set for the analysis of reported financial outcomes in Chapter Two. Indeed, the 1955 general election was immediately followed by a deflationary mini-budget and the following spring, Butler's successor as Chancellor (Harold Macmillan)[21] announced a plan to cut £100m from total spending in FY 1956/57.[22] And in 1957, after Macmillan had succeeded Eden as prime minister following the crisis surrounding the failed Anglo-French attempt to re-take the Suez Canal from Egypt, the government announced the end of conscription to the armed forces by 1962, meaning a loss of half of army personnel, a third of the air force and a tenth of the navy. That policy was intended to cut costs and reflected Macmillan's long-standing belief that most spending on defence was ineffective. The year after that, Macmillan's successor as Chancellor (Peter Thorneycroft) and two other Treasury ministers (Enoch Powell and Nigel Birch) resigned after Macmillan rejected their proposals to cut spending by about £153m in 1958/59 to protect the currency, which would have meant unemployment rising in the run-up to a general election (see Lowe (1989); Cooper (2011)). This event is a notable case of a Chancellor's efforts for spending squeeze being overcome by counter-pressures from the prime minister and cabinet and is the only instance in the entire century considered by this book in which a Chancellor resigned after failing to get spending cuts through cabinet. Like the Labour ministerial resignations over Gaitskell's spending cuts in 1951, this episode resonated in the Conservative Party and helped shape 'Thatcherism' a decade or more later.

Even so, some candidates for spending cutbacks that had escaped the 'Butler squeeze' were targeted during this period. One case in point is the removal of 'pensioners' tobacco tokens' (mentioned in Chapter Five), a measure introduced by Hugh Dalton in 1947 to soften the blow of a doubling in tobacco tax in that year, and finally abolished in 1958 after years of campaigning by the Treasury, despite the electoral sensitivity of removing 'grey' benefits in the run-up to a general election.[23] But as we saw in Chapter Two, such political

---

[21] T273/331 Draft of a letter from Harold Macmillan to the Prime Minister, 10 November 1955: 'If unpleasant decisions are to be taken, the earlier in our period of office we take them, the less difficult they will be.'

[22] T233 1456 1956 Review of Government Expenditure £100m cut. Notable cuts included government armaments factories, public buildings, civil defence, strategic food stocks, bread and milk subsidies, emergency oil storage and distribution, plus increases in passport fees and school meal charges.

[23] By the time these tokens were withdrawn, some 2.6 million pensioners (roughly half of all pensioners) were claiming them as self-certified 'habitual smokers', implying an annual loss of

efforts did not result in reported financial outcomes that registered as a spending squeeze on the thresholds used here.

However, what does show up in Chapter Two is a revenue squeeze in 1960/61, coming immediately after the Conservatives' third successive election victory in 1959, which saw their parliamentary majority increase to one hundred seats, despite a slight decline in their vote share. A month before the 1959 general election, Peter Thorneycroft's successor as Chancellor (Derek Heathcote Amory) presented a classic pre-election 'giveaway' budget, which among other things cut the standard rate of income tax by some seven percentage points (more than double Butler's giveaway in 1955), and also cut beer duty and the higher rates of Purchase Tax. In the election campaign the Conservatives pointed to Labour's plans for higher spending (especially on retirement pensions), estimated them as implying an increase of some £1bn over the course of a parliament, and warned the voters of higher taxes to fund these spending promises if Labour was elected. That tactic forced the Labour leader (Hugh Gaitskell) to pledge not to raise taxes, and thereby opened up scope for the Conservatives to query how the promised extra spending would be funded.

After the Conservatives' re-election, continuing inflationary pressures linked to a balance of payments deficit led to a post-election revenue squeeze (which the Labour Opposition decried as a repeat of 1955, with a giveaway pre-election budget followed by tax increases immediately after the election).[24] The post-election 1960 budget raised tobacco taxes and increased Profits Tax from 10 per cent to 12.5 per cent, and in the following year's budget, [John] Selwyn Lloyd, Heathcote Amory's successor as Chancellor (and the fifth Conservative Chancellor in a decade) sharpened the squeeze by raising Profits Tax by a further 2 per cent and increasing indirect taxes (for example on fuel, car licences, and TV advertisements), as well as cutting spending and raising Bank Rate. In the same year, 1961, the compulsory National Insurance contributions became earnings related (up to a threshold) for the first time, to accompany a new graduated state retirement pension, making those contributions more like income tax, and that meant a huge jump in revenue in the short term before the costs of the new graduated pension started to be incurred (Chote, Emmerson and Simpson (2003): Chapter 5). On top of that, a major currency crisis in the summer of 1961 led to a further emergency budget, along with a package of other measures

tobacco duty of about £16.5m. The length of time it took to withdraw that benefit reflects ministers' concerns to ensure that no pensioner of any description could claim to be worse off as a result of the policy change. (T223/137 Future of the Tobacco Token Scheme for Old Age Pensioners.)

[24] Hugh Gaitskell, HC Deb 4 April 1960, *cc.*76–9.

intended to stabilize the currency by combating inflation, including the exercise of a newly enacted power to impose surcharges on customs and excise duties by delegated legislation[25] and a measure of non-fiscal austerity in the form of a pay freeze for all public sector workers that heralded a new phase of attempts to develop a coordinated incomes policy under both Conservative and Labour Governments (Evans and Taylor (1996): 122).

## 6.4 The Two Labour Squeezes of the 1960s

The pattern of squeezes in the 1950s—heavily governed by the need to protect the currency in the fixed exchange rate system, against a background of low unemployment and inflationary pressures—continued under the Labour Government elected in 1964 under the leadership of Harold Wilson, one of the spending rebels in Labour's 1951 budget battles.

The Conservatives' 1963 budget had reduced income taxes at the lower levels and announced plans to scrap income tax (known as Schedule A) on owner-occupiers of residential property in 1964—the year in which the next general election had to be held according to electoral law. But National Insurance contributions were also raised in 1963 and in the general election year of 1964 (in the face of a major anticipated balance of payments deficit that would require loans from the IMF to stabilize the currency) the pre-election budget by the then Conservative Chancellor (Reginald Maudling) did not follow the pre-election giveaway pattern of 1955 and 1959. Indeed Maudling increased taxes on tobacco and alcohol before the election, while announcing increases in virtually every domain of public expenditure premised on highly optimistic expectations of 4 per cent annual growth in GDP over five years. In the event, the Conservatives narrowly lost the 1964 general election to Labour, which won a miniscule overall majority of only four.

James Callaghan, the incoming Labour Chancellor, dramatically deepened Maudling's tax squeeze in an emergency budget a month after the election. The new government declared this budget to be necessary to tackle a balance of payments deficit that they put at some £800m (a figure claimed to be exaggerated by the Conservative opposition)[26] and to levy over £400m in extra taxes. Those extra taxes were intended to fund some £345m of extra

---

[25] The power had been enacted in the 1961 budget, along with a similar power to surcharge employers' National Insurance contributions that was scrapped the following year.

[26] Reginald Maudling, HC Deb 12 November 1964, c.1201:

The Government talk about . . . a deficit of £800 million . . . [that] is the highest possible figure they could choose from a range of figures . . . of the figure of £800 million something like a half . . . is not trade deficit, but either overseas investment . . . or repayment of existing, outstanding overseas debt, including the North American loan.

public spending the Party had promised in the election campaign, notably higher retirement pensions and welfare payments, plus other measures such as raising the school leaving age from fifteen to sixteen and abolishing the NHS prescription charges that the Labour Government had finally rejected in 1951 and which the Conservatives had subsequently imposed.[27] That emergency 1964 budget levied surcharges on most imports, and brought about a big rise in road fuel tax, a steep rise in National Insurance contributions, and a rise in income tax rates to take effect the following April. These measures helped the government to negotiate loans totalling £857m from the IMF in 1964 and 1965.

With an overall majority of four, Wilson's Government never expected to survive a full electoral term, and faced problems both of parliamentary management and of aligning fiscal policy to the electoral cycle. The government's second budget in 1965 continued the revenue squeeze with further increases in taxation of about £250m, including tax rises on tobacco, alcohol, and vehicle licences, reduction of income tax allowances, and a new capital gains tax replacing an earlier system for taxing short-term gains. Those tax increases coincided with cuts in defence spending, which included withdrawing from Aden, phasing out a major aircraft carrier programme, cancelling a big contract for a new fighter aircraft (TSR-2) intended to save some £35m, and a defence review intended to contain future defence spending at roughly the FY 1964/65 level.

Labour did badly in local government elections in 1964 and lost a by-election that cut its overall majority to only two. By 1966 its majority dropped to one and the prime minister called a general election at which the Party faced the voters having raised taxes but also increased welfare spending while cutting defence—meaning it had applied a tax squeeze to fund a spending increase, the opposite of spending squeezes to fund tax cuts.

In the election campaign, Labour claimed credit for halving the balance of payments deficit while maintaining full employment and thus successfully managing a severe economic crisis, which it blamed on its predecessor's economic mismanagement and on speculation by international financiers, summed up as the 'Gnomes of Zurich', in a famous and much quoted phrase coined by the Labour heavyweight George Brown. The Party manifesto claimed any cut in taxation would be irresponsible at that time,[28] but the Chancellor presented a 'mini-budget' at the start of the election campaign in which he said 'I do not foresee the need for severe increases in taxation.'[29] He

---

[27] Labour Party 1964 election manifesto 'The New Britain', http://www.politicsresources.net/area/uk/man/lab64.htm.

[28] Labour Party 1966 manifesto 'Time for Decision', http://www.politicsresources.net/area/uk/man/lab66.htm.

[29] HC Deb 1 March 1966, c.1116.

also presented plans for subsidizing mortgage payments by house-buyers on incomes too low to benefit from the tax relief then applying to mortgage interest payments, to be funded by a new tax on betting and gaming to be introduced after the election.

This approach paid off electorally in that there was a 3 per cent swing to Labour in the 1966 election, which increased its overall majority to a comfortable ninety-six. And a post-election Budget continued the revenue squeeze by announcing measures designed to increase revenue by a further £386m in FY 1966/67.[30] Those measures included the promised new betting tax, but most of the extra revenue was to come from a new payroll tax on employers in services and construction (Selective Employment Tax) which, unlike the Betting Tax, had not been mentioned either in the pre-election mini-budget or the Party's 1966 manifesto. That new payroll tax, which was intended to raise some £240 a year and was paid by employers through the National Insurance system,[31] was a variant of an earlier idea of a surcharge on employers' National Insurance payments which the previous Conservative Government had given itself powers to bring into effect by order, but never did. Another serious balance of payments crisis occurred in mid-1966, leading to an emergency summer package of measures including a policy of general wage standstill and subsequent restraint (backed up by statutory powers for government to hold down wages) and a 10 per cent surcharge on surtax for higher incomes. But the 1967 budget did not deepen the tax squeeze, and although the budget speech mentioned a possible squeeze on public spending, the Chancellor boldly stated: 'I sum up the prospects for 1967 in three short sentences. We are back on course. The ship is picking up speed. The economy is moving. Every seaman knows the command at such a moment, "Steady as she goes".'[32]

That famous or notorious claim was soon overtaken by events in the form of yet another major currency crisis in late 1967, which forced a devaluation of the currency in November (along with a commitment to cut defence spending and capital spending of state-owned enterprises, an immediate review of public spending to make further cuts, and a 'Letter of Intent' to the IMF pledging to limit net borrowing and therefore to raising taxes). It also ended Callaghan's Chancellorship (Callaghan, along with Wilson, had repeatedly ruled out devaluation as an option in the same way that Cripps had done in the 1940s), and heralded a new phase of squeeze in which the emphasis shifted to restraining public spending as well as raising taxes.

On the spending side, in January 1968 the prime minister (who, it will be recalled, had resigned from the Labour Government in 1951 over Gaitskell's

---

[30] Budget Statement, HC Deb 3 May 1966, c.1459.
[31] Budget Statement, HC Deb 3 May 1966, c.1457.   [32] HC Deb 11 April 1967, c.1010.

cuts in health spending[33]) announced the results of the post-devaluation spending review. This announcement reflected high political cost because the cutback package broke or at least postponed several promises made in Labour's 1964 and 1966 election manifestos, notably in education, health, and housing. The new Chancellor Roy Jenkins expanded on those plans the following day, foreshadowing a 'hard budget'[34] to accompany the spending cuts, to be followed by 'two years of hard slog'.[35]

The spending cuts were concentrated on defence in the medium term (accelerating the closure of military bases in the Middle East, Far East, and South East Asia, cancelling a major new fighter aircraft (the F111), phasing out an aircraft carrier force, and building fewer nuclear submarines), but the costs of cancelling contracts meant there would be no net savings in defence spending in FY 1968/69. On the civil spending side, further uprating of welfare benefits was postponed until 1969, and education spending was cut by delaying capital spending in higher education and postponing for two years (to 1973) the rise in the school leaving age which the Party had promised in its 1964 manifesto. Civil defence was to be cut back completely to a 'care and maintenance' basis, and planned spending on roads and housing was to be reduced (the latter in spite of Labour's promise in its 1966 manifesto to make housing its 'first priority'). Further—crossing another important political Rubicon for the Labour Party—some selectivity was to be introduced into health and welfare benefits by 'clawing back' an amount equivalent to announced increases in Family Allowance (welfare payments to mothers with children) from standard-rate income taxpayers. Finally, the charges for NHS prescription medicines that Labour had promised to abolish in its 1964 election manifesto (and had done so in 1965) were to be reintroduced, albeit with numerous exemptions.

Jenkins' 1968 budget proceeded to institute another major revenue squeeze, with tax increases intended to raise almost an extra £1bn a year. The Conservative Leader of the Opposition (Edward Heath) claimed that amount was 'more than two and a half times the maximum which any Chancellor of the Exchequer has ever imposed in one Budget before'[36] and pointedly contrasted those tax increases with James Callaghan's statement before the 1966 general election (as mentioned earlier) that he foresaw no need for major tax increases. On the direct tax side, the squeeze took the form of the extra charges on standard-rate taxpayers to recover the cost of increased Family Allowances,[37] a special one-off levy on higher investment incomes and an increase in the rate of Corporation Tax from 40 to 42.5 per cent.

[33] HC Deb 16 January 1968, cc.1577–1619.    [34] HC Deb 17 January 1968, c.1790.
[35] HC Deb 17 January 1968, c.1805.    [36] HC Deb 19 March 1968, c.303.
[37] HC Deb 19 March 1968, c.295.

On top of that, the payroll tax (Selective Employment Tax) was raised by some 50 per cent and there was a swathe of indirect tax rises, on tobacco, spirits, fuel, vehicle tax, and Purchase Tax.

Jenkins followed up this 'hard budget' the following year by more tax increases aimed to raise an extra £340m a year—including higher rates of road fuel tax, Selective Employment Tax, and Corporation Tax (the latter raised from 42.5 per cent to 45 per cent, a rate the government claimed to be in line with that charged by other competitor countries in the developed world at that time).[38] The 1969 budget speech also announced a plan to raise National Insurance contributions to pay for a major increase in state retirement pensions, such that pensions would be some 20 per cent higher in real terms by the time of the following election than when the government had taken office.[39] Jenkins' 1970 budget, introduced two months before the prime minister called a surprise early general election in mid-1970, effectively ended the revenue squeeze, though not by as much as his party colleagues were said to have wanted. Jenkins' pre-election budget left indirect taxes, the payroll tax, and Corporation Tax unchanged, but substantially raised the thresholds for income tax and surtax, which he claimed would benefit some 16.5 million voters.[40]

The Wilson Government was defeated in the 1970 general election, confounding opinion poll predictions, and the Conservatives (supported by the Ulster Unionists) won an overall majority of thirty-one. The Conservative election manifesto made much of what was claimed to be £3bn of extra taxes imposed by the Labour Government, contrasted that increase with what was claimed to have been a £2bn reduction in taxes under Conservative rule between 1951 and 1964, and promised to cut taxes, giving first priority to income tax reductions (promises denounced by Labour as 'irresponsible tax bribes' and 'crude electoral manoeuvres' likely to worsen inflation).[41] On the spending side, the Conservatives highlighted Labour's failure to achieve its 1966 election promise to build 500,000 houses a year by 1970, which had been a casualty of the post-devaluation spending cuts package of 1968, and promised to do better.[42] It is debatable how far these fiscal squeeze-related issues affected the election result as against other factors in play, notably the anti-immigration rhetoric of Enoch Powell, then a leading figure in the Conservative party (Hansen 2000), rising prices, the announcement of adverse balance of payments and unemployment figures just before the election, even

---

[38] HC Deb 15 April 1969, c.1026.   [39] HC Deb 15 April 1969, c.1014.
[40] Budget Statement, HC Deb 14 April 1970, c.1252.
[41] Labour Party 1970 Manifesto, 'Now Britain's Strong—Let's Make it Great to Live in', http://www.politicsresources.net/area/uk/man/lab70.htm.
[42] Conservative Party 1970 Manifesto, 'A Better Tomorrow', http://www.conservativemanifesto.com/1970/1970-conservative-manifesto.shtml.

matters such as the defeat of the England football team in the World Cup before the election. All that can be said is that the Labour incumbents' campaign cannot have been helped by the tax and spending squeeze imposed during 1968 and 1969.

## 6.5 Conclusions

As in previous chapters, we conclude by assessing the four squeezes that have been qualitatively described here in the light of the three sets of issues raised in the opening chapter about the politics of fiscal squeeze.

### 6.5.1 *Tax and Spending, Depth and Duration, Blame and Control*

Although, as noted at the outset, the four fiscal squeezes described in this chapter all took place against a broadly similar economic background—of low unemployment accompanied by inflation and repeated balance of payments crises threatening the currency in the 'Bretton Woods' era of fixed exchange rates—their political characteristics were different, and that underlay the different balance between revenue and spending in the various squeezes. The 1950s Butler squeeze, like the Geddes Axe of the 1920s, was designed to restrain spending so that taxes could be cut to satisfy those voters who wanted lower taxes, whereas, as already noted, the first Labour squeeze of the 1960s (arguably begun by the Conservatives' 1963 budget) represented the opposite approach, of raising taxes to pay for election promises of increased spending. That government faced the voters in 1966 having raised both taxes and spending, while claiming to have dealt effectively with an economic crisis that it blamed on its predecessors.

However, the other two squeezes considered in this chapter—the Heathcote Amory/Selwyn Lloyd revenue squeeze of the early 1960s and the Jenkins revenue and spending squeeze of 1968–69—presented a more problematic mix of revenue and spending for the parties concerned. The first involved a right-of-centre government imposing significant tax increases to check inflation and stabilize the currency, while the second involved a left-of-centre government both imposing swingeing tax increases and reversing election promises it had made to increase spending in several electorally important domains such as housing and education. There were 'exogenous' forces in the sense of pressure on the currency that prompted both of those squeezes and helped to shape the balance of revenue increases and spending cuts, which in both cases cut across what might be assumed to be the normal predilection of right-of-centre parties to squeeze by cutting spending and left-of-centre parties to do so by raising taxes.

On the issue of blame versus control which we raised in Chapter One, in none of these cases does there seem to have been any serious move to pass the poisoned chalice of selecting spending cuts to an outside committee like the Geddes and May Committees of the 1920s and 1930s. Indeed, as in the case of the post-1945 Labour Government discussed in Chapter Five, this was an era in which all the main elements of economic and financial administration—monetary policy, economic forecasting, and tax and spending decisions—were directly in the hands of ministers rather than delegated to others who could take or share the blame.

### 6.5.2 Loss, Cost, and Effort Involved in These Episodes

As in previous chapters, Table 6.1 summarizes our assessment of the extent of loss imposed on citizens and voters, the extent of reputational cost and stress incurred by governing politicians, and the degree of effort exerted by the state machine in handling the squeeze.

The Butler squeeze of the 1950s does not seem to rate at more than a moderate level on the spectrum we identified in Chapter One relating to three dimensions of intensity of fiscal squeeze. There were some significant

Table 6.1. A qualitative classification of imposed loss, political cost, and state effort associated with 1950s and 1960s fiscal squeezes

| | Low | Moderate | High | Overall classification |
|---|---|---|---|---|
| 1953–55. Squeeze Type: Soft Revenue/Soft Spending Conservatives 10/1951–5/1955 | | | | |
| Loss | [1] | [1] | | Moderate |
| Cost | [4] | [1], [2] | | Moderate |
| Effort | | [1], [2], [3] | | Moderate |
| 1960–61. Squeeze Type: Hard Revenue Conservatives 8/1959 onwards | | | | |
| Loss | | | [1] | High |
| Cost | | [1], [2] | [3] | High |
| Effort | | [1], [3] | | Moderate |
| 1964–67. Squeeze Type: Hard Revenue | | | | |
| Labour 10/1964–3/1966 | | | | |
| Loss | | | [1],[3] | High |
| Cost | [2] | [1], [2] | | Low/Moderate |
| Effort | | | [2] | High |
| Labour 3/1966 onwards | | | | |
| Loss | [3] | [1] | [2], [3] | Moderate |
| Cost | [1] | [1] | [1] | Moderate/High |
| Effort | | | [1] | High/Moderate |
| 1968–69. Squeeze Type: Hard Revenue | | | | |
| Labour 3/1966–6/1970 | | | | |
| Loss | | [1] | [1] | High |
| Cost | [2] | | [1], [2] | High |
| Effort | | [1] | | Moderate |

Note: Numbers in square brackets refer to categories in Table 1.2, Chapter One.

extra charges (NHS prescriptions, school meals, and transport), but the revenue hit fell far short of some others imposed in the century and although Butler's early moves included imposition of extra import controls and a doubling of Bank Rate, non-fiscal austerity in the form of rationing fell away during this period. As far as political cost is concerned, we saw earlier that the incumbent politicians at first struggled to deliver on their tax-cutting election promises and even briefly imposed a special Excess Profits Tax early in the electoral cycle, but they had readily available scapegoats in the form of the previous Labour Government, and by the end of the electoral cycle had succeeded in cutting the standard income tax rate by some two percentage points and raising tax thresholds. In terms of effort by the state machine, the changes required to shed wartime programmes to make room for tax cuts went well beyond the incremental level, but the ending of the Korean War meant a 'peace dividend' that limited the effort required at the end of the period.

The other three squeezes discussed in this chapter seem to have involved a greater degree of imposed losses in terms of extra taxes or charges, for instance, with three tax-raising budgets in a row between the graduation of National Insurance payments in 1961 and the income tax increases of 1964, the two successive tax-raising budgets under the first Labour Government and the later tax rises after devaluation in the 1968 and 1969 budgets. An element of non-fiscal austerity also applied in the form of policies of pay restraint under both Conservative and Labour Governments, the latter case ultimately involving statutory powers to restrain wage increases along with price increases.

In terms of cost to the reputation of incumbent politicians, the Jenkins squeeze of 1968–69 (even though it only just registers as a squeeze on our method of counting from reported financial outcomes, as explained in Chapter Two) seems to rate high, and the Conservative tax squeeze of the early 1960s also seems relatively high. In the latter case, a right-of-centre government was approaching the end of its electoral term with a succession of tax-raising budgets, while in the case of the Labour Government of the late 1960s, a left-of-centre government was reining in types of spending that it had promised to increase, as well as imposing swingeing tax increases in the run-up to an election and re-imposing the NHS prescription charges it had promised to abolish in 1964. In both of those cases too, the government concerned had been in office for more than one electoral term and so could less plausibly put the blame onto its predecessors for the relevant squeezes.

For the effort imposed by the state machine, all of these squeezes seem to go well beyond the minimal level we identified in Table 1.2 in Chapter One, but arguably the greatest effort was associated with the Labour squeeze of 1964–67, particularly with all the new taxes (such as Selective Employment Tax, Corporation Tax, Capital Gains Tax) that were brought in over that period, as well as the development of non-fiscal austerity in the form of wage standstill policy (along with price control) in the mid-1960s.

### 6.5.3 *Electoral and Other Consequences*

In both the Butler squeeze of the mid-1950s and the Callaghan squeeze of 1964–67, the incumbent government concerned managed to reap overall electoral credit and convincingly win the post-squeeze election, even though other factors undoubtedly came into play in both cases. In contrast, the Heathcote-Amory/Selwyn Lloyd tax squeeze of the early 1960s and the Jenkins revenue and spending squeeze of the late 1960s were followed by electoral defeat for the incumbents.

The difference in electoral outcomes between those two sets of squeezes partly fits with a pattern of 'exogenous shocks' in the sense of outside pressures on the currency cutting across the 'normal' electoral cycle of fiscal squeeze and relaxation discussed in the first chapter, in which parties in government seek to raise taxes and/or cut spending early in their electoral term and reverse that position as the next election approaches. The 1950s Butler revenue squeeze was concluded early enough to be followed by a pre-election giveaway budget in 1955, a tactic the Conservatives successfully repeated in 1959—a 'political business cycle' effect that can partially explain the Conservatives' re-election in 1955, and contrasts sharply with the much more muted pre-election giveaway in 1964 following the revenue squeeze of the early 1960s.

On the Labour side, however, the Wilson Governments had to face the voters in 1966 and 1970 after pressures on the currency cut across the normal 'political business cycle', but with very different electoral outcomes. In the first case, it decisively won the election after only seventeen months in office with spending increases but no significant tax giveaways to moderate its revenue squeeze (and consequently had to place heavy emphasis on diverting the blame to the the previous government and on the machinations of 'Gnomes of Zurich' international financiers). In the second case it lost the election after imposing 'two years of hard slog' that included cutting back on promised spending increases. So those electoral outcomes only partly fit 'political business cycle' expectations, but they are also consistent with the 'asymmetrical punishment' suggestion in Chapter One that if other things are equal, right-of-centre parties might experience more electoral punishment for tax increases, while left-of-centre parties might experience greater electoral punishment for spending cuts.

The longer-term consequences of these episodes are again debatable. Even though the Labour Party lost the 1970 election, and political scars were certainly left by the 1968–69 fiscal squeeze that continued to show in left–right divisions in the Party in the 1970s, there was no breakaway party as in 1931, and the Party returned to government under the same leader less than four years later, albeit with a much more left-wing manifesto. On the policy side, the most obvious consequence of the Butler squeeze of the 1950s was the abandonment or scaling back of food subsidies and of other measures associated with wartime planning such as strategic reserves and storage systems. The 1968 spending cuts led to the accelerated abandonment of much of the visible trappings of a global or imperial defence power 'East of Suez' (though it might be argued that, as with the Geddes cuts of the 1920s, these military assets may have been outdated for the strategic era that was to come and their abandonment did not in fact prevent future military involvement in the Middle East).

Another policy legacy of this era was the adoption of NHS prescription charges, at first by the Conservatives and later by Labour (albeit with a raft of exemptions that narrowed the effect of such charges), which remained in force, in England at least, under the two subsequent Labour Governments. Means testing was also applied for the first time in this period by a Labour Government to Family Allowance welfare payments, with increases for those at the lower income levels but not for standard rate income tax–payers—arguably a forerunner of the 'Child Benefit Tax Charge' introduced for higher rate taxpayers in the early 2010s.

In general, what the episodes discussed in this chapter bring out is that fiscal squeezes do not have common political consequences in terms of post-squeeze credit and blame, even when those squeezes have a broadly similar background (in this case of recurring balance of payments deficits and currency management problems). Blame politics really did matter in those electoral outcomes, in the extent to which incumbents could plausibly deflect blame to predecessors or outside forces ('Gnomes of Zurich') and in the extent to which they could align fiscal and electoral cycles.

# 7

# The 1970s Fiscal Squeeze

## Stagflation, Recession, Currency Crisis, and Political Crisis

### 7.1 Background: The Period in Perspective

Like the 1920s, the 1970s was for the UK a decade of intractable economic problems combined with high electoral turbulence. One of the economic problems faced by governments in the 1950s and 1960s (as noted in Chapter Six), namely the management of the currency in a fixed-exchange rate system, changed its character with the abandonment of the 'Bretton Woods' system in the early 1970s in favour of a system of floating currencies. But that certainly did not mean that exchange rates ceased to be a political problem for governments, as this episode shows.

Moreover, as can be seen from the tables in the Appendix to this book, two other economic conditions dramatically worsened. In contrast to the low unemployment of the previous three decades, mass unemployment returned, with unemployment going over a million for the first time since the 1930s. Further, whereas unemployment had been associated with falling prices in the 1920s and 1930s, inflation spiked up dramatically from the low single-figure annual price rises of much of the 1950s and 1960s into double digits, peaking at over 20 per cent in the mid-1970s.

Associated with that inflation were high levels of trade union militancy, another marked feature of this decade. And a key factor behind the inflation spike was a huge rise in global oil prices, which increased six-fold between the early and mid-1970s, and by the late 1970s were some seventeen times early 1970s prices. The result was a combination of recession and inflation ('recesso-petroflation', as some termed it) in the UK and other oil-importing countries. Oil and gas were discovered in British (mainly Scottish) waters under the

North Sea in the 1960s, but it was not brought ashore in large quantities until the later 1970s. Production was still extremely limited in the eventful year of 1976, though it was to rise sharply by the end of the 1970s.

In politics, the 1970s was a decade marked by four general elections (as in the 1920s). Almost four years of majority Conservative Government (1970–74) were followed by three years of minority or bare-majority Labour Government (1974–77), which were in turn followed by a Labour–Liberal pact from 1977 to 1978,[1] then a minority Labour Government again until it lost office to the Conservatives in 1979. As in the 1960s, the 'blame game' over fiscal squeeze in much of the 1970s consisted of the Labour Government aiming to blame their Conservative predecessors (and then the global situation) for fiscal squeeze, while the Conservatives blamed the Labour Government for mismanaging the economy and allowing pay settlements to blow out.

We saw in Chapter Two that historical financial statistics point to three episodes of fiscal squeeze in the 1970s. The first, a hard revenue squeeze between 1973/74 and 1975/76 began in the last year of the Heath Conservative Government and was extended in the first year of the subsequent Labour Government, in the latter case involving tax increases to finance increased government spending and in that sense resembling the mid-1960s Labour revenue squeeze discussed in Chapter Six. That tax squeeze was followed by a year of hard spending squeeze accompanied by soft revenue squeeze, and then by a hard spending-only squeeze, in both cases associated with a deep currency crisis and financial bailouts from the US Government and the IMF. An element of non-fiscal austerity also figured in this case, in the form of efforts to cap wages by both Conservative and Labour Governments and very high interest rates (the highest in the twentieth century) in the late 1970s.

## 7.2 The Early-to-Mid-1970s Revenue Squeeze

Alongside pledges to take the UK into the European Economic Community (EEC), as the European Union was then named, and regulate labour unions, the Conservatives' 1970 general election manifesto promised to cut income tax and abolish Selective Employment Tax, the payroll tax introduced by the Labour Government in 1966. It declared that taxes could be cut without worsening public services or benefits as a result of economic growth, better management, and cutting back on 'unnecessary' government spending. 'In

---

[1] Not a coalition but a 'confidence and supply' arrangement, with the Liberals supporting the Labour Government on confidence and appropriation motions in the House of Commons, in the same way that the Ulster Unionists supported the Conservatives up to 1974.

the thirteen years of Conservative prosperity we cut tax rates by £2,000 million—as well as doubling expenditure on the social services. We have done it before: we can do it again.'[2]

The route to that hoped-for 'better tomorrow' proved to be rocky. The Heath Government found itself facing a recession, with unemployment over a million for the first time since before World War II, along with rising inflation and bitter battles with labour unions over regulation and wage demands that led the government to U-turn away from its initial free-market stance and set up politically contested statutory controls over wages and prices. But the Conservatives did indeed cut the standard rate of income tax in 1971, raised tax thresholds, and introduced Value Added Tax (to replace Purchase Tax, the sales tax introduced in World War II, and Selective Employment Tax, the payroll tax imposed in 1966, as discussed in Chapter Six). The Labour opposition declared 'total and unremitting opposition'[3] to the new tax, but VAT was an accompaniment to the UK's entry into the EU, and Labour's 1974 manifesto did not include proposals to abolish the tax.

By 1973 the Conservative Chancellor, Anthony Barber, was claiming, 'We have reduced taxation on a scale unprecedented in our history. Taxation as a proportion of Gross Domestic Product has been cut from 35 to 30 per cent.' Barber's claim did not take account of successive increases in compulsory National Insurance contributions (not officially counted as a 'tax') to pay for annual uprating of pension and social security benefits, nor of sharp increases in user charges for NHS medicines, school meals, and rents for local authority housing, but it broadly accords with the reported financial outcomes discussed in Chapter Two and the more detailed figures given in the Appendix.

Up to 1973, that reduction in income and other taxes was not accompanied by significant cutbacks in government spending. Indeed, such spending rose markedly in the early 1970s, and the gap between spending and taxation was covered by increased borrowing on a scale which the Opposition claimed to have exceeded that which occurred during World War II: '... under this government, expenditure has risen more rapidly than at any time in our history'.[4]

The position changed dramatically in 1973. In that year, a balance of payments surplus that had followed the 1967 devaluation (described in Chapter Six) turned into a large trade deficit, the inflation rate rose to 10 per cent despite elaborate statutory control of wages and prices, and the government became locked into conflict with trade unions over wage demands. The

---

[2] 1970 Conservative Party General Election Manifesto, 'A Better Tomorrow', http://www.conservativemanifesto.com/1970/1970-conservative-manifesto.shtml.
[3] Harold Wilson, HC Deb 21 March 1972, c.1395.
[4] Harold Wilson, HC Deb 6 March 1974, c.283.

result was an energy shortage caused by a coal miners' strike that led to the imposition of a three-day working week and rolling power cuts in early 1974. And in October 1973, after the Yom Kippur war, the OPEC oil-exporting countries restricted oil supplies, producing a quadrupling of oil prices over the next year and recession across the oil-importing countries.

The Heath Government responded to these developments by a mini-budget in December, imposing extra taxes on higher earners and land developers and announcing plans for 20 per cent cuts in capital spending and 10 per cent in general procurement spending in most policy domains in FY 1974/75, though it spared public housing and (most unusually for a spending squeeze) avoided cuts in public service employment.[5] The Opposition claimed the government was using the OPEC oil price hike as a smokescreen for what it would have had to do anyway to correct the financial consequences of tax cuts funded by borrowing.

That revenue squeeze increased sharply after Heath's Conservative Government called and unexpectedly lost a general election in February 1974 on the issue of 'who governs Britain?' in relation to its dispute with the coal miners that had led to the three-day working week mentioned earlier. After the Conservatives failed to agree terms for a coalition with the Liberals, a minority Labour Government led by Harold Wilson took office.

Labour went into the election with a manifesto heavily influenced by left-wingers within the Party, committing itself to 'a fundamental and irreversible shift in the balance of power and wealth in favour of working people and their families', 'far greater economic equality—in income, wealth and living stand-ards', 'drastic redistribution of income and wealth' through an annual wealth tax, cuts in defence spending to the European average, the abolition of NHS prescription charges, further state intervention in and ownership of industry, and renegotiation of the UK's terms of entry into the EEC, followed by an in/out referendum on membership of the Community.[6]

In his post-election budget, the new Labour Chancellor, Denis Healey, announced plans to raise public spending by about £700m in FY 1974/75 (to increase pensions and welfare benefits by almost 30 per cent, subsidize basic foods, and spend more on public housing, all of which had been prom-ised in Labour's manifesto) but also increased taxes by approximately double that amount. That steep tax hike—for which the new government blamed its Conservative predecessor for its debt-funded tax cuts—comprised extra indir-ect taxes on road fuel, alcohol, and tobacco, and higher direct taxes, while the general rate of VAT was cut from 10 to 8 per cent. The direct tax increases

---

[5] HC Deb 17 December 1973, *cc*.952–79.
[6] Labour Party manifesto February 1974, 'Let Us Work Together—Labour's Way Out of the Crisis', http://www.politicsresources.net/area/uk/man/lab74feb.htm.

comprised a higher rate of Corporation Tax, a rise in the standard rate of income tax by an amount similar to the Labour income tax increases of 1950 and 1964, reversing the Conservatives' cuts, and a steep increase in the top tax rate from 75 to 83 per cent (or 98 per cent in the case of investment incomes). Later Healey (1990: 402) claimed the combination of increased taxes on higher earners combined with pay restraint for ministers meant that his own real take-home pay as Chancellor fell to only half what he had been earning as Defence Minister the previous decade.

After barely eight months in office (during which it ended the miners' strike with an above-inflation pay settlement, repealed the Conservatives' trade union legislation, and retained a seat in the only by-election of the Parliament), the Labour Government was re-elected in a second general election in 1974 with the slimmest of overall parliamentary majorities (of three) and deeply divided between right- and left-wing factions. Labour campaigned on a manifesto seeking a mandate for the policies it had advocated in its February manifesto, albeit with no explicit repetition of its earlier proposals for a wealth tax or 'radical redistribution' of income and wealth, and indeed no mention of extra taxes at all.[7]

There was no pre-election give-away budget, but in a second budget immediately after the general election (the third budget in less than a year), Healey raised taxes on road fuel further (by levying VAT on petrol at a new rate of 25 per cent), as well as introducing new taxes on the profits of oil companies, capital transfers, and land development (something the previous Conservative Government had planned). He also announced plans to phase out the massive deficits incurred by state-owned enterprises as a result of previous price restraint 'as fast as possible', implying big price rises for utilities.[8]

The revenue squeeze continued with the 1975 budget, which raised the basic and higher rates of income tax by an extra two percentage points (but not the highest rate, which was already 98 per cent and thus effectively at a confiscatory level), lifting the basic rate of income tax to 35 per cent from the 30 per cent at which it had been left by the Conservatives. Moreover, with inflation well over 20 per cent, most income tax thresholds were raised by only about half that inflation rate. That pattern of 'fiscal drag' (later described by the Labour Chief Secretary to the Treasury, Joel Barnett (1982: 23) as a 'stealth tax') continued in later budgets until a Labour backbench revolt led to statutory price indexation of income tax allowances in 1977, and indeed revenue from income tax and National Insurance contributions increased more rapidly than the rate of inflation, while the opposite applied to excise

[7] Labour Party manifesto October 1974, 'Britain will Win with Labour', http://www.politicsresources .net/area/uk/man/lab74oct.htm.

[8] HC Deb 12 Nov 1974, *c*.268.

duties).[9] At the same time, the higher 25 per cent VAT rate that had been imposed on petrol in the November 1974 budget was applied to other goods deemed to be 'luxuries' (such as TVs), vehicle excise duties were raised, and taxes on alcohol and tobacco were sharply raised as well.

However, the 1975 budget also marked a politically significant transition from the revenue-only, tax-to-spend fiscal squeeze of the previous year, which had been accompanied by an increase in public spending of about 10 per cent, to the first explicit mention of public spending cuts. Challenging the Labour left, Healey declared for the first time in his 1975 budget statement that spending cuts had become 'inevitable'[10] and announced (for FY 1976/77) a 3 per cent cut in planned spending on defence, a 10 per cent cut in planned capital spending, and a 1.5 per cent cut in planned increases in civil expenditure (with numerous 'ring-fenced' areas, so as not to breach Labour's electoral promise to increase current spending on social security).

In addition to Labour's explicit political choices to increase retirement pensions, housing subsidies, and food subsidies, public spending was also being driven upwards by a system of planning public expenditure in volume-terms (rather than cash) which the Conservatives had introduced a decade or so earlier, following the 1961 Plowden Report,[11] arising from earlier concerns about failures to forecast and plan public spending over time. Both Denis Healey and his Chief Secretary, Joel Barnett, seem to have viewed that system as contributing to the breakdown of spending control by the Heath Conservative Government, through 'encouraging [politicians] to concentrate attention on the relatively distant future while the short-term situation was getting out of control',[12] which postponed planned cuts to the end of the planning cycle. Healey expressed doubts about this system in his 1975 budget statement,[13] and began to abandon it in the following year, when the revenue-only squeeze to finance higher public spending turned into a combined tax and spending squeeze.

## 7.3 1976 and After: Spending Squeeze in Political, Monetary, and Fiscal Crisis

Our analysis of financial outcome data in Chapter Two showed up two further fiscal squeezes associated with the Labour Government of the 1970s—FY

---

[9] HC Deb 15 April 1975, c.286.    [10] HC Deb 15 April 1975, c.294.

[11] *Control of Public Expenditure*, Cmnd 1432 1961 (London: HMSO). See also Mackenzie (1963); Lowe (1997).

[12] Memo by Joel Barnett, Chief Secretary of the Treasury, June 1976, 'Secret: Public Expenditure—the 1976 Survey', T371/106, 'Public Expenditure 1977–78: Chancellor's Statement 22nd July 1976 on Public Expenditure Reductions'.

[13] HC Deb 15 April 1975, c.279.

1976/77, which involved a hybrid squeeze (hard on spending, soft on revenue) that accompanied two major international bailout loans, and the following year, when the hard spending squeeze continued but revenue fell as well as expenditure and indeed fell by slightly more than spending.

This period has attracted far more discussion than the squeeze episode described in section 7.2, owing to the political drama associated with a major currency crisis and the high degree of conflict engendered within a left-of-centre party in government as it moved in stages over the course of a year (in February, July, and December) from an initial tax-and-spend stance to the adoption of significant spending cuts for 1977/78 and 1978/79 (see Burk and Cairncross 1992; Latham and Prowie 2012). Most of the political players and the then Permanent Secretary of the Treasury (Douglas Wass) also published accounts of this episode (Barnett (1982); Callaghan (1987); Dell (1991); Donoughue (1987); Healey (1990); Wass (2008)). Building on our analysis in Chapter Two, three features of this episode can be noted at the outset.

First, there were substantial falls in recorded spending relative to GDP in 1976/77 and 1977/78 (1.5 and 3 percentage points respectively). And while there was certainly some 'cosmetic' element in those recorded changes (on which we comment later) those spending falls also undoubtedly reflected major political cost to the incumbents, as we shall show later.

Second, this squeeze episode occurred during a fiscal crisis—that is, a struggle to finance a substantial budget deficit in the face of a steep decline in the currency on the international markets—and was accompanied by a major international bailout with strings attached that came to be a byword for fiscal squeeze. It is true that the degree of 'exogeneity' involved in this episode is disputed: most accounts of the period suggest that at least part of the dramatic fall in the currency from March 1976 reflected a deliberate policy by the central bank to contrive a fall in sterling by cutting interest rates and selling the currency, though who exactly knew what when, and how far any depreciation of the currency was intended to go, is still contested (see Hickson (2005: 74–8); Fay and Young (1978)). But even so, a key part of the drama was played out on the currency markets in a way that did not apply to the earlier revenue squeeze episode, when the pound had been relatively stable.

It was far from the first time that the UK had borrowed from the IMF to stabilize its currency, which happened several times in the 1950s and 1960s, and perhaps most notably by the previous Labour Government in 1967, as discussed in Chapter Six. But the scale of the bailout far exceeded any previous IMF loan to the UK (or indeed to any other country at that time) and the degree of conditionality attached to it was also greater than that applying to the 1967 IMF loan, adding to its political significance.

Third, like all the other post-World War II squeeze episodes (from the 1940s to the 1990s at least), this squeeze was conducted in an era of inflation.

Indeed, it was the most inflationary of all those post-World War II episodes, and consequently offered the greatest opportunity for revenue squeeze through 'fiscal drag', as mentioned earlier (i.e., not indexing tax thresholds to take account of inflation as money incomes rose) and for spending squeeze through widespread application of cash limits on spending and other limits on indexation of expenditure—both of which are marked features of this episode.

## 7.4 The Turning Point: 1975–76

In the crisis year of 1976, Harold Wilson's third Labour Government had been in office for two years. Its parliamentary majority of three disappeared in that year as a result of defections and by-election defeats, but it might plausibly have been able to 'muddle through' towards a general election expected in 1978 or 1979. By that time, the economy was expected to be out of the deep recession associated with the OPEC oil price shocks, the government's efforts to get the inflation rate down below 10 per cent by 'social contract' deals with labour unions (which had replaced the earlier Conservative Government's statutory price and wage controls) might have been expected to have borne some fruit, and revenues from the developing North Sea oil and gas fields would be rising sharply, giving room for tax cuts or spending increases that would help to improve Labour's re-election prospects.

In the event, the Labour Government found itself in a dramatic crisis. It began to shift from the initial revenue squeeze to raise public spending to a squeeze on spending in the autumn of 1975, when (following months of talks between the Treasury and the IMF[14]) the Labour cabinet agreed to apply to the IMF for a stand-by loan to support the currency, which had fallen sharply since 1971. Since the IMF, probably under US influence, had become more sceptical of Keynesian-type expansionary fiscal policy than it had been a few years earlier and was likely to demand spending cuts as a condition of a major loan, the Chancellor presented the cabinet with a spending plan that involved no cuts in planned public expenditure for the next financial year (1976/77), but reductions in planned increases in public spending of the order of 1bn in 1977/78 and £2.4bn in 1978/79. These proposals were opposed on the left by Labour heavyweights Tony Benn and Anthony Crosland, even though the latter had argued in a much-quoted 'party's over' speech earlier that year that local government spending needed to be cut. But the cabinet as a whole

---

[14] For example, the Chancellor and Treasury officials met with two senior IMF officials in April 1975 to discuss the terms of a possible loan. T364/50 International Monetary Fund including Letter of Intent.

approved Healey's spending plan and in return the IMF approved a stand-by loan of some US $2bn from the start of 1976 (Hickson (2005: 58–9)).

Those cuts in planned future spending were announced early in February 1976 in a White Paper on Public Expenditure to 1979/80.[15] Written for several audiences (Labour's left-wing Tribune Group as well as the IMF), the White Paper was carefully packaged as a plan to hold public spending broadly constant in real terms over four years, in contrast to what had happened over the previous few years. It began by stating that voters' expectations of better public services and welfare programmes had not been matched by economic growth or willingness to pay more taxes, such that in the previous three years, national output had risen by less than 2 per cent while public expenditure had grown by nearly 20 per cent and the ratio of public expenditure to GDP had gone up from 50 per cent to 60 per cent. The White Paper partially blamed the world recession for that outcome and declared there were signs that the recession was bottoming out, meaning that its plan to stabilize public spending at its 1976/77 level for some years would cause the public expenditure to GDP ratio to fall again when economic growth returned (and implying that there might be some fiscal relaxation as the next general election approached, as did indeed happen).

But that White Paper, comprising the fiscal package agreed by the cabinet to accompany the January IMF loan, came to grief on the floor of the House of Commons as a result of a left-wing Labour backbench revolt after a debate on 9 and 10 March. The voting outcome was messy and complicated, with an Opposition motion to reject the White Paper defeated but the Chancellor's motion to approve the White Paper also defeated, by twenty-eight votes. That vote left fiscal policy in confusion and indeed raised constitutional questions as to whether the Labour Government should resign at that point, but the government succeeded in winning a confidence vote the next day.

Less than a week afterwards (on 16 March), the prime minister, Harold Wilson, suddenly announced his retirement at the age of sixty, a bombshell announcement that came out of the blue and is still the subject of numerous conspiracy theories (see, for instance, Wright 1987; Leigh 1988), though the mainstream explanation is that it reflected Wilson's developing health problems. There then followed three weeks of policy paralysis in government as Labour's left-wing heavyweights (Michael Foot and Tony Benn) battled in party leadership elections against figures from the centre-right (James Callaghan, Denis Healey, Roy Jenkins, and Tony Crosland) in three successive ballots. Healey's chances were damaged by the conflict over his public expenditure plans, and Callaghan, who had been the first Chancellor in the Labour

---

[15] *Public Expenditure to 1979–80*, Cmnd 6393 (London: HMSO, 1976).

Government of the 1960s (as discussed in Chapter Six), was eventually elected at the third ballot. Callaghan defeated Michael Foot (who had led in the first ballot) by some thirty-nine votes, but his victory was hardly a walkover, and his cabinet consequently included some key figures from the left of the Party (such as Tony Benn and Peter Shore) in major ministerial positions.

Just two days after Callaghan became prime minister following his election as Labour leader, the Party lost its fragile majority in Parliament with the resignation of one of its MPs[16] to join the English National Party. One seat short of an overall majority, Callaghan struck a deal with the Scottish National Party and Plaid Cymru, promising legislation to introduce devolved assemblies in Scotland and Wales in exchange for parliamentary support from those parties. And the day after Callaghan's election, the Chancellor introduced what he described as an 'almost neutral budget',[17] reiterating the policy proposed in the February Expenditure White Paper of holding public spending at current levels for several years but also declaring that 'we have set ourselves against short-term cuts in spending in the current year'[18] (a stance which led to attacks from the Opposition Conservatives under their new leader Margaret Thatcher as avoiding tough decisions in reducing the deficit: 'a big borrower's budget from a soft-options Chancellor'[19]).

But in the summer of 1976 the fiscal squeeze moved from reining in future planned increases in public spending to plans for deeper spending cuts in FY 1977/78 along with a further revenue squeeze. As already mentioned, the currency had fallen precipitously on the international money markets since early March. It continued to slide after Callaghan's election, despite the government's reiteration of its policy to stabilize public expenditure as the recession ended. In June it hit what was then a record low against the US dollar, dropping from $2.40 in early 1975 to under $1.60 at one point, and it went on falling until October. Accordingly, in mid-1976 the government faced the options of letting the pound going into free fall, imposing severe import restrictions despite the UK's entry to the EEC, or going for a bailout deal with economic allies to prop up the currency while a further fiscal squeeze was applied to meet the conditions for a bigger IMF bailout loan later in the year.

The battle between right and left in the Labour Party turned on the choice between the second and third option, with Callaghan and Healey opting firmly for the third, while the Labour left (led by Tony Benn and Peter Shore) and the Trades Union Congress argued for the second. Despite the

[16] John Stonehouse, a former cabinet Minister, who was then in prison awaiting trial for insurance fraud after extradition from Australia. The Conservatives later won Stonehouse's former constituency in a by-election.
[17] HC Deb 6 April 1976, c.280.     [18] HC Deb 6 April 1976, c.267.
[19] HC Deb 6 April 1976, c.289.

ideological differences between the UK Labour Government and Gerald Ford's Republican Administration then in office in the United States, the US Treasury Secretary agreed in June to part-fund a short-term stand-by loan of $5.3bn to support the pound. But this bailout was only a temporary stopgap: the money had to be repaid by December and by September the UK government had drawn so heavily on this loan that it could only repay it by borrowing from another source, namely the IMF.

Going for a major IMF loan led to repeated battles within the Labour cabinet and later in the Party's annual conference during two phases of decision to tighten the fiscal squeeze in July and December 1976. In July the government went beyond the cuts in planned increases in future spending that had been proposed by the February Expenditure White Paper to announce a further £1bn of cuts in planned expenditure in 1977/78 accompanied by a surcharge on employers' National Insurance contributions that was expected to bring in another £1bn in revenue in 1977/78. And in December, as part of a bailout package agreed with the IMF, the government announced a further £1bn reduction in planned spending for 1977/78 and a £1.5bn reduction in planned spending in 1978/79.[20]

Treasury files from the period show how officials and ministers worked over the hot summer of 1976 to arrive at that July fiscal squeeze package. The Treasury extended cash limitation of budget allocations (a powerful way of reining in spending at a time of high inflation) from a measure used mainly for capital projects to a much larger swathe of public expenditure (Hickson 2005: 58), a move Healey later described as highly successful.[21] And an extra £1bn of proposed spending cuts for 1977/78 was presented by the Chancellor to the House of Commons on 22 July 1976, which was reported in the press to have been the subject of some seventeen hours of cabinet discussion,[22] indicating the level of friction and political stress involved in the process.

Before that July statement, the prime minister, James Callaghan, was reported to have met with seventy junior ministers to explain the proposed cuts and call for government unity—an approach that evidently had the desired political effect, since there were no resignations either from the cabinet or from lower ministerial ranks at this point. The parliamentary vote on the public spending package was tight because the Conservatives under Margaret Thatcher chose to welcome the 'belated' plan to cut public sector borrowing but to attack the specific means chosen, and the Scottish National Party's then ten MPs voted against the government with the Conservatives.[23]

---

[20] Letter of Intent sent by the Chancellor to the IMF, 15 December 1976: 5–6.
[21] HC Deb 29 March 1977, c.269.   [22] T371/171 Public Expenditure 1977–78.
[23] The SNP's then leader, Donald Stewart, declared: 'The outlook for the United Kingdom is grim...We are weighted down by England's bankruptcy. In a free Scotland it would be different...' (HC Deb 22 July 1976, c.1291).

But the July fiscal squeeze package was not the end of the process. In September the government formally applied to the IMF for a loan of nearly $4bn (at least $30bn today) on top of the $2bn the IMF had provided in January. That was then the largest amount ever requested from the IMF, which had to obtain extra funds from the US and Germany to raise the sum required, and the last time any Western country went to the IMF for a loan until Iceland, Hungary, and Belarus did so in 2008. The bailout plan was opposed by the left in cabinet, because in return for the IMF loan a cap had to be agreed on public sector borrowing, requiring further spending cuts on top of those already planned—a far cry from the absence of any serious conditions attached to the IMF loan at the time of the sterling devaluation in 1967. The bid for a further IMF loan also led to strife in the Labour Party's annual conference in September, when Callaghan made a speech containing a famous passage written by his son-in-law Peter Jay: 'We used to think that you could spend your way out of a recession by cutting taxes and boosting government spending. I tell you in all candour that that option no longer exists.'

That third stage of fiscal squeeze in 1976 culminated in a formal application for the further IMF loan in mid-December, after a battle in cabinet early that month, when proposals from ministers on the left (Tony Benn and Peter Shore) for import quotas were finally rejected in favour of the IMF bailout option. That bailout involved a ceiling on borrowing that required a further reduction of £1bn in 1977/78 spending plans and £1.5bn in spending plans for the following year—plus further increases in alcohol and tobacco taxes, as announced by Denis Healey just before the Christmas holiday.[24] A key feature of the package—almost a fifth of the total—was the announcement of an intention to sell government stock in the state-owned oil company BP while retaining a majority shareholding.

In this squeeze episode, sharply contrasting with those of the 1920s and 1930s, as well as most of the other post-World War II episodes, social security spending was not cut. The Labour cabinet decided at the outset against spending cuts in this domain, in part reflecting the Party's inherited political baggage over that issue from 1931.[25] It also gave priority to overseas aid and to some industrial spending, increasing funding for public venture capital in industry and to the nationalized British National Oil Corporation while cutting back on capital spending by other state-owned enterprises. And as already mentioned, another distinctive feature of this squeeze is that there was no

---

[24] Treasury's spin doctors suggested the package should be presented 'as an adjustment to policies which are already on the road to being successful, not as a response to a "crisis"' (memo by P.V. Dickson and J. Anson, December 1976, T371/171 Public Expenditure 1977–78).
[25] Joel Barnett (1982: 64 and 98) comments on the references back to 1931 that were made by Labour Party figures at the time.

major cut in defence spending, unlike in the 1920s squeeze and all the other post-World War II spending squeezes.

The Treasury's approach, as in the case of the Geddes Axe in the 1920s, was to start by looking at what could feasibly be cut without legislative change (and that was arguably an even more important consideration in this episode, given that the Labour Government had lost its overall majority in Parliament).[26] As a result, many of the cutbacks comprised delays or deferrals of existing capital projects, imposing moratoria on new spending and limiting new commitments in areas such as road building. Consequently, capital spending fell sharply, with deep cuts in public sector net investment from 1976 onwards.

Cuts in housing expenditure (which, as noted earlier, Labour's February 1974 manifesto had promised to increase) figured large in those reductions, and central government housing expenditure relative to GDP fell from around 6.7 per cent in 1974 to 2 per cent by 1979. Indeed, in a memo written ahead of the July squeeze package, considering cuts that could feasibly be made in 1977/78, the Chief Secretary (Joel Barnett) saw housing as offering the greatest scope for spending reductions without legislation, since there were some large items that could be cut back quickly.[27] The following month, a Treasury official (Nicholas Monck) described housing, along with regional and industrial policy, as the spending domain presenting the greatest political difficulties for the Labour cabinet.[28] Monck was referring to a reduction in planned local authority council house building from 10,000 to 6–7000 starts per month in England (with similar reductions in Scotland and Wales) which was part of the spending reduction package and was described by Monck as 'politically the most explosive component', indicating the political costs involved to Labour ministers.

In the same vein, the July 1976 spending cuts package for 1977/78 included an accelerated phase-out of the food subsidies promised by Labour in its February 1974 election manifesto. And whereas social security was 'ring-fenced' in this episode, education spending was cut sharply, as with all of the other spending squeeze cases examined in this book except for the 1940s and 1990s. Education spending was cut by nearly 1 per cent of GDP, falling mainly on spending on schools and the further education colleges that were

<hr/>

[26] Memo by Joel Barnett, June 1976, 'Secret: Public Expenditure—the 1976 Survey', T371/106, 'Public Expenditure 1977–78: Chancellor's Statement 22nd July 1976 on Public Expenditure Reductions'.

[27] Memo by Joel Barnett, June 1976, 'Secret: Public Expenditure—the 1976 Survey', T371/106, 'Public Expenditure 1977–78: Chancellor's Statement 22nd July 1976 on Public Expenditure Reductions'.

[28] Letter from N. Monck, Treasury, to J.A. Marshall, Cabinet Office 14 July 1976 T371/106, 'Public Expenditure 1977–78: Chancellor's Statement 22nd July 1976 on Public Expenditure Reduction'.

then funded by local authorities. Cuts were also applied to spending on police, fire services, and local authority garbage collection and sewerage services. Civil service employment started to fall from a high point through staffing reductions, mainly achieved by a hiring freeze.

The overall result in reported financial outcomes, as discussed in Chapter Two, was a very hard expenditure squeeze in 1977/78, with a fall in public spending of 3.7 per cent in constant prices and some three percentage points relative to GDP. But by no means all of those dramatic reductions came from the cuts mentioned above, and some of them seem to have come from convenient if not creative accounting. Douglas Wass (2008: 331), the then Permanent Secretary of the Treasury, notes that part of that large fall in reported public expenditure in 1977/78 came from an increase in foreign currency borrowing by state-owned industries and from a fall in refinancing of export credits (as a result of private banks being persuaded to refinance such credits). Joel Barnett (1982: 124–6), Chief Secretary of the Treasury at that time, also comments extensively on the effort and ingenuity (in that case said to have come from Harold Lever, the Chancellor of the Duchy of Lancaster) that went into the export refinancing switch and other related changes to produce reductions in reported public spending and the estimated Public Sector Borrowing Requirement.

## 7.5 The Final Phase: 1977–78

After the fiscal dramas of 1976, there was a modest economic recovery the following year (albeit with continuing high unemployment and balance of payments deficits), inflation started to fall, and after its low point in October 1976, the currency began to recover on the international markets as North Sea oil and gas came on stream. As noted earlier, in March 1977, the Labour Government, with no overall majority, avoided defeat on a 'no confidence' motion by securing a one-year 'confidence and supply' agreement with the Liberal Party in exchange for accepting some Liberal proposals.

As announced by Healey the previous year, 1977 saw the first big privatization of recent decades, in the form of a sale of 66 million BP shares in 1977 that realized £564m towards the planned cuts of £3bn. The 1977 budget (dubbed by Margaret Thatcher as 'an IMF budget',[29] reflecting the government's borrowing cap agreed as part of the IMF bailout) further raised taxes on road fuel and vehicle licences, and though it raised income tax thresholds to the point of taking some 845,000 people who would otherwise have paid tax out of the

---

[29] HC Deb 29 March 1977, c.294.

net, critics pointed out that the government's previous tax changes had brought over a million people into the income tax net and that the much-trumpeted increase in tax thresholds did no more than correct for inflation.[30]

The month after the 1977 budget the Conservatives won by-elections in two out of three previously Labour-held constituencies, and another previously Labour-held seat fell to the Conservatives early the following year. With a general election expected in the autumn of 1978, when the Lib–Lab pact was due to expire, the government began to moderate the spending squeeze in the autumn of 1977. In October the Chancellor announced that some £1bn was to be added back to expenditure plans for 1978/79, mainly consisting of an extra £400m for construction and over £300m for raising the rates of child benefit in 1978. The 1978 budget also raised income tax thresholds further, introduced a new lower tax rate of 25 per cent on the first £750 of taxable income (though the changes still left the real level of income tax thresholds lower and the standard rate higher than they had been at the start of 1974), and announced a further uprating of retirement pensions to take effect in November, claiming that the real level of such pensions had increased by some 20 per cent over the life of the government.

Despite this relaxation in the fiscal squeeze, unfavourable opinion polls persuaded Callaghan to remain in office as head of a minority government rather than call a general election when the Lib–Lab pact ended in 1977, in the hope that an economic upturn and further tax cuts could boost Labour's chances in a general election the following year. But a winter of industrial disputes sparked by the government's public sector pay caps hampered the Labour campaign, and the government lost control of the election date after a referendum on Scottish devolution in March 1979 (when the numbers approving the devolution proposal fell short of the threshold required for enacting the legislation). At that point, Margaret Thatcher tabled a parliamentary motion of no confidence in the Labour Government, which was supported by the Scottish National Party and carried by a single vote.

As a result, the Labour Government could neither hold an election at the time of its own choosing nor bring out a giveaway pre-election budget, and Denis Healey merely introduced a 'caretaker budget' raising all tax thresholds by the rate of inflation. With the Liberals damaged by allegations that their former leader, Jeremy Thorpe, had conspired to murder a former gay lover, the subsequent general election in May 1979 turned into a straight fight between Labour and the Conservatives, producing a Conservative majority of forty-four and the largest swing between the two parties since 1945.

---

[30] (John Stokes), HC Deb 29 March 1977, c.315.

## 7.6 Conclusion

The later squeeze episode in this chapter generated political drama at a level at or close to that of 1931. Joel Barnett (1982: 23), the Chief Secretary of the Treasury from 1974 to 1979, argued that the UK experienced special fiscal difficulties after 1974 as a result of Denis Healey's decision to react to the massive oil price hikes of that time by maintaining plans for increased spending and borrowing to cover the gap (in contrast to the spending-cuts policies followed by countries like Germany and Japan in response to the oil price rises). Given that the UK saw virtually no economic growth between 1974 and 1977, Barnett argued, the decision to maintain expenditure necessitated very big tax increases to avoid even larger borrowing. As in previous chapters, we conclude by assessing the squeezes that have been qualitatively described here in the light of the three sets of issues raised in the opening chapter about the politics of fiscal squeeze.

### 7.6.1 *Tax and Spending, Depth and Duration, Blame and Control*

As we have seen, the 1970s comprise a number of different episodes of fiscal squeeze, according to our analysis in Chapter Two. One, relatively little discussed, was the revenue squeeze running from 1973/74 to 1975/76, sparked off by a right-of-centre government at the end of a debt-fuelled boom but mostly taking place under a left-of-centre government which chose to raise taxes sharply to allow for an increase in public spending, mainly on housing and welfare.

The later Labour squeezes comprised a combination of a spending and revenue squeeze in 1976/77, followed by a notably hard spending squeeze of 1977/78 to 1978/90, associated with an international bailout of 1976, which involved the deepest cuts in civil expenditure since the 1930s, along with some tax increases. Some elements of non-fiscal austerity applied as well, in the form of historically high interest rates for much of the period, and wage caps of one kind or another (statutory in the case of the Heath Government 1972–74 and part of a 'social contact' between the subsequent Labour Government and the labour unions, but with wage caps set well below the inflation rate for public sector workers in the final squeeze episode).

All three governments in this period sought to lay part of the blame for the fiscal squeezes they enacted on world economic conditions (the oil price hike and the world recession of that time) and the Labour Government in its first term in part blamed its predecessor's financial management for necessitating fiscal correction through steep tax increases. But as in the 1950s and 1960s, all three governments retained direct control of most of the principal instruments of austerity policy (interest rates, the economic forecasting accompanying fiscal changes, and choices over spending cuts and tax rises) rather than seeking to limit blame by passing any of those instruments to arms-length bodies.

### 7.6.2 Loss, Cost, and Effort Involved in These Episodes

Following the format of previous chapters, Table 7.1 is a summary assessment of how the fiscal squeeze episodes discussed in this chapter rate in terms of the three qualitative elements of intensity of squeeze discussed in Chapter One.

The revenue squeeze begun by the Heath Conservative Government seems to have involved non-trivial losses, if only because it came on top of non-fiscal austerity in the form of high inflation and unemployment accompanied by wage caps. The state machinery was certainly heavily engaged with handling strikes (as in the 1920s period) and related issues of regulating trade unions, but fiscal issues more narrowly do not seem to have exposed it to more than moderate effort. Political costs to the incumbents seem to have been fairly high, in that the government found itself squeezing spending and raising taxes (albeit mostly on non-core voters) in what turned out to be the run-up to an election and at least went against the spirit of the Party's 1970 manifesto pledge to cut rates of surtax.

**Table 7.1.** A qualitative classification of imposed loss, political cost, and state effort associated with 1970s fiscal squeezes

| | Low | Moderate | High | Overall classification |
|---|---|---|---|---|
| 1973–75. Squeeze Type: Hard Revenue | | | | |
| Conservatives, 6/1970–2/1974 | | | | |
| Loss | | [1], [2] | [3] | High–Mod |
| Cost | | [1] | [1], [2] | High–Mod |
| Effort | | | [1], [2] | High |
| Labour, 2/1974–10/1974 | | | | |
| Loss | [3] | [2] | [1], [2] | Moderate |
| Cost | [4] | [1] | | Moderate |
| Effort | | [1], [2] | [1] | Moderate/high |
| Labour, 10/1974 onwards | | | | |
| Loss | | [1], [2] | | Moderate |
| Cost | [2] | [1], [2] | | Moderate |
| Effort | | [3] | [1] | Moderate |
| 1976. Squeeze Type: Hard Spending/Soft Revenue Labour, 10/1974 onwards | | | | |
| Loss | | [1] | [1] | High/moderate |
| Cost | | [1], [2] | | Moderate |
| Effort | | [1] | | Moderate |
| 1977–78. Hard Spending—Labour, 10/1974 onwards | | | | |
| Loss | | [1] | [1] | High |
| Cost | | [1] | [1] | High |
| Effort | | | [1], [3] | High |

*Note:* Numbers in square brackets refer to categories in Table 1.2, Chapter One.

For the first Labour revenue squeeze, imposed losses seem to have been at least moderate, given the heavy extra taxation commented on by Joel Barnett (albeit with some of it falling on non-core voters, and offset in part by extra spending on food subsidies). The exertions required of the government machine also seem to have been at least moderate, but the political costs to the incumbents seem to have been relatively low, with those revenue squeezes in part foreshadowed and at least not ruled out by the Party's 1974 election promises.

As time went on in the subsequent stages of the Labour squeezes, those political costs arguably rose as it became less possible to blame the squeeze on the previous government and the losses imposed seem to have risen as well through effects such as fiscal drag and extra taxes on items such as petrol. But the 1977/78–1978/79 hard spending squeeze seems to be a clear case of high loss or effort on all three of the qualitative elements of fiscal squeeze intensity.

That was the first substantial reduction in civilian spending for two decades and differed from the 'two years of hard slog' post-devaluation Jenkins squeeze of 1968–69, discussed in Chapter Six, both in the depth of the spending cuts imposed and in their composition. As we saw in Chapter Six, the Jenkins squeeze had focused heavily on cutting defence, while in this episode defence was cut only lightly and the cuts therefore fell on civilian spending, excluding current spending on social security but including several items that had figured prominently in Labour's 1974 manifestos.[31]

Further, while the Jenkins squeeze of 1968–69 was certainly far from conflict-free, this episode witnessed a deep political crisis going along with a financial crisis, involving both a leadership contest following a sudden prime ministerial resignation and a battle running over nine months or so between rival views of how to deal with a fiscal crisis, further splitting a fragile and divided party barely able to muster a majority in Parliament for its legislation.

### 7.6.3 Electoral and Other Consequences

The fiscal squeezes described in this chapter seem to have produced uneven electoral punishment from voters. The Heath Conservative Government lost the snap election following its emergency mini-budget of December 1973 that marked the end of its period of direct tax cuts funded by borrowing, but voters were arguably at least as concerned to punish that government for its handling of industrial relations as for its fiscal record. The subsequent Labour Government did not suffer electoral punishment for its early revenue squeeze designed to fund higher public spending.

---

[31] The Chancellor noted: 'Almost all of the spending cuts ran against the Labour Party's principles, and many also ran against our campaign promises' (Healey (1990: 401)).

It was the fiscal squeeze episode of 1976–78 (accompanied as it was by the biggest rise in both unemployment and inflation since World War II) that produced the most dramatic electoral punishment, in the form of a 5.2 per cent vote swing from Labour to the Conservatives, after which Labour was out of power at central government level for eighteen years. The Liberal Party, which had propped up the Callaghan Labour Government in 1977–78, also experienced electoral punishment in the form of a 4.5 per cent loss of vote share and the loss of two out of its then eleven parliamentary seats. The October 1974 and May 1979 election outcomes are both compatible with the 'asymmetrical punishment' idea explored in Chapter One, that left-of-centre governments may be more liable to electoral punishment for spending cuts than for tax increases.

Indeed, as argued earlier, on top of that electoral defeat, the 1976 battle over spending cuts and the IMF bailout exacerbated an existing division in the Labour Party, resulting in a short-term victory for the right over fiscal policy but also helping to sow the seeds for the victory of the left in the Party in the 1980s, when it was powerful in local government and controlled many of the big cities but was out of office at central government level. The schism that arose within the Labour Party over that final episode was arguably more serious than the decade-long split between Bevanites and Gaitskellites following the imposition of charges for NHS dentures and spectacles in Labour's 1951 budget, because the conflict was not contained within the Party (as happened after 1951). Instead, it led to the formation of a breakaway centrist party as a result of the defection of four leading Labour frontbench 'moderates' to form a new Social Democratic Party in 1981 (which later merged with the Liberal Party in 1988 to form the Liberal Democrats of the present day). In that sense the political consequences involved in that final episode seem to be more like those of 1931 than 1951.

In terms of other consequences too, it is the final squeeze episode discussed in this chapter that seems to have left more of a legacy than the earlier ones, even though the spending cuts were partly cosmetic, proved relatively short-lived, and aggregate spending soon went back up again, in contrast to the cuts of the 1920s. But as we have seen, the 1976–78 episode saw a major Rubicon crossed in the institutional control of public expenditure, in the form of a big extension of cash limits as a means of controlling a wide swathe of public spending, linked to regular in-year reporting of departmental expenditure in cash. The 'Plowden' system, of medium-term multi-year volume-terms planning of public expenditure allied with economic forecasting, lingered on alongside the cash limits regime until 1982 when the Thatcher Government formally killed it off,[32] and multi-year expenditure planning was destined to

---

[32] *The Government's Expenditure Plans 1982–83 to 1984–85*, Cmnd 8484 1982 (London: HMSO).

reappear in a different form some decades later. But it can be argued that it was this squeeze episode that reinstated cash limits as the basis of managing public spending for the next thirty years.

Finally, this episode also involved policy developments of long-term consequence. The outcome of the long left–right battles within the Labour Party in 1976 put paid for at least a generation to the idea of dealing with fiscal and monetary problems by imposing exchange and import controls command economy-style, put forward by politicians who remembered the application of such measures during and after World War II. It represents the last time up to the present day that such an approach was seriously considered. And the major privatization that was central to Denis Healey's 1976 fiscal adjustment package—the massive sale of stock in the former state-owned oil company BP in 1977—probably unintentionally blazed a trail for the spate of privatizations of former state-owned enterprises under the Conservatives that were to ensue in the following decade. Of course there had been some denationalizations (for example, of steel and road transport) under the Conservatives in the 1950s, but the major public share flotation involved in the BP sale was the first significant Labour privatization and arguably represented a new way to sell state assets, proving in every sense to be the start of something big.

# 8

## Rolling Back the State? Fiscal Squeeze, Thatcher-Style

### 8.1 Background: The Period in Perspective

Like the Labour squeeze associated with the 1976 IMF bailout, the story of 'Thatcherism'—the policies of the Conservative majority-party governments led by Margaret Thatcher in the 1980s—has been told frequently and from many different angles. As with the 1970s episode, many of the leading players published memoirs, and archives for much of the period were available at the time of writing. This chapter does not seek to offer any new interpretation of the much-discussed topic of Thatcherism in general, only to look at that period through the lens of 'fiscal squeeze', to compare it with the other episodes covered in this book.

As we saw in Chapter Two, reported financial outcome data show up two main fiscal squeeze episodes in the 1980s. One was a hard revenue squeeze after the 1979 election, some of which seems to have come from an abrupt near-doubling of VAT rates in 1979 under Margaret Thatcher's first Chancellor (Geoffrey Howe) and more from a deeply controversial budget in 1981 which sharply raised taxes, in the depths of what was then the most severe recession since World War II. The other episode is a longish (five-year) 'soft' squeeze on both revenue and expenditure under Margaret Thatcher's second Chancellor (Nigel Lawson) that shows up in the financial outcome numbers from 1983/84. That second episode occurred during a long period of economic growth (albeit with turbulence in both politics and financial markets), as the deep recession triggered by a steep increase in the world oil prices in 1979 gave way to economic recovery from 1982/83 and developed into a financial boom.

As with several of our other cases, this era brings out the limitations of using reported aggregate financial outcome data as the sole indicator of the political effort going into fiscal squeeze, for several reasons. One is that undeniable efforts by ministers to cut public spending in the Thatcher Government's first term (following 1979 election pledges to do so) did not produce an overall fall in expenditure in the reported outcome figures shown in Chapter Two. That is because the early 1980s recession greatly pushed up welfare spending (and related employment measures for training and work experience) as unemployment rose by a million to hit 2.5 million in 1981, more than doubled between 1979/80 and 1982/83, and reached levels not seen since the 1930s. At the same time, the economy shrank (with GDP contracting by about 2 per cent in 1980), such that, far from falling, government spending rose relative to GDP. So the early Thatcher period is a case where cyclically adjusted figures may give a better indication of the efforts going into restraining spending.

A second point relating to the reported revenue numbers in this case is that North Sea oil came fully on stream during this period. That development had various effects, including turning the pound into a petrocurrency in the government's first term, with severe effects on manufacturing. But from a fiscal squeeze perspective the important consequence is that it gave the government a major new source of tax revenue in the early 1980s (amounting to something like half the yield from income tax), greatly increasing government revenue and making room for cuts in business and personal taxes that would otherwise have been far more difficult. So there is room for argument as to how far revenue increases derived from newly exploited natural resources really amount to a 'squeeze'.

A third issue with reported financial data as indicators of fiscal squeeze concerns the asset sales for which the Thatcher Government became internationally famous (though it followed in the wake of the previous Labour Government's big sale of BP stock in 1977, discussed in the Chapter Seven). The 'privatization swag', as the government's critics termed it,[1] had the effect of lowering spending by reducing the need for borrowing, and it is also debatable how far asset sales really amount to a squeeze on spending. For all these reasons, it is important to look behind those aggregate outcome figures in Chapter Two.

## 8.2 The First Thatcher Squeeze

The 1979 election produced an overall majority of forty-four for the Conservatives, who had promised the voters 'substantial economies' in public spending, to be achieved among other things by scrapping 'expensive socialist programmes' like land nationalization and outsourcing the work done by heavily-unionized direct labour organizations in local government.[2] The

---

[1] (Neil Kinnock), HC Deb 17 March 1987, c.833.
[2] Conservative Manifesto 1979, http://www.politicsresources.net/area/uk/man/con79.htm.

Conservatives also promised a switch from taxes on earnings to taxes on spending, with cuts in income tax at all levels, including the topmost rates and the tax surcharge on income from savings and investment. (The Liberals also campaigned for income tax cuts in the 1979 election, proposing a basic rate of 20 per cent and top rate of 50 per cent.)

The Conservative manifesto also reflected a commitment to 'monetarism' in the form of targets for limiting the growth of the money supply by restricting public and private debt. Such targets had been adopted in effect under the previous Labour Government, and indeed that approach is traced by some scholars back to the late 1960s, contrary to the view that monetarism only appeared in the Thatcher era (Davies 2012). But the process of setting and applying those targets was now formalized, elaborated in new arcane jargon and reflected acceptance of monetarist doctrine by some leading Conservatives, including Sir Keith Joseph and Margaret Thatcher.

Monetarist concerns to limit government borrowing (Miller (1981)) meant more pressure to apply fiscal squeeze, albeit through a justification different at least in detail from the pre-World War II ideas about balanced budgets that were discussed in Chapters Three and Four (Neild (2012)). And the higher interest rates that were another part of the monetarist medicine in the early years of the Thatcher Government also pushed up public spending by increasing the costs of debt servicing, as well as constituting an element of non-fiscal austerity.

Those 1979 election promises to cut spending and taxes had some resemblance to the 'set the people free' platform on which the Conservatives campaigned in 1951, as described in Chapter Six. And there were other parallels with the early 1950s. Like its Conservative predecessor of 1951, the Thatcher Government comprised many ministers who had been in the 1970–74 Heath Government only five years earlier and who could draw on what they had learned from that experience in a way not open to those governments with little previous ministerial experience, for example in 1924, 1997, or 2010. Also comparable with the early 1950s was the fact that the new government's fiscal stance was affected by several 'post-dated cheques' left by the previous Labour Government in the form of catch-up public sector pay settlements (which the Conservatives had promised to honour in their 1979 manifesto, and which sharply pushed up the public sector pay bill between 1979/80 and 1980/81). Moreover, as with the early 1950s, the Labour opposition was divided, partly in consequence of ongoing conflicts associated with the 1976 fiscal squeeze.

But there were also differences between 1979 and 1951. At forty-four, the Conservative Government's parliamentary majority was much larger than in 1951 and the Labour opposition was arguably more divided. As mentioned in Chapter Seven, whereas the split between the Bevanites and the Gaitskellites originating in the battles over spending cuts in 1950/51 had been contained within the Party, the 1980s were more like the 1930s for Labour in that the divisions led to the formation of a breakaway Social Democratic Party, set up in 1981 by four ex-Labour ministers disaffected with what they saw as excessive domination of the Labour Party by the far left. Twenty-eight Labour MPs (and one Conservative) eventually defected to the new party, which scored dramatic victories in two by-elections in 1981–82, formed an electoral alliance with the Liberals, and deeply split the left-of-centre vote.

Further, the economic background after the 1979 election differed greatly from that of the 1950s. As already mentioned, the North Sea oilfields came into full production in the 1980s, giving the Conservatives a huge new revenue source not available to their 1950s predecessors (a revenue squeeze can still be identified for 1980/81 even when oil revenues are excluded, but the squeeze is much less deep when calculated that way). But oil also provided a major exogenous shock, in that a large spike in world oil prices only weeks after the Conservatives won government triggered recession across the developed world, increasing UK unemployment by a million and a half, particularly in manufacturing. That unemployment, together with the Thatcher Government's emphasis on the contested doctrine of monetarism ('sado-monetarism', as its opponents dubbed it), produced political conflict and criticism over the government's efforts to contain public spending in the early 1980s recession that seems to have gone much deeper than in the early 1950s. Perhaps the high point of such criticism was a statement in *The Times* newspaper in March 1981[3] signed by 364 academic economists (including most of the officeholders of the Royal Economic Society, and five of the post-World War II Chief Economic Advisers to the Government) highly critical of the government's 1981 budget and of Margaret Thatcher's often-repeated claim that there was no real alternative to the government's policies.[4] The degree of opposition within the economics profession to the 1981 revenue squeeze seems to have gone much deeper than in the squeezes of the 1950s, 1960s, and even 1970s, and is arguably more comparable to the disputes over the ideas of 'expansionary fiscal contraction' associated with fiscal squeeze across the eurozone in the 2010s (Needham and Hotson (2014)).

As the Conservatives had done in 1951, the new government began trying to squeeze public spending as soon as it took office. One of its early tactics (reminiscent of that adopted by the 1954 Swinton Committee described in

---

[3] 'Monetarism Attacked by Top Economists', *The Times*, 30 March 1981, p. 1 (continued p. 15).

[4] The letter was immediately used by the Labour opposition as political ammunition against the government. Unusually, it provoked a formal rebuttal from the Treasury, arguing that, 'although the 364 economists assert that there are alternative policies, they are unable to specify any…agreed alternatives'. ('Treasury Denies Economy Damaged by Policies', *The Times*, 31 March 1981, p. 3).

Chapter Six) was to ask all departmental ministers to say what would be needed to reduce their 1979/80 staff costs by 10 per cent, 15 per cent, or 20 per cent by the end of 1981/82. That led to a plan developed at the start of the government's life imposing ambitious targets for cuts in civil service headcount from over 730,000 in 1979 to 630,000 by 1984.

Similarly, following an idea originally floated by Nigel Lawson and others in the 1970s, the government developed a four-year plan (the Medium Term Financial Strategy) for public spending to 1983/84. Intended as a commitment mechanism, the Strategy was described by the Chancellor as 'a logical development of the "letters of intent" which our Labour predecessors had been obliged to send to the IMF' (Howe (1994): 169). Championed by Nigel Lawson, then Financial Secretary of the Treasury, and eventually published alongside the 1980 budget, the MTFS aimed not just to reduce the previous Labour Government's plans for spending increases but also to squeeze spending in constant-price terms, cutting it by some 4 per cent between 1980/81 and 1983/84.

Within that total, the plan was to increase defence and law and order spending, raise spending on health by an amount similar to that planned by the previous Labour Government (that is, about 2 per cent a year, offset by higher prescription charges and other charges, including on overseas health 'tourists' using the NHS and on insurance companies for NHS treatment of road traffic accident victims). Overall education spending was to be cut but school rolls were falling at that time, such that spending per pupil would still increase. Civil service staffing and overseas aid were among the areas selected for big cuts.

Related to those plans, two politically important spending changes were introduced in the post-election 1979 budget.[5] One was a reduction of the real value of sickness, unemployment, and other social security benefits (first by raising them by five percentage points less than the rise in the price index and later, in 1982, subjecting them to income tax). The other was the breaking of what had been a double lock on pension payments introduced by the previous Labour Government. That 'double lock', meaning that state retirement pensions were to be increased according to the rate of price or earnings increase, whichever was the higher, was broken in the post-election budget, which changed the system to uprating on the basis of price indexation alone. But, important as these changes may have been in the long term, neither served to reduce overall spending immediately. Rising unemployment in the government's early years drove up expenditure on benefit payments and special employment measures. And high inflation in the early years of the Thatcher

---

[5] T366/456, Approach to the Second 1979 Budget, Treasury note, 4 April 1979.

Government (in 1980 inflation was running at about 22 per cent on the measures used at that time) meant that breaking the double lock on pensions only began to bring down spending relative to GDP when price rises started to fall behind earnings growth during the economic recovery a few years later.

For these and other reasons, those 'substantial economies' in public spending promised by the Conservatives failed to materialize in the first few years after 1979 and the targets of Lawson's 1980 Medium Term Financial Strategy were dramatically missed. A key political turning point in that process seems to have come in 1982, in the form of a cabinet revolt over a review for options for significant cuts in public spending relative to GDP in a low-growth environment that was leaked to the media and provoked major political attack from opposition parties claiming the government was contemplating a wholesale demolition of the welfare state (Lawson (1992): 189). But the government did deliver on its promise to switch the relative tax burden from earnings to consumption, albeit in the context of an overall tax squeeze that had certainly not been trailed in the 1979 Conservative manifesto and which produced high political conflict, not only between government and opposition but also within the Party and the cabinet.

The Treasury's 1979 post-election briefing (with two separate versions to cover the eventuality of a Conservative or Labour victory) pointed out that there had been a notable shift from indirect to direct taxes as a result of 'inertia policies' that had raised direct tax levels from a quarter to a fifth of average earnings in the 1970s Labour squeeze, while reducing the relative share of indirect taxes based on nominal rates for the same reason.[6] The Treasury expected the Conservatives if elected to go for a higher unified VAT rate (unifying the 'standard' rate and the 'luxury' 25 per cent rate mentioned in Chapter Seven) of about 12.5 per cent, and Labour to opt for a unified VAT of about 10 per cent.

But the new Chancellor, Geoffrey Howe, opted for a rate of some 15 per cent.[7] According to his memoirs, Howe (1994: 130) argued that the government's first budget presented the only political chance for such a big tax hike, although Margaret Thatcher was reluctant to agree to raise VAT above 12.5 per cent. The post-election 1979 budget duly enacted a dramatic shift from direct to indirect taxation by all but doubling the (standard) VAT rate at a stroke while cutting the standard rate of income tax from 33 to 30 per cent and the top rate of tax (on earned income) from 83 to 60 per cent.

While that post-election move substantially altered the tax structure (and created its own winners and losers) it does not show up as a revenue squeeze

---

[6] T366/525, Treasury Post-Election Briefing for the Labour Party, April 1979.
[7] Note of a meeting between the Chancellor and Treasury officials to discuss the budget, 9 May 1979, T366/456.

for 1979/80 in Chapter Two, because the 1979 budget intended the extra yield from increased VAT (plus increases in fuel duty and Petroleum Revenue Tax) to be more than offset by reduced yield from lower income tax rates and higher thresholds.[8] Outside the formal realm of taxation, NHS prescription charges were more than doubled (and were doubled again the following year) and the Chancellor's budget speech announced a plan for asset sales amounting to approximately £1bn in 1979, pointedly declaring, '... we shall follow the example of the previous administration'. Neither of the latter two measures had been foreshadowed in the 1979 Conservative manifesto, which did not feature the word 'privatization' or mention the asset sales for which the Thatcher Government later became internationally famous.

As well as the 'headwinds' already mentioned that pushed up public spending in the Thatcher Government's early years (high welfare spending as a result of the recession, high debt servicing costs, and the manifesto commitment to honour catch-up public sector pay settlements agreed by the previous government), there were other forms of resistance within the Party and the cabinet. Some of the government's early ideas for increasing charges to offset spending proved impractical or hit a political brick wall, and the Chancellor was defeated by Margaret Thatcher and others in an attempt to resist a NATO target of increasing defence spending by more than the rate of inflation (Howe 1994: 144). The Financial Secretary to the Treasury, Nigel Lawson, recalled in his memoirs that though the Chancellor secured cabinet agreement to a reduction in total planned public expenditure for 1981/82 in July 1980, the autumn bilateral discussions between the Treasury and spending ministers failed to produce agreement on ways to realize such cutbacks, and one of the major savings proposed, namely to abandon annual uprating of retirement pensions for inflation, was of the 'political boomerang' nature that was predictably later overturned in cabinet as electorally toxic (Lawson (1992): 59–60).

Perhaps the most public and dramatic political reversal over spending restraint in the government's first few years was a proposal to charge parents for school transport (a measure the Treasury had frequently floated to ministers in the 1950s), estimated to save about £50m a year.[9] The plan was defeated in the House of Lords in 1980 by opponents from across the political spectrum including such Conservative grandees as the Duke of Norfolk and Lord 'RAB' Butler, who as Chancellor had presided over the mid-1950s fiscal squeeze (James (1997): 195–7). A plan for charging insurance companies for NHS treatment of road traffic victims also came to nothing.

---

[8] Budget statement, HC Debs 12 June 1979, c.251 and 261.
[9] Paper circulated by the Chief Secretary of the Treasury (John Biffen) as background for the cabinet's discussion of the 1980 Public Expenditure Survey, July 1980, CAB 129/204/14.

In the run-up to the 1981 budget the Treasury detected doubts or resistance among Conservative backbenchers to other spending cuts, including criticism of a perceived tendency to target capital spending for cutbacks, resistance to cuts in defence spending, pressure for increases in child benefit payments, and resistance to proposals to trim the next uprating of retirement pensions by 1 per cent.[10] And as already mentioned, there was a major cabinet row over a review of options for public spending cuts in 1982 which forced the government to retreat and deny that it was considering radical options for reducing welfare state expenditure.

At the same time, efforts to limit the budget deficit (which had risen from the cap of 3.75 per cent of GDP agreed in the 1976 IMF loan agreement discussed in the previous chapter to 5.5 per cent in 1978/79 and about 6 per cent in 1980/81) led to continuing efforts to increase tax revenue. Those efforts included successive hikes in indirect taxes on fuel, alcohol, tobacco, and vehicles at about twice the rate of inflation, higher rates of compulsory National Insurance contributions for three years in succession, and new taxes on North Sea oil production in 1980, in just the sort of revenue-raising mini-budget the Conservatives had condemned during the Labour years and resolved to eschew (Lawson (1992): 60; Howe (1994): 190).

The high point of the revenue squeeze arguably came in the controversial 1981 budget, in the form of complete non-indexation of personal income tax thresholds and allowances for that year—partly to create room for more tax breaks for companies aimed at helping employers at a time when the government was facing severe political criticism over the rise in unemployment. There had been debates within government over whether to increase the basic rate of income tax or freeze tax thresholds, with the prime minister and Chancellor opting for the latter as the least electorally damaging (Howe (1994): 204). But freezing tax thresholds and allowances effectively increased income tax rates (and raised tax revenue by some £2bn) through 'fiscal drag' at a time when annual inflation was about 20 per cent. There was even a one-off 2.5 per cent windfall tax on bank deposits in the same year, a measure that a left-wing Labour Chancellor might have adopted with enthusiasm (it resulted in the resignation of one PPS, Tim Renton) and which reflected the 'desperate circumstances' (in Lawson's (1992: 62) words) the cabinet felt itself to be in.

The degree of political effort that went into this much-discussed revenue squeeze went far beyond the 'inertia' level discussed in Chapter One and indeed must rank alongside episodes such as 1931 and 1976, in that manifesto promises had to be set aside and significant political capital expended to pass the necessary legislation. The tax increases in the 1981 budget flew in the face

---

[10] T414/374 Spring Budget 1981, Budget briefs, 20 February 1981, comment on 'outside representations—political groups'.

of the Conservatives' 1979 election pledges to cut taxation and pressures from parts of the Party to abolish domestic rates, the local property tax. It went against established Keynesian economic doctrine and the views of many respected economists that fiscal squeeze together with a tight money policy would exacerbate the recession as well as pressures for a fiscal expansionism by business groups and trade unions. It provoked fierce and continuing political attack from the Opposition[11] and many other critics as unemployment soared and communities were blighted by industrial closures.

The non-indexation of income tax allowances also reflected high political effort in that it went against an explicit statutory requirement to index such allowances, the so-called 'Rooker-Wise amendment', which had been written into the 1977 Finance Act as a result of a backbench revolt, mentioned in Chapter Seven, against the previous Labour Government's practice of revenue squeeze through 'fiscal drag' (raising tax allowances by less than the inflation rate). The Thatcher Government therefore had to legislate to set aside that indexation requirement in its 1981 Finance Bill (Lawson (1992), Chapter 9). Threats of a Conservative backbench revolt against an increase in tax on diesel in the Finance Bill also forced the government to cut the proposed increase in diesel taxation by half and make up the revenue foregone by higher taxes on betting and tobacco.

Although the 1981 budget did not involve the long-drawn-out cabinet wrangling over spending cuts packages that took place under Labour Governments in 1931 and 1976 (indeed there was no detailed prior consideration of the budget prior to the cabinet meeting on the morning of the budget itself), the prime minister was said to have been aghast at the political prospect of the steep tax increases proposed,[12] and the cabinet was divided over the plans (Lawson (1992): 64) says they were 'roundly attacked' by 'the usual wets'). It is not hard to understand those political anxieties. By March 1981 the government was extraordinarily unpopular in opinion polls, with only 16 per cent of IPSOS-Mori poll respondents expressing satisfaction over the way it was running the country. Other indications of the government's political unpopularity were the loss of over 1000 Conservative seats in 1981 local government elections and the fact that the Conservatives sank to third place in the opinion polls for a time after the formation of the Social Democratic Party in 1981. Even the rioting that broke out in several deprived urban areas

---

[11] For instance, the Labour leader, James Callaghan, described the 1980 budget as, '...three years of austerity and industrial decline on the basis of a stagnating economy combined with shifting the burden from the healthy to the sick and from the rich to the poor'. (HC Deb 26 March 1980, c.1492). The Labour MP Jack Straw described the budget as 'vicious and wicked' (HC Deb 26 March 1980, c.1508).
[12] Stephanie Flanders (2006) 'Were 364 Economists All Wrong?', http://news.bbc.co.uk/1/hi/programmes/newsnight/4803858.stm, accessed July 2015.

in England between April and July of that year (including Brixton, Handsworth, Southall, Toxteth, Hyson Green, and Moss Side) seems to have been sparked in part by discontent over government fiscal policies in the face of recession and unemployment.

The combination of the revenue squeeze that reached its peak in the 1981 budget and the effects of mass unemployment on public spending meant that both revenue and overall government spending in fact rose as a proportion of GDP over the first term of the Thatcher Government, despite the government's efforts, manifesto promises, and ambitions—a fact that was not lost on its critics in the run-up to the 1983 general election.[13] However, in the general election of 1983 the Thatcher Government managed to avoid the electoral punishment that (as of 1981) might have been and was predicted for a government that had raised taxes and presided over steeply rising unemployment.

Several reasons have been given for the lack of electoral punishment in this case. One factor stressed by observers such as Peter Riddell (1987: 4), is that the political opposition was more divided than at any time since the 1920s. The breakaway centrist party, the Social Democrats, came within 700,000 of Labour's total vote in the 1983 general election, deeply splitting the anti-Conservative vote, even though the SDP only won six seats. The defection of many Labour 'centrists' to the SDP left the Labour Party itself dominated by the left and campaigning on a far from 'centrist' manifesto that included unilateral nuclear disarmament and Britain's departure from the European Union.

Another factor stressed by commentators such as Andrew Marr (2007) is a form of 'heresthetic', as mentioned in Chapter One, in this case taking the form of the diversionary effect of an extraneous crisis over the invasion of the Falkland Islands (Malvinas)—remote and sparsely populated islands in the South Atlantic which were a British Crown dependency but claimed by Argentina in a long-running territorial dispute—by General Galtieri's military government in Argentina in April 1982. Argentina's invasion followed reductions in UK defence expenditure in the South Atlantic, and thus was partly prompted by the Thatcher Government's efforts to cut spending. The invasion triggered high-risk military operations by the UK to recapture the islands with a combined-operations task force. Some claim the unexpected war provided a powerful diversion from the 'blame game' over the government's handling of tax, unemployment, and recession, suddenly boosting its popularity as a result of support from most of the tabloid press that dramatically changed Margaret Thatcher's fortunes as a political leader. But this view is

---

[13] (Austen Mitchell) HC Deb 15 March 1983, c.181.

contested by those observers (notably Sanders et al. (1987)) who note that, from the low point of March 1981, the Conservatives had recovered their lead in the opinion polls and their support was accelerating before the Argentine invasion, such that the so-called 'Falklands factor' was worth only a few points at most in the polls.

A third view, advanced by David Sanders and others (Sanders et al. (1991); Dunleavy (1991: 123)), is that the distributive effects of the Conservatives' economic policies (such as income tax cuts, council house sales, trade union reforms) on median or swing voters over this period account for the absence of severe electoral punishment in 1983, though some (such as Kempley (2010)) have objected that those policies created large numbers of losers as well as winners, such that the split on the left and the division of the Opposition is a more convincing explanation of the electoral outcome. In addition, as noted earlier, about half the extra taxation raised in the 1981 budget comprised a one-off windfall tax and new taxes on oil production, meaning that any losses they imposed on key or median voters were far less visible than changes in income tax, National Insurance, and the major indirect taxes. Further, it can also be noted that the revenue squeeze was accompanied by increasing expenditure and also by tacit abandonment of the tight money policy associated with the government's initial enthusiasm for monetarism, to the point that observers such as Robert Neild[14] have argued that the net effect of the 1981 budget was expansionary.

For those or other reasons, March 1981 proved to be the low point of the Conservatives' popularity and their opinion poll ratings subsequently began to climb. It is true that unemployment went on rising (albeit at a declining rate from 1982), remained very high by historical standards, and indeed did not fall until 1986. But just as the 364 economists signed their famous letter, the recession was bottoming out. By 1982/83 GDP had begun to rise, while (partly due to a fall in world oil prices) inflation fell to half the rate it had been in 1980. Those developments eased the upward pressure on public spending and thereby cut the budget deficit. So the 1982 and 1983 budgets relaxed the earlier revenue squeeze (even though they did not wholly reverse it) and eased restrictions on consumer credit as well.

Accordingly, while most of the tax reduction in the 1982 budget was directed to creating more tax breaks for business (for example by reducing a surcharge on National Insurance contributions by employers, an easy-to-collect payroll tax that had been introduced by the previous Labour Government), that budget raised personal income tax thresholds and allowances by slightly more than the inflation rate while leaving the standard tax rate

---

[14] Quoted by F. Williams, 'The Economic Mirage—by "Rebel" Professors,' *The Time*, 30 March 1984.

unchanged at 30 per cent and raising most excise taxes only in line with inflation. The next budget, before the 1983 general election, was not a pre-election giveaway on the same scale as the Conservative budgets of 1955 and 1959 and contained no eye-catching cuts in income tax rates, but it raised tax thresholds and allowances by well above the inflation rate. It also added other pre-election sweeteners, such as raising pensions to a level that allowed the Party to claim it had delivered on a 1979 manifesto pledge to protect the real value of pensions, as well as raising child benefit and extending tax relief on mortgage payments for first-time home-buyers.

Whatever accounts for the 1983 electoral outcome, this major revenue squeeze episode (as well as the rise in unemployment to levels previously thought to be politically unsustainable in the government's first term) is notable for the absence of severe retrospective punishment from the voters. Instead of sharing the electoral fate of the previous Labour Government, the Conservatives only saw their overall vote share fall by 1 per cent or so, and under the first-past-the-post electoral system the split on the left between Labour and the SDP had the effect of increasing the Conservatives' parliamentary majority by some sixty seats. Any electoral punishment for revenue squeeze was muted and indeed the outcome in this case amounted to de facto electoral reward.

## 8.3 The Later Thatcher Episode: Squeezing in Recovery

The second fiscal squeeze in the 1980s that shows up from the reported financial outcomes data analysed in Chapter Two was very different from the Thatcher Government's first-term squeeze. It included a long-drawn-out 'soft' spending squeeze between 1983/84 and 1988/89, producing a balanced budget in 1987–88 and government spending falling relative to GDP but not in constant prices. Along with the soft spending squeeze went a soft revenue squeeze, in that revenue rose in real terms but not relative to GDP. But as mentioned earlier, the special conditions producing that revenue outcome mean it is debatable how far that 'squeeze' involved pain inflicted on mainstream voters.

Within that overall picture, a closer analysis reveals an uneven time-pattern related to the election cycle, with spending cut in real terms as well as relative to GDP (that is, 'hard' in our terminology) in most policy domains in 1985/86 and 1988/89, but much less severe cuts in all areas of current spending except defence in FY 1986/87 ahead of the 1987 general election. On the revenue side, the only area in which there are signs of the electoral cycle punctuating the soft squeeze is that of taxes on income and wealth, the revenue from which fell in 1986/87 and 1987/88 while rising in real terms for all the other years of the episode.

This second Thatcher squeeze involved an exceptionally long period of continuous economic growth (indeed, the longest continuous period of growth for over half a century at that time, ending only in 1990), mostly combined with low inflation. A squeeze on public spending began barely a month after the 1983 general election, with the new Chancellor, Nigel Lawson, announcing cuts in planned spending that led to accusations that the Conservatives had misled the voters in that election (given that the Party's 1983 manifesto had not explicitly indicated that public spending would be cut).[15]

The plan for public spending to decline relative to GDP as GDP grew was a strategy that Nigel Lawson first formulated publicly in 1983 and described as more politically 'realistic' than the frustrated attempts to cut real public spending in a recession in the Thatcher Government's first term (Lawson (1992): 191). That approach was enshrined in another Medium Term Financial Strategy announced in 1984, aiming for public expenditure to remain relatively flat in constant-price terms at 1984/85 levels while GDP rose.[16] Moreover, during this economic growth period, the strategy adopted by the Thatcher Government of uprating pensions and other welfare benefits in line with prices but not earnings meant that over the years spending on such items—40 per cent or more of overall government expenditure—fell relative to (rising) GDP. At the same time, reported unemployment began to fall towards the end of the government's second term (although the official numbers were heavily disputed), which served to reduce spending on welfare and related work programmes. Further, the accounting practice of counting the proceeds of asset sales through privatization (running at approximately £5bn a year at this time) as negative public expenditure also contributed to the reported spending outcomes shown in Chapter Two, such that the depth of this spending squeeze episode would be about one-eighth lower without such asset sales (see HM Treasury (1994) Table 1.1: 8).

On the revenue side, yields rose overall in constant-price terms, but the Chancellor (Nigel Lawson) repeatedly claimed, for example in his 1988 budget speech, that 'income tax has been reduced in each of the last six budgets—the first time this has ever occurred'.[17] The standard rate of income tax was indeed

---

[15] The election manifesto said, 'We shall maintain firm control of public spending and borrowing...Less spending by government leaves more room to reduce taxes on families and businesses.' But it did not mention any specific spending reductions. Conservative Election Manifesto 1983, 'The Road to Recovery', http://www.politicsresources.net/area/uk/man/con83.htm.

[16] *Financial Statement and Budget Report* 1984 HC 304 1983–4: 8–9.

[17] Nigel Lawson, budget speech, HC Deb 15 March 1988, c.1006.

cut from 30 to 25 per cent in stages between 1983 and 1988 and in 1986 the government claimed credit for raising the main thresholds and allowances by 20 per cent above the rate of inflation.[18] Moreover, Lawson claimed credit over this period for abolishing several taxes introduced by Labour over this period (including the National Insurance payroll surcharge, the income tax surcharge on investment income, Development Land Tax, and tax on lifetime gifts) and reduced or abolished higher rates of income tax and inheritance tax, in the face of strong protests by opposition parties about what they saw as the distributional unfairness of such changes.

So why did overall revenue increase in constant-price terms at this time? One reason, already mentioned, was the effect of North Sea oil in adding an extra £6bn or more a year to the revenue base (for example, a much-trumpeted but unexpected budget balance achieved in 1987–88 was mostly down to oil revenues exceeding expectations by some £2.5bn). A second was the effect of falling unemployment, which halved between 1986 and 1989. And a runaway debt-fuelled consumer boom coming towards the end of the period (despite the government's earlier professed belief in monetary restraint) boosted revenue in various ways, for example, in VAT receipts from imports bought on credit.

Moreover, along with the successive reductions in income and corporation tax rates highlighted by Nigel Lawson went some notable (if perhaps less noticeable) increases in other taxes, including higher compulsory National Insurance contributions by employees and employers, higher excise taxes, particularly on road fuel, and (a sign of things to come in future decades) new taxes on pension funds in 1987. Over this period numerous tax offsets or allowances were also removed or reduced, notably investment allowances (removed in 1984) that enabled firms to set investment against Corporation Tax, the removal of tax relief on non-charitable gifts by covenant in 1988 and on life insurance premium payments in 1984, and less generous tax allowances for company-provided cars and other in-kind benefits.

Less clear as a factor that might account for the growth of revenue in real terms during this period is the so-called 'Laffer curve' effect mentioned in Chapter Two, in which reduction of nominal tax rates is said (within bounds) to have the effect of increasing tax paid as a result of making tax avoidance and evasion less worthwhile. Such effects were certainly claimed by the Thatcher Government, for instance, over the much greater yield from inheritance taxes in the late 1980s levied at much lower nominal rates than the Capital Transfer Tax introduced by its Labour predecessor in the 1970s.[19] To the extent that 'Laffer curve' effects contributed to real-terms revenue

[18] Nigel Lawson, budget speech, HC Deb 18 March 1986, c.182.
[19] Budget speech HC Deb 17 March 1987, c.826.

increases during this period, that again makes it problematic to construe that outcome as a tax squeeze in a meaningful sense. And even if this period did constitute a tax squeeze in a meaningful sense (albeit of the soft variety), it was decidedly different in style and content from previous revenue squeeze episodes (including 1980/81 to 1981/82) discussed earlier in this book.

The long period of economic growth that accompanied the soft squeeze on revenue and spending in the Thatcher Government's second term and the beginning of its third term was punctuated by at least four major shocks affecting revenue or spending or both, but none of those shocks had a sufficiently deep or long impact either to trigger recession or to undermine the conditions for that real-terms revenue increase and relative reduction in spending. On the political front, the two major shocks were the cost of the unexpected Falklands War of 1982, and a bitter and unexpectedly drawn out coal miners' strike in 1984/85 which threatened power supplies and forced the government to borrow an extra £2.75bn to cover the extra public expenditure associated with the strike.[20] On the economic and financial front, one of the major shocks was a market collapse in 1986 which took oil prices back down to their 1973 levels and thereby unexpectedly halved the UK's tax take from North Sea oil (from £11.5bn in 1985/86 to approximately £6bn the following year), such that the government had to resort to other taxes and extra borrowing to fill the gap. The other shock was a world stock market crash in 1987, which was feared by some at the time to presage a 1930s-type world slump but in the event did not do so.

Politically, the Thatcher Government during this period was challenged on the left by trade unions, notably in the public services and state-owned enterprises and especially by coal miners in the 1984/85 strike. The government was also challenged by several local authorities controlled by the Labour left, particularly in London and some other major cities, which opposed the government's successive attempts to limit local authority spending. But while these challenges put significant pressure on the Thatcher Government—notably in public order policing during the 1984/85 coal miners' strike and in battles with local authorities including the outright abolition of the Greater London Council in 1986—they do not seem to have seriously threatened that government electorally in its second term and may even have boosted the Conservative vote. And there was nothing quite comparable to the 'austerity' debates of the early 1980s described earlier, in which the government's fiscal and monetary stance had been argued to be counterproductive and a recipe for producing mass unemployment by serious professional economists as well as by the Conservatives' normal political enemies.

[20] Budget speech HC Deb 19 March 1985, c.783.

The Thatcher Government was certainly accused during this time by its political opponents of fiscal and economic mismanagement in various ways— notably, of 'frittering away'[21] the once-for-all revenues from North Sea oil on current spending rather than devoting those revenues to investment; of selling public assets to produce once-for-all revenue at the cost of sacrificing long-term income streams (Neil Kinnock, the Labour leader at this time, compared it to selling an owner-occupied house to live in rented accommodation);[22] and of promoting a consumer boom based on unsustainable levels of debt. The government's critics also argued that it had done too little to reduce unemployment, particularly in former mining and manufacturing areas; that it had not increased health care spending sufficiently to prevent waiting lists for treatment from lengthening; that despite its tax-cutting rhetoric, the tax burden on the average household actually rose by about 10 per cent between 1979 and 1987 as a result of increased National Insurance contributions, VAT hikes, and increases in domestic rates (the local property tax); and that by the later 1980s retirement pensioners were far worse off as a result of the 1979 move to remove the link with earnings.[23]

However, the Thatcher Government again did not suffer substantial electoral punishment in the 1987 general election after this four-year 'soft' squeeze. After a pre-election budget (described by the leader of the Opposition as a 'bribes budget'[24]) which cut the standard rate of income tax from 29 to 27 per cent and was presented with triumphalist rhetoric about steady growth, low inflation, and fiscal prudence, the Conservatives secured a third victory with a comfortable overall majority, albeit with a slight loss in vote share, a loss of some twenty-one parliamentary seats and a further geographical polarization between the Conservatives' electoral heartlands in the South of England on the one hand, and Scotland, Wales, and Northern England on the other.

So again, any electoral punishment for this second-term 'soft' squeeze was quite muted. And the final post-election budget of the 'soft squeeze' period, in 1988—introduced among tempestuous scenes in the House of Commons as opposition parties protested about what they saw as its social unfairness— applied the previous recipe with even sharper effect. It continued the pattern of cutting income tax rates for the sixth year in succession (with the basic rate of income tax cut from 27 to 25 per cent, and all higher rates of income tax

---

[21] A phrase used by the then acting Liberal leader, Jo Grimond, commenting on the 1980 budget. See HC Deb 26 March 1980, c.1499.

[22] HC Deb 17 March 1988, c.1021.

[23] Neil Kinnock, leader of the Opposition, claimed that in 1988 a single pensioner would gain an 80p pension increase as against £7.20 under the pre-1979 'double-lock' system. HC Deb 17 March 1988, c.833.

[24] HC Deb 17 March 1987, c.829.

above 40 per cent abolished), while some tax allowances were removed and the overall tax burden was not planned to fall relative to GDP.[25]

## 8.4 Conclusions

Margaret Thatcher expressed an ambition to 'break the mould' of British politics and that phrase (much used at the time) has often been applied to her government by commentators (for example, Dransfield and Dransfield (2003): 143). But whether it broke the mould of fiscal squeeze is debatable. Following the pattern of earlier chapters, we conclude with an assessment of the two Thatcher squeeze episodes in the light of the three sets of issues about the politics of fiscal squeeze that we raised in Chapter One.

### 8.4.1 *Tax and Spending, Depth and Duration, Blame and Control*

As we have seen, the Thatcher fiscal squeeze episodes comprised a short but deep revenue squeeze associated with rising expenditure in a deep recession and a longer 'soft' squeeze on both revenue and expenditure, accompanying economic growth. And to the extent that the metrics of squeeze from reported financial outcomes are meaningful for these episodes, they do not indicate that the Thatcher squeezes were 'off the map', as is so often implied by those who consider the 'Iron Lady's' Government to have been a unique one-off political era. Politically painful as it undoubtedly was at the time, the early 1980s revenue squeeze was not the most severe such squeeze in peacetime over the century (it was exceeded by the squeeze of 1919–21, and that was not able to draw on oil). And though the soft squeeze on spending in the later 1980s was comparatively long, the annual reductions it involved were not greater than the spending squeezes of 1953–55, 1977–78, or 2013 and are dwarfed by the spending squeezes of 1919–21, 1923–25, and 1946–49. Indeed, if we take out the proceeds of privatization, the annual average fall in spending relative to GDP is 1.3 per cent rather than the 1.6 per cent shown in Chapter Two, roughly similar to the spending cuts enacted in the 2010s, to be described in Chapter Ten. In short, those Thatcher Government squeeze episodes appear in comparative perspective to lie in the upper to middle range. But they are not off the scale.

When it comes to handling the blame for fiscal squeeze, too, the Thatcher Government chose, like its Labour predecessor, to keep direct control of the levers of fiscal and monetary policy rather than to deflect blame by delegating

---

[25] Budget speech HC Deb 15 March 1988, *c*.996 and 1006.

such functions to others (though it did so in other domains, such as regulation of utilities). Again like its Labour predecessor, it was inventive in the way it presented and packaged figures, and made much of blaming the previous incumbent for creating the need for its first-term fiscal squeeze, as well as world political and economic events such as the OPEC oil price hike and the war with Argentina. But that too seems more normal than exceptional.

### 8.4.2 Loss, Cost, and Effort Involved in These Episodes

We noted at the outset that the 1980s Thatcher Government episodes are cases in which the metrics used in Chapter Two to pick up 'squeeze' are arguably more problematic than in the previous five chapters. When we look at them through the prism of imposed losses, political cost to incumbents, and effort required of the state machine, as shown in Table 8.1, it is the early 1980s episode that appears to rate high on all three of these dimensions, for reasons given earlier.

In that episode, the Thatcher Government indeed had to expend political capital by breaking election promises, had to work the state machine well beyond its established routines in conditions of high conflict (for instance, in developing its privatization programme, unpicking the 'lock' on pension and benefit uprating, and developing measures such as the bank windfall tax), as well as imposing losses on median or core voters (notably by freezing tax thresholds in 1981) to raise revenue in what it saw as 'desperate circumstances'.

By contrast, the mid-to-late 1980s episode of 'double soft' squeeze looks more like medium or even low political effort on the scale we introduced in

**Table 8.1.** A qualitative classification of imposed loss, political cost, and state effort associated with 1980s fiscal squeezes

| | Low | Moderate | High | Overall classification |
|---|---|---|---|---|
| **1980–81 Squeeze Type: Hard Revenue** | | | | |
| Conservative 5/1979 onwards | | | | |
| Loss | [2] | [1], [2] | [1], [2] | High |
| Cost | | [1], [2] | [1], [4] | High |
| Effort | | [3] | [1], [2] | High |
| **1983–88 Squeeze Type: Soft Revenue/Soft Spending** | | | | |
| Conservative (until 6/1983) | | | | |
| Loss | [3] | [1] | [1] | Moderate |
| Cost | | [1], [2], [3] | | Moderate |
| Effort | | [1] | [1], [2] | Moderate/High |
| Conservative 6/1983 onwards | | | | |
| Loss | [3] | [3] | | Moderate |
| Cost | [1] | [2] | | Low |
| Effort | | [1], [2] | | Moderate |

Note: Numbers in square brackets refer to categories in Table 1.2, Chapter One.

Chapter Two. As we have seen, imposed losses in this episode were variable (hitting some voters hard while benefiting others), but many of those losses seem to fall into the 'moderate' category of Table 1.2, as 'stealth taxes' outside the headline rates of income tax, or 'stealth' benefit cuts such as the cumulative effects of the changes in pension uprating as inflation fell and economic growth resumed. Incumbents were not forced into breaking explicit election promises and could shape the timing of fiscal squeeze to the electoral cycle. More was required of the state machine in fiscal policy over this period than minor adaptations of existing routines, but the effort required arguably fell well short of that involved in cases such as the development of a new system of mass income taxation in World War II.

### 8.4.3 *Electoral and Other Consequences*

As we have seen, the electoral outcomes in this case run counter to the 'asymmetrical punishment' hypothesis discussed in Chapter One, in that a right-of-centre party escaped severe electoral punishment for a hard revenue squeeze, in quite special circumstances that included a major breakaway party splitting the left-of-centre vote (and for some the presumed 'heresthetic' effect of the Falklands War).

The electoral outcome of the second squeeze episode in 1987, when the Conservatives also escaped serious electoral punishment (losing some twenty-one seats on a miniscule 0.2 per cent swing), is arguably rather less of an anomaly. As we saw, the fiscal squeeze in that case was soft on both the revenue and spending side (even then, reflecting items like increased oil revenue and massive asset sales that arguably cushioned its effect on voters at large), and was moderated to fit the electoral cycle.

However, one notable electoral effect that occurred at that time that arguably had major long-term consequences, albeit hard to attribute as between fiscal squeeze and other factors in play at that time, is the decline of the Conservatives as a major political party in Scotland over this period (from twenty-two to ten of the then seventy-two Scottish parliamentary seats between 1979 and 1987, and from 31.4 to 24 per cent of the Scottish vote over the same period). How far the accompanying political pressures for constitutional change in the form of Scottish self-government and independence can be put down to the effects of Thatcherite fiscal squeeze is a major imponderable.

Beyond electoral effects, the 'Thatcherite' fiscal squeeze episodes discussed in this chapter seem to have had several other longer-term consequences. Its use of asset sales to reduce government borrowing requirements, itself borrowed from Labour's sale of BP shares in 1977, set a pattern for all subsequent governments to date (albeit under changing accounting rules) and led to a remarkable long-term decline in the net worth of the public sector relative to GDP. Its dramatic run-down of civil service employment in favour of more outsourced public service delivery also constituted a policy broadly continued under all subsequent governments (Hood and Dixon 2015). Its tactic, particularly in the soft revenue squeeze of 1983–89, of raising revenue in real terms but not relative to GDP by cutting or at least not increasing basic income tax rates while increasing revenue from indirect taxes and other less visible 'stealth' tax measures, also entered the political playbook of all its successors up to 2015. And the tactic underlying the soft spending squeeze of the Lawson Chancellorship—of raising spending, particularly on welfare, in line with inflation but below the rate of earnings growth over a relatively long period—set the pattern for the long-drawn-out 'boiling frogs' approach to spending cuts adopted in the 1990s and 2010s episodes, discussed in Chapters Nine and Ten.

# 9

# Fiscal Squeeze in the 1990s

## Tales of the Unexpected

### 9.1 Background: The Period in Perspective

The politics of the fiscal squeeze episode of the 1990s is distinctive and perhaps surprising in at least three ways. First, a Conservative Government not expecting to be re-elected (following the downfall of Margaret Thatcher, who was deposed as Conservative leader in 1990) turned out to be just as effective as the government of the 'Iron Lady' in the previous decade, if not more so, in restraining government spending in general and spending on administration costs in particular. Second, a split and fractious Conservative Party, which after re-election in 1992 proceeded to tear itself apart over the UK's membership of the European Union before going down to one of its biggest ever general election defeats in 1997, somehow managed to apply a surprisingly collective approach to containing the growth of public spending. And third, the squeeze was prolonged at the end of the period by a Labour Government elected by a landslide (bigger than what the Party had achieved in 1945) that had politically committed itself before the 1997 election to stick to its Conservative predecessor's plans for spending restraint for two years.

The economic background to this squeeze episode (in contrast to those of the 1920s, 1930s, and 1970s) resembled the second Thatcher episode discussed in Chapter Eight, in that it comprised a period of steady economic growth coming after a severe recession that began in 1990 and was exacerbated by the first Gulf War in 1990–91. That recession was shallower than that of the early 1980s in terms of fall in GDP, but produced similar levels of unemployment and lasted longer, confounding successive Treasury forecasts of early recovery that proved politically embarrassing to the incumbents. In the later 1980s the Thatcher Government congratulated itself on having permanently recast the public finances in a new balanced-budget mode, with public debt reduced to levels not seen since before World War I. But the early 1990s, recession, combined with a public spending blowout in the run-up to the 1992 general election, caused the budget deficit to leap from just over 1 per cent of GDP in 1990/91 to over 7 per cent in 1993/94—back to the 1970s levels that the Conservatives claimed their 'rolling back the state' policies had left behind.

However, when the economic recovery finally began, a mix of continuing growth and falling inflation made it possible for that unexpectedly re-elected Conservative Government to follow a tactic similar to that developed by Chancellor Nigel Lawson in the mid-to-late 1980s episode, cutting public spending relative to GDP (but not in constant prices) over successive years, broadly by uprating social welfare and other spending in line with the price index but by less than the increase in real GDP. At the same time, the unexpected collapse of the Soviet Union in 1991 reduced the perceived need for extra military and security spending (in contrast, say, to the late 1940s and the early 1950s discussed in earlier chapters, when the advent of the Cold War and the Korean War meant sharp upward pressures on military spending).

On the tax side, the pattern was again in some ways redolent of the second 1980s squeeze described in Chapter Eight. Revenue presented the mirror image of what happened to public spending, rising over the period as a whole in real terms but not relative to GDP as the economy grew. Within that overall pattern, there were 'hard' revenue spikes in the mid-1990s and again in 1997/98, in the first case reflecting swingeing post-1992 election VAT increases combined with a freeze on direct tax thresholds and allowances for two successive years, and in the second case reflecting post-1997 election tax changes by the newly elected Blair Labour Government, including a one-off utilities windfall tax. Taxes on road fuel also rose sharply over the period as a whole, eventually producing a dramatic fuel tax revolt by oil tanker drivers blockading refineries in 2000 which thereafter made governments more wary of imposing extra taxes on fuel. And both the Major and Blair Governments introduced new taxes over the period, many of which were dubbed 'stealth taxes' by their political opponents.

As before, this chapter aims to look behind the numbers we set out in Chapter Two and the data appendix. But since official archives for this period were not open at the time of writing, the account is based on public sources (speeches, media reports, politicians' memoirs), supplemented by a few inter-views with some of those involved in the Treasury at that time. We begin in 1992/23, when the Conservatives, re-elected but then seriously weakened by a major currency crisis that fatally damaged the then Chancellor's career, moved from pre-election tax giveaways funded by borrowing to a soft spend-ing squeeze linked to a revenue squeeze that was 'hard' for two successive years in the mid-1990s before being relaxed for the 1997 election. Finally, we turn to the continuation, indeed intensification of that squeeze for a time after 1997 under the subsequent New Labour Government headed by Tony Blair.

## 9.2 The Road to 1992: Recession, Tax Revolt, and Leadership Switch

In the early 1990s, the Conservatives, in office for over ten years, were nearing the end of their third term in deep political difficulties over economic management. Inflation, which had been markedly reduced in the earlier period of Conservative Government, rose again from the late 1980s, and was running at about 10 per cent in the early 1990s. And after the 'Lawson boom' of the later 1980s, described in Chapter Eight, 1990 saw the start of another major recession that lasted longer than that of the early 1980s and was only slightly smaller in its effects on output and unemployment. The latter again rose to three million and so was only just below the peak of the early to mid-Thatcher period. Similar recessions proved electorally fatal to right-of-centre political leaders or parties on the other side of the Atlantic, namely President George H.W. Bush in the United States and Brian Mulroney's Conservatives in Canada, who were both defeated by opponents attacking their economic record in the early 1990s.

Further, on top of the political problems associated with approaching a general election in such conditions, the incumbent Conservatives faced more specific electoral difficulties associated with the introduction of an unpopular new tax. After eleven years as prime minister (the longest tenure in the twentieth century), Margaret Thatcher was ousted in 1990 in a leadership challenge following a political crisis caused by the replacement of the traditional local property tax by a poll tax (Butler, Travers, and Adonis 1994). That switch in local taxation went back to Conservative ambitions to scrap the old system of local taxation (announced as long ago as the party's 1979 general election manifesto) and it had been intended to create more winners than losers, particularly among swing voters. But in the event it provoked a major tax revolt, including riots and civil disobedience, and came to be seen as fatal to the Conservatives' chances of re-election.

Facing the prospect of electoral defeat, Conservative MPs ousted Margaret Thatcher and the Party leadership was eventually won by a 'dark horse' candidate, John Major (then Chancellor of the Exchequer, most of whose ministerial experience had been as Chief Secretary of the Treasury under Nigel Lawson). Major appointed Norman Lamont, who had organized his leadership election campaign, to take his place as Chancellor, and the new government swiftly announced the demise of the poll tax, to be replaced by a variant of the previous local property tax system combined with a 2.5 per cent increase in VAT to cover the funding gap left by the abandonment of the poll tax.

With a new leader and the decision to scrap the poll tax announced, the Conservatives' poll ratings improved (the Party was sixteen percentage points behind Labour in the month before John Major became prime minister, but led by three points the following month) and the Major Government claimed credit for military success in the first Gulf War and for securing two opt-outs for the UK in the 1992 EU Maastricht Treaty (including an opt-out from the single currency). Labour and the Conservatives were running level at about 40 per cent each in the polls in March 1992, but a final poll of polls just ahead of the 1992 general election gave Labour a narrow lead and the outcome was widely predicted to be either a narrow Labour victory or a hung Parliament and a minority Labour Government.

On the fiscal policy front, the Conservatives' 1992 electoral strategy included a dramatically tax-cutting giveaway budget before the election. The budget cut income tax from 25 to 20 per cent for the first tranche of taxable income, electorally outflanking Labour's proposal for a similar change,[1] and was combined with a heavy assault on Labour's plans for taxation and expenditure. Given that Labour was behind the Conservatives in the opinion polls at that time on economic and financial competence (though it led in many other policy domains), Labour's Shadow Chancellor, John Smith, sought to make the Party's fiscal plans credible to voters by bringing out a 'shadow budget' early in the election campaign, to demonstrate the afford-ability of Labour's election promises. That shadow budget included plans to increase income tax and compulsory National Insurance contributions for higher earners (partially reversing the tax cuts for top earners introduced in 1988) to reduce taxes on those on lower incomes. The Party claimed such measures would make eight out of ten taxpayers better off.

At first this tactic appeared to pay off for Labour in the election campaign, but six days after the Shadow Budget appeared, the Conservatives produced 'costings' of Labour's plans, proclaiming an impending tax 'bombshell' ('The Price of Labour: £1250 a Year for Every Family')[2] and splashed that '£1250 a year per family' figure on billboards across the country in poster campaigning. In the event, while the pollsters and the exit polls predicted a Conservative defeat, the Conservatives unexpectedly secured a small but clear overall fourth-term victory of twenty-one seats, comparable to the margin of their victory in 1951.

---

[1] This 20 per cent lower rate band was claimed to be the first step towards a standard rate of 20 per cent. See Norman Lamont, Budget Statement, HC Deb 10 March 1992, c.761.

[2] Nigel Lawson (1992: 201) says similar costings of the Labour Opposition's pledges to reverse spending cutbacks had been drawn up under his Chancellorship for the 1987 election, but that those costings were hardly (if at all) used in that campaign.

## 9.3 The Turning Point: 1992–93

Faced with the challenge of how to tackle a mounting budget deficit having cut income tax rates, and of delivering on electoral promises most of its ministers probably never expected to have to keep, the Major Government swiftly moved from pre-election tax-cutting largesse to post-election fiscal squeeze. Two months after the election, the cabinet adopted a new way of controlling public spending and a new medium-term spending plan which was redolent of the Medium Term Financial Strategies of the 1980s described in Chapter Eight.

The new arrangements, introduced by Norman Lamont based on work done by the Treasury's public spending team, were intended to avoid repeating the pattern of the later 1980s, in which (as noted earlier) the reduction of public spending relative to GDP during economic growth had been quickly reversed with the onset of recession. During the boom the government had accepted higher spending in constant price terms provided that the public spending/GDP ratio was falling. According to Lamont (1999: 301–2), the new spending-control arrangements were intended to avoid repeating that pattern, and also to adapt to a changed political dynamic within the cabinet, from a position in which Prime Minister Margaret Thatcher had mostly sided with her Chancellor in efforts to impose restraint on spending ministers in cabinet battles to one in which John Major was more inclined to side with spending ministers against the Chancellor.

To deal with the first issue, Lamont reclassified public spending by dividing it into cyclical and non-cyclical public spending, with increases in the latter to be restricted to less than the long-term rate of growth in the UK economy as a whole, and the former intended to shrink in boom years to offset its growth during recessions (Lamont (1999): 300). According to Lamont, John Major refused to contemplate cuts in spending in constant-price terms, so Lamont pressed for a highly restrictive three year target for non-cyclical spending ('the New Control Total'), with a real-terms freeze over the following two years and growth limited to 1 per cent per year thereafter. The cabinet agreed in principle to this target in July 1993—but that left open all the subsequent autumn negotiations over individual spending settlements.

To deal with those negotiations, Lamont initiated a new cabinet committee procedure for handling departmental spending bids, that was a variant on the use of such committees in earlier eras and particularly of the so-called 'Star Chamber' system of adjudicating spending conflicts in a cabinet committee that had been adopted in 1982 but fell into disuse as spending control relaxed in the late 1980s (Thain (2010): 51–2). As with earlier spending control arrangements, the new system introduced in 1993 began with an overall total for spending agreed by cabinet in advance of later bilateral negotiations between the Treasury and spending departments. What was different was that that envelope now comprised the non-cyclical element of spending, the 'New Control Total'. The later political process consisted of departmental spending bids for funding from that total being considered by a special cabinet committee called 'EDX'. EDX included the Chief Secretary of the Treasury, some non-spending ministers and a few experienced cabinet heavyweights and was chaired by the Chancellor himself (in a departure from the system operating since the early 1960s when a second cabinet minister in the Treasury, the Chief Secretary, had dealt with the nitty-gritty of bilateral spending negotiations with departments each autumn). As with the 'Star Chamber' system of the 1980s, ministers could not join the Committee until they had agreed their own spending plans, meaning that 'holdouts' could expect to face a relatively unsympathetic committee of ministers who had already settled their budgets, and with a smaller pot of available cash left in the New Control Total (Thain and Wright (1995): 294–306).

A few months after the election, a severe currency crisis dramatically changed the political backdrop to fiscal policy. In September 1992, the pound, along with the Italian lira, suddenly crashed out of the European Exchange Rate Mechanism (ERM)—a system of fixed exchange rates that was a precursor of the euro, and which the UK had entered in 1989 under John Major's Chancellorship. That currency collapse took place in conditions of panic and recrimination, after the Treasury had spent some £27bn of reserves in an unsuccessful attempt to keep the currency above its then agreed lower limit relative to the Deutschmark.

Many have commented on the economic effects of this currency collapse, with some arguing that the discipline imposed by ERM membership had benefits to the UK that outlasted the UK's membership of the ERM and others arguing that the cut in interest rates and currency devaluation that followed exit from the ERM boosted the UK economy (Budd 2004; Stephens 1997). But irrespective of any such economic effects, the episode had lasting and damaging political consequences for the Conservatives in general and more particularly for the prime minister and Chancellor. The Party's 1992 election manifesto had stated unequivocally that 'membership of the ERM is . . . central to our counter-inflation discipline', and pledged that, 'In due course, we will move to the narrow bands of the ERM'. The dramatic and ignominious collapse of a major plank of economic policy destroyed what had previously been a clear Conservative lead over Labour on economic competence in the opinion polls for more than a decade (Green and Jennings 2016), and in that sense can be seen as the equivalent for the Conservatives of what the 1976 IMF bailout had been for Labour.

Support for the Conservatives in Gallup polls plunged from 43 per cent in September to 29 per cent in October, opening up a strong Labour lead which persisted with only brief interludes for the next fourteen years. More particularly, the currency's exit from the ERM severely damaged the political career of the Chancellor, who, unlike James Callaghan after the devaluation of 1987, remained at the Treasury for a further six months despite widespread calls even in the Conservative press for his departure (Castle 1992). According to Lamont, the main reason for his continuance at the Treasury was to serve as a lightning rod to divert blame for the ERM fiasco away the prime minister, who as Chancellor had enthusiastically led the UK into the ERM.[3] Lamont was finally sacked after a disastrous by-election defeat for the Conservatives the following May.

After the ERM debacle, the government tried to regain the political initiative by turning its 1992 autumn expenditure statement into a mini-budget. Following one four-hour cabinet meeting and two other shorter ones, that Autumn Statement was peppered with energetic rhetoric about stimulating investment and growth by protecting capital spending,[4] but what the figures showed was a plan to keep overall expenditure virtually flat in real terms. That Statement marked the start of the 'soft' expenditure squeeze beginning in 1993 that we noted in Chapter Two. The squeeze involved holding down the non-cyclical part of public spending to less than the long-term rate of GDP growth as the economy recovered, and indeed adopting a standstill in such spending in real terms for 1993/94. Lamont failed to get cabinet support for big cuts in defence spending after the collapse of the USSR, but the cabinet agreed to a measure of non-fiscal austerity in the form of a 1.5 per cent cap on public sector pay rises, and cabinet ministers, senior civil servants, judges, and senior military officers received no pay increase at all.

Even then, the short-term effect of the spending plans, coupled with high cyclical spending resulting from the recession, meant a likely budget deficit of 7 to 8 per cent of GDP in 1993/94 (a number not revealed in the Autumn Statement, and not greatly different from what had occurred under the Labour Government of the 1970s (Lamont (1999): 333). And it was that expected deficit that seems to have triggered a squeeze on the revenue side as well for the following year's budget. So instead of the Labour 'tax bombshell' presaged by the Conservatives in the 1992 election campaign, the 1993 budget contained a Conservative 'tax bombshell'.

The 1993 budget reflected a strategy (probably reflecting the outcome of political negotiations over spending rather than a formula agreed in advance by cabinet) to reduce the deficit by two years of hard tax squeeze combined

[3] Norman Lamont (1999: 369) writes: 'The PM had made it emphatically clear to me that he did not want me to resign [after the ERM episode] ... "You are a lightning conductor for me," he said.'
[4] HC Deb 12 November 1992, c.995. Lamont (1999: 307) later observed 'that sounded good but was actually rather specious', because of the plasticity and arbitrariness of what counted as 'capital' as against 'current' spending.

with a soft spending squeeze. That budget was also notable for the fact that it planned staged tax increases over three years rather than all at once—the revenue equivalent of the 'boiling frogs' approach discussed in Chapter One. The tax changes seem to have been intended to raise extra revenue approximating to that of Geoffrey Howe's 1981 budget discussed in the previous chapter, increasing revenue by 1 per cent of GDP as well as in constant prices (a 'hard' tax squeeze in our analytic terminology).[5] Measures to take effect in 1993/94 included freezing income tax allowances and the threshold for inheritance tax (as had been applied in the 1981 budget, albeit at a much higher rate of inflation), reducing tax offsets for mortgage interest payments, and increasing taxes on alcohol, tobacco, gaming machines, and fuel. Also—taking a step which resembled Denis Healey's sale of BP shares in 1977 in that it opened up a precedent that would be seized upon and taken much further by the next government—tax credits which pension funds could claim from dividend payments on which tax had already been paid were reduced by five percentage points, intended to boost the tax take by some £1bn a year.

For the later part of the multi-year 'tax wedge' plan for increasing revenue built into this budget, measures to take effect in FY 1994/95 included higher compulsory National Insurance contributions for employees (but not employers) and—most controversially—levying VAT on domestic energy bills for the first time, at 8 per cent. Further, the Finance Bill provided for a further major increase in VAT on domestic energy from 8 to 17.5 per cent in the following year (FY 1995/96), with accompanying but non-specific promises of compensation for those who would be particularly hard hit by this tax hike.

Reflecting on the political calculations that lay behind this 'tax wedge' strategy, Norman Lamont (1999: 336 and 345) writes that this tax squeeze was dictated by the limits of what the cabinet was prepared to accept in spending cuts, and that the scale of the revenue increases needed could only be realized from 'big-ticket' items such as National Insurance contributions, income tax, or VAT. Raising income tax rates was ruled out because it would run contrary to a central plank of Conservative policy since 1979, and when it came to possible VAT increases, the political judgement was that there were no obviously less unpopular alternatives to levying VAT on energy bills. Moreover, Lamont and his colleagues thought there was a greater risk of Conservative backbench revolts if VAT was applied to a range of other items that had previously been exempt rather than concentrated on domestic energy.

Lamont's memoirs also reflect on the blame risks that were run by the staged ('boiling frogs') approach to tax increases adopted in the 1993 budget. By comparison with the one-shot 'surgery without anaesthetics' approach (as in

---

[5] The budget speech declared an intention to raise revenue by £6bn in 1994/95 and by £10bn in 1995/96: HC Deb 16 March 1993, *c*.175.

the 1981 budget), 'The stringing out of the tax increases meant that criticisms of the Conservatives "breaking their election promises" were regularly repeated throughout the rest of the Parliament and were still fresh in voters' minds at the subsequent (1997) general election' (Lamont 1999: 357).[6] Further, phasing the imposition of VAT on energy bills ran the political risk that the second stage could be reversed at a later date by a backbench revolt. And that was exactly what did happen in 1994, in the form of an amendment to the Finance Act allowing a further vote on the second stage of the VAT increases, when the second proposed increase (to 17.5 per cent) was defeated by Conservative backbenchers. As a result, the eventual fiscal squeeze was much less severe than Lamont originally planned in 1993.

## 9.4 The Later Conservative Squeeze, 1993–97

Norman Lamont was succeeded in mid-1993 by Kenneth Clarke, a highly experienced minister who had headed three major departments during the Thatcher and Major Governments and had also been a key member of the EDX committee. Clarke's political position within the Party differed from that of his predecessor in several ways (in that he was pro-EU and more to the left) and he described himself and his Chief Secretary from 1994 (Jonathan Aitken) as 'poachers turned gamekeepers' who had been in charge of big spending departments but neither of whom espoused what he called 'the slash and burn approach to public spending'.[7]

Nevertheless, Clarke broadly continued with the soft spending and revenue squeeze initiated by his predecessor over the course of the four subsequent budgets of the Major Government. In his November 1993 budget,[8] Clarke announced plans to reduce the deficit over the course of the Parliament (to the point where borrowing would equate only to government's capital spending by FY 1996/97) and to eliminate government borrowing entirely by the end of the century. In his first year as Chancellor, he said that about half of the cuts in the deficit came from changes in public spending plans and the other half

---

[6] Indeed, the 1997 Labour general election manifesto declared:

There have been few more gross breaches of faith than when the Conservatives...promised, before the election of 1992, that they would not raise taxes, but would cut them every year; and then went on to raise them by the largest amount in peacetime history...Since 1992 the typical family has paid more than £2,000 in extra taxes...breaking every promise made by John Major at the last election.

1997 Labour Party manifesto, 'New Labour Because Britain Deserves Better', http://www.politicsresources.net/area/uk/man/lab97.htm.
[7] HC Deb 28 November 1995, c.1057.    [8] HC Deb 30 November 1993, c.926.

from increased taxes,[9] but in his later years as Chancellor, relatively more emphasis was laid on reductions in planned spending.

That spending squeeze was carefully packaged politically as one that provided extra real-terms spending in the most electorally salient policy domains—notably in the key party battlegrounds of education, healthcare, and policing, but also including training and science—at the expense of savings in domains that were seen as less electorally salient for swing voters. Accordingly, in the non-cyclical parts of public spending, there were notable 'cuts', mostly in the form of reductions in planned increases, in defence, roadbuilding and transport, local government, public sector running costs, and parts of social security (the latter including the imposition of tighter tests for invalidity payments and the introduction of a new taxable incapacity benefit).

Cuts in government running costs—a classic 'valence' issue in electoral competition—figured large in credit-claiming passages in three of Clarke's four budget speeches. For instance, in 1994 he declared that cost reductions had focused on 'cutting the back office and protecting the front-line delivery of our key public services',[10] introducing a front-line/back office distinction that had been less prominent (though by no means completely absent) in earlier spending squeezes but which became familiar in later decades and indeed led to a complete reclassification of 'running costs' in the 2000s. By 1996, Clarke claimed to have reduced central government's running costs by no less than 8 per cent in constant prices since 1992[11]—a remarkable result which contrasts sharply with the failure to cut those costs under the Thatcher Government in the previous decade (Hood and Dixon (2015): 74–5). At the same time, the cyclical parts of public spending (notably on unemployment benefits and employment programmes) fell as a result of falling unemployment, while a reduction in the inflation rate (for example in 1994) meant that spending in several years undershot what had been planned. The effect of all these changes, as we saw in Chapter Two, was not to cut public spending in constant-price terms (except in a single year, 1996/97), but to slow its growth while GDP grew, such that the ratio of spending to GDP fell, and government borrowing fell by almost a half between 1993 and 1996.

In addition, a long-term cost-reducing change to retirement pension eligibility was announced during this period which, as with the de-linking of pension payments to earnings by the Thatcher Government in 1979, had a delayed but substantial impact. That was the announcement in the 1993 budget that state retirement pension entitlement ages for men and women (sixty-five and sixty, respectively, at that time) would be equalized at sixty-five

---

[9] HC Deb 29 Nov 1994, c.1082.     [10] HC Deb 29 November 1994, c.1084.
[11] HC Deb 26 November 1996, c.163.

from 2010[12]—something that had not been mentioned in the 1992 Conservative manifesto but which was justified as a way of making the social security budget grow at more affordable rates in the long-term, while honouring manifesto commitments to protect the real value of pensions and benefits. (The same budget speech also announced a long-term plan to introduce a system of electronic charging for motorways when the technology permitted it,[13] a policy proposal first floated in the 1960s but which had not yet happened at the time of writing.)

On the revenue side, as already mentioned, the planned second stage of the controversial imposition of VAT on domestic energy bills, legislated for in the 1993 Finance Act, was derailed by a backbench revolt in 1994. That revolt left VAT on energy at the first-stage level of 8 per cent rather than 17.5 per cent, and thereby removed £3bn or so of extra revenue that the second-stage increase had been expected to bring in, while adding to spending by a careful package to compensate electorally important losers, notably retirement pensioners, from the second-stage VAT charge that never happened. But nevertheless, Clarke's first budget raised taxes substantially by freezing income tax and inheritance tax thresholds, while further cutting tax offsets from mortgage interest payments, beginning a policy of increasing road fuel duties and tobacco taxes each year by at least 5 per cent and 3 per cent, respectively, in constant-price terms. It also announced two new taxes, Air Passenger Duty (a levy on passengers departing from UK airports) and a tax on insurance premium payments.

Clarke's second budget in 1994 held income tax rates constant while raising thresholds and allowances by the rate of inflation, introduced more above-inflation increases in road fuel and tobacco taxes, and announced another new tax, Landfill Tax on waste disposal, to start in 1996. But (in a pattern that was to recur in the 2010s) tax revenue outcomes fell below what had been planned, both on VAT and on direct taxes, in 1994/95 and 1995/96.

As the next general election approached, Clarke's third and fourth budgets in 1995 and 1996 cut taxes overall, in both cases widening the 20 per cent rate band, raising direct tax allowances by slightly more than the inflation rate in 1995 and by much more the following year, and cutting the standard rate of income tax by one percentage point in each year, from 25 per cent to 23 per cent between 1995 and the pre-election budget of late 1996. Presenting that 1996 budget, Clarke claimed credit for introducing the lowest standard rate of income tax for nearly sixty years,[14] but still applied the real-terms 'accelerator' to road fuel and tobacco taxes and left the standard rate of income tax above the Conservatives' often-announced goal of 20 per cent.

---

[12] HC Deb 30 November 1993, c.929.    [13] HC Deb 30 November 1993, c.932.
[14] HC Deb 26 November 1996, c.172.

What is therefore noticeable about the financial year (1996/97) leading up to the 1997 election is that the 'hard' revenue squeeze of the previous two years turned into a soft squeeze for the election year, but there was also a notable reduction in spending in that financial year (much but not all of it due to the reduction in cyclical social security spending associated with falling unemployment). The reported numbers indicate only a fairly modest 'electoral cycle' effect, and indeed according to Prime Minister John Major (2000: 689) in his memoirs, the pre-election budget disappointed Conservative backbenches who wanted a pre-election bonanza along the lines of the 1992 budget or some of the Conservative pre-election budgets of the 1950s.

## 9.5 Another Turning Point: Pre-1997 Election Bear Traps and Labour 'Prudence'

As mentioned at the outset, the squeeze episode described in this chapter was unusually long-drawn-out partly because one party's outline plans for spending restraint and limiting borrowing were matched by a successor in government from a different party, albeit with important changes in the composition of spending. Indeed, that party convergence may help to explain why spending actually fell in that election year.

The Party convergence came about because after 1992, Labour's electoral strategy involved adopting a 'centrist' stance designed to appeal to swing voters by accepting many of the changes made by the Conservatives since 1979—particularly when Tony Blair succeeded Neil Kinnock as Labour leader in 1994 and rebranded the Party as 'New Labour' to signify a political stance somewhere between the Conservative and harder left positions. And in fiscal policy the Labour leadership in the run-up to the 1997 election was at pains to avoid risking a repeat of the Conservatives' successful 'Labour's tax bombshell' election tactic of 1992 in response to Labour's shadow budget of that time. Lavish promises to increase spending on public services might run the political risk that the Conservatives would counter with dramatic estimates of the tax costs of such promises.

Accordingly, even although Labour was well ahead of the Conservatives in the polls in the run-up to the general election, its Shadow Chancellor, Gordon Brown, promised early in 1997 that Labour if it won government would broadly match the aggregates of the Conservatives' announced spending plans for its first two years in office—a promise reiterated in the 1997 Labour manifesto.[15] Brown also committed Labour to matching the Conservatives'

---

[15] 1997 Labour Party manifesto, 'New Labour because Britain deserves better', http://www. politicsresources.net/area/uk/man/lab97.htm.

inflation target and to following a so-called 'golden rule' of borrowing only for 'investment' over the course of an economic cycle (a 'rule' that left it unclear how precisely 'investment' or 'economic cycle' were to be defined and by whom). Moreover, the Labour manifesto promised not to increase standard or higher rates of income tax during the following Parliament (whereas the Liberal Democrats proposed an extra one per cent on the standard rate of income tax to fund improvements in education and a new 50 per cent top rate of tax for top earners). Indeed, some of the Labour leader's statements during the election campaign were construed as meaning there would be no tax rises at all if Labour won government.[16]

In the event, as already noted, Labour won the May 1997 general election with its greatest ever landslide in terms of parliamentary seats. But far from relaxing fiscal squeeze, the new government tightened it on the tax side as well as continuing restraint on public spending increases over the next two financial years which in the event meant rather lower spending on health and education than the Conservatives had planned. Gordon Brown, the new Chancellor, announced a five-year deficit reduction plan in his first budget two months after the election. That plan was designed to give effect to the Party's announced intention to meet current spending from taxation over the economic cycle, to correct what Brown described the following year as 'a substantial structural deficit in excess of 2 per cent of national income'[17] that the Labour Government had inherited, and to achieve budget balance by 2000.

On the tax side, following the Party's election pledges, no changes were made to the basic or top rates of income tax, and VAT on domestic energy bills was cut from the 8 per cent imposed by the Major Government in 1994 to 5 per cent (said to be the lowest rate compatible with European Union legislation). In addition, the main rate of Corporation Tax was cut from 33 to 31 per cent—the lowest rate since the tax was introduced, and lower than equivalent rates in France, Germany, Japan, and the United States. But overall tax revenue was substantially raised in several ways, producing a hard revenue squeeze in the new government's first financial year (1997/98).

One of those ways, foreshadowed in Labour's 1997 election manifesto, comprised a one-off 'windfall' tax on profits made by the privatized utilities in the first four years after privatization, intended to raise nearly £5bn over three years and to fund a new welfare-to-work programme. A second comprised removal or reduction of tax allowances, including a further reduction of tax relief on mortgage interest payments, which disappeared altogether in the 1999 budget. The most notable tax offset to be removed in 1997 applied to

---

[16] (William Hague), HC Deb 17 March 1998, c.1113.
[17] HC Deb 17 March 1998, c.1099.

pension funds, which until that time could claim back tax on dividends they received from UK companies, to offset the Corporation Tax those companies had already paid on their profits.

As noted earlier, Norman Lamont had cut these tax credits from 25 to 20 per cent in 1993, and Gordon Brown's first budget abolished them entirely, arguing that they distorted firms' incentives to invest and were not needed for pension saving because many pension funds were in surplus at that time, with numerous employers taking 'holidays' from their pension fund contributions at a time of booming stock markets. The removal of those offsets (a classic 'stealth tax', unintelligible to laypersons, not foreshadowed in the Labour manifesto and buried in the small print of the budget statement) reduced pension funds' income by a figure widely claimed by lobbyists and media reports to be around £5bn a year but which was estimated by the Pensions Policy Institute (2005) as no more than £3.5bn. Along with a stock market collapse in 1999 the tax change was used by many companies to justify closing their defined-benefit (final salary) pension schemes, though the removal of this major tax offset did not increase the tax take by that amount because Corporation Tax was reduced at the same time.

A third category of tax increases in that first Labour budget comprised higher indirect taxes, including continuing and increasing the 'escalators' on road fuel tax and tobacco tax initiated by the previous government (that is, annual tax rises well above the rate of inflation), and increasing stamp duties on higher-value real estate transactions (the tax payable to make transfers of ownership of property valid in law). All the taxes in that third category were increased in the first two New Labour budgets, and together with the pension fund 'raid' mentioned above, led to repeated opposition accusations of 'stealth taxation'. More dramatically, after the raised road fuel tax accelerator had helped to produce a 40 per cent increase in fuel prices between early 1999 and mid-2000, the fuel tax rises led to a tax revolt in the form of direct action by fuel tanker drivers in 2000. The protestors blockaded six of the UK's eight fuel refineries in September of that year, causing half of the country's filling stations to shut and leading the government to announce a freeze of fuel taxes.

The new government's pledges to match Conservative spending plans also led to numerous political tensions. On the spending side, one of the 'bear traps' that the previous Conservative Government laid for Labour ahead of the 1997 election was to announce a plan to abolish a higher single-parent rate of income support and child benefit for future claimants if those claimants did not seek work. In the face of this challenge to show it was not 'soft' on welfare claimants, the Blair Government chose to stick to this planned cut, despite (or perhaps because) of Labour backbench protests, with some forty-seven Labour MPs voting against this measure in November 1997 in the first significant backbench revolt of the Labour Government (Brown 1997).

The Labour leadership had also agreed a year before the 1997 election to develop rather than abolish the previous government's creation of a 'jobseeker's allowance' benefit that linked unemployment benefits to demonstrable search for work, a principle that was taken further in the welfare-to-work 'New Deal' programme to be funded from the windfall tax on the privatized utilities and which also entailed a controversial review of disability benefits and the possibility of linking such benefits more narrowly to willingness and ability to work (Peck 1998).

Another notable policy change on the spending side in 1997 related to university funding and charges. Labour's 1997 election manifesto had included a declaration that 'the costs of student maintenance should be repaid by graduates on an income-related basis', and in response to a report on the subject commissioned by the Conservatives in government but published after the election, the new Education Minister (David Blunkett) announced the scrapping of maintenance grants for university students, which government had provided since the early 1960s, to be replaced by means-tested student loans, with maintenance grants only for the poorest students. Blunkett also announced top-up fees for university tuition (of £1000 a year but subject to means testing on the basis of parental income, such that only two thirds of students would pay). The leading Conservative Sir Keith Joseph had proposed such a change but failed to enact it as Education Minister under the Thatcher Government in the mid-1980s.

After the fiscal squeeze in the early new Labour years, a move to greater largesse for the years 1999–2002 was signalled in 1998 with a 'comprehensive spending review' announcing plans for major increases in future spending on electorally sensitive public services such as health and education,[18] and in the following year, the government announced that the double lock on retirement pensions (linking rises to earnings as well as prices) that the Conservatives had abolished in 1979 would return in 2000, as well as lowering rates at the bottom end of the income-tax scale. So by the time of the 2001 general election the fiscal squeeze was over and the government's agenda had shifted to improving the quality of public services and getting 'more for more'.

## 9.6 Conclusion

As before, we conclude by looking at this episode in terms of the three sets of issues about the politics of fiscal squeeze that we raised in Chapter One.

---

[18] 'Modern Public Services in Britain: Investing in Reform', Comprehensive Spending Review: New Public Spending Plans 1999–2002, Cm 4011 1998, London: HMSO.

### 9.6.1 *Tax and Spending, Depth and Duration, Blame and Control*

Our analysis of financial outcome data in Chapter Two showed the fiscal squeeze episode of the 1990s—in the later years of John Major's Conservative Government and the first two years of Tony Blair's 'New Labour' Government— was distinctive in at least two ways. It is the longest continuous squeeze episode over the century as a whole, comprising altogether seven years of 'soft squeeze' on both the revenue and spending side. That is substantially longer than the second Thatcher squeeze of the 1980s, discussed in Chapter Eight, and contains individual years of 'hard' squeeze sandwiched (in a manner modulated to fit the electoral cycle) within a longer period of soft squeeze. While the period as a whole has features of the 'boiling frogs' approach we discussed in Chapter One, when we look more closely we can see that the frog was taken somewhat off the boil at some points and the heat turned up sharply at others.

Second and relatedly, it is the first squeeze episode at least since World War II in which overall plans for spending restraint adopted by one party in government were implemented by a successor government from a different political party. As far as blame management is concerned, neither of the governments involved chose to 'outsource' the identification of spending cuts along the lines of the Geddes and May Committees of the 1920s and 1930s, but both moved to distance themselves from direct control of other potentially blame-attracting aspects of policy. Given the blame associated with unreliable (usually over-optimistic) Treasury economic forecasting that underlay spending and taxing plans, Chancellor Norman Lamont made use of some independent political forecasters—a move destined to be taken much further in the 2010s. And in contrast to the actions of the 1945 Labour Government, whose first nationalization had been that of the Bank of England, immediately after the 1997 election Chancellor Gordon Brown outsourced the process of setting Bank of England interest rates to an expert committee (the Monetary Policy Committee) tasked with achieving specified inflation targets.

### 9.6.2 *Loss, Cost, and Effort Involved in These Episodes*

As already noted, the 1990s fiscal squeeze described in this chapter is the longest-drawn-out episode in the whole period covered by this book, but it seems hard to argue that it also involved the greatest political stress and effort on the part of officeholders or the greatest losses imposed on the population. As in previous chapters, Table 9.1 gives a summary rating of the intensity of the squeeze for the two governments involved on the spectrum we discussed in Chapter One.

**Table 9.1.** A qualitative classification of imposed loss, political cost, and state effort associated with 1990s fiscal squeezes

|  | Low | Moderate | High | Overall classification |
|---|---|---|---|---|
| 1993–2000 Squeeze Type: Soft Spending/Soft Revenue | | | | |
| Conservatives 4/1992–5/1997 | | | | |
| Loss |  | [1], [2] | [1] | Moderate |
| Cost | [1] | [1], [2] | [3] | Moderate |
| Effort |  | [1], [2], [3] | [1] | Moderate |
| Labour 5/1997 onwards | | | | |
| Loss | [3] | [1], [2] |  | Moderate |
| Cost | [1] | [1], [2] |  | Low |
| Effort |  | [1] | [1] | Moderate |

Note: numbers in square brackets refer to categories in Table 1.2, Chapter One.

Certainly, there were some significant losers in this squeeze episode, under both governments, such as those disadvantaged by the changes in welfare policies and by the 1993 budget that froze tax thresholds and imposed VAT on fuel and power. But even the two post-election budgets—the 1993 'tax wedge' budget and the 1997 'windfall tax' budget—do not seem to have matched the losses imposed by the 1981 budget, and some of the extra taxes imposed in the post-election 1997 budget, notably the utilities windfall tax, did not fall visibly or directly on mainstream voters. Further, as we have seen, for much of the episode, under both the Conservatives and Labour, steady economic growth meant spending could be increased in constant-price terms while declining relative to rising GDP, and that revenue rose in real terms though not as a proportion of GDP. Those are much more benign conditions than applied to several of the eras described in earlier chapters, and without accompanying non-fiscal austerity in the form of rationing or wage caps that applied to some previous squeezes. Moreover, even though privatization proceeds were starting to fall off at this time, this episode also reflected revenue raising or spending reduction through selling assets and exploiting oil reserves which we noted in Chapter Eight as features of the Thatcher squeezes of the 1980s and which limited the direct and immediate pain imposed on voters.

As for political costs to incumbents, this period of fiscal squeeze certainly involved political effort over both tax and spending. But again it seems hard to rate these squeezes at the same level on our spectrum as cases such as 1931 or 1976. Even for the Major Government, the post-ERM dramas of the 1992 Autumn Statement and March 1993 budget did not involve an outright breach of manifesto promises, though they certainly included tax increases and spending cuts about which the 1992 Conservative manifesto had been notably silent. (That manifesto, an unwieldy document running to almost 30,000 words, promised tax cuts and contained only a vague statement about maintaining 'firm control of public spending',[19] so the post-election VAT hike in particular inevitably invited accusations of misleading the voters.)

For the continuation of the squeeze under the subsequent New Labour Government, it can be argued that political costs for incumbents rated rather lower than for the Major Conservative Government. Some of that government's approach to handling the squeeze consisted of 'inertia strategies', such as continuing with accelerators on indirect taxes on fuel and tobacco, staying with the previous government's spending targets, and broadly matching the previous government's policies on lone parent benefits and welfare to work.

Some of the policies accompanying the spending squeeze in the early years of New Labour—such as the imposition of university tuition fees and restriction of benefit increases to single parents—certainly provoked political conflict and backbench revolts, but the government's parliamentary majority was so large that such conflict did not pose political threats to its future at the same level as (say) those of the early 1930s or mid-1970s. Moreover, again in contrast to those episodes, the timing of the New Labour squeeze went with the electoral cycle rather than against it, with the squeeze ending well before the 2001 general election.

As for the effort required from the state machinery in applying the fiscal squeezes discussed in these chapters, that too seems to have gone well beyond the incremental level under both governments—for instance, in the crafting of the 'New Control Total' and 'EDX' machinery in the early 1990s, remarkable reductions in running costs and plans for long-term pension changes under the Major Government, and the changes in funding higher education, the 'welfare-to-work' regime, the crafting of new taxes including the utilities windfall tax, and the development of the comprehensive spending review system under the Blair Government.

### 9.6.3 *Electoral and Other Consequences*

How far does this episode support the idea that fiscal squeeze can ordinarily be expected to be followed by electoral punishment of incumbents? On the face of it, the Conservatives' massive electoral defeat in 1997 seems to support that expectation. The Major Government that applied the squeeze over 1993–97 was heavily punished by the voters amid widespread claims of 'underfunding' of public services, and its Labour successor that took the brakes off public spending before the subsequent general election (and promised further increases in a second term) was rewarded with comfortable re-election. And—especially with Norman Lamont's 'tax wedge' in his 1993 budget—the

---

[19] 'The Best Future for Britain', 1992 Conservative Party manifesto, http://www.conservativemanifesto.com/1992/1992-conservative-manifesto.shtml.

1997 electoral outcome is also consistent with the 'asymmetrical punishment' suggestion considered in Chapter One, namely that right-of-centre parties may be particularly vulnerable to electoral punishment for tax squeezes.

Still, it seems implausible to attribute that 1997 electoral outcome to fiscal squeeze alone. As already noted, it was the perceived debacle of the pound exiting the ERM in 1992 that seems to have been the key factor in the Conservatives' loss of their previous poll lead on economic competence, rather than the fiscal squeeze measures alone.

Moreover, while quality of electorally salient public services such as education and healthcare whose funding had lagged behind the rate of economic growth certainly seems to have been a key issue in party competition for votes, Labour's 1997 decision to match the Conservatives' spending plans meant it was not promising the voters to let rip with public spending, at least for the following two years. And most of those commenting on the 1997 election see the outcome as a product of a combination of factors rather than a single one—for instance, a 'time for a change' factor in the replacement of a very long-tenure government perceived to have run its course by a repositioned 'centrist' Labour Party under energetic and carefully orchestrated leadership; voter reaction against the Conservatives' internal divisions over the European Union which had led to recurring friction and disunity within the Major Government; and perceptions of Conservative 'sleaze' arising from a succession of well-publicized scandals over financial and other misconduct by Conservative MPs and ministers (Butler and Kavanagh 1997). Fiscal squeeze seems only to have been part of the mix.

Going beyond electoral effects, these squeezes left some long-term institutional and policy consequences behind them. As we saw, some major institutional changes were made in the management of public spending in the 1990s. The specific machinery of EDX and the 'New Control Total' adopted in 1992 did not outlive the Major Government, but the general pattern of punishing 'holdouts' in spending negotiations by subjecting them to scrutiny by ministers who had already settled re-emerged under the Conservative–Liberal Democrat coalition government in the 2010s. And the distinction made in 1992 between cyclical and non-cyclical expenditure and the subjection of the latter to top-down control limits proved to be the basis of all subsequent public expenditure control regimes up to the time of writing.

Going beyond those institutional changes, we have seen that these fiscal squeezes also included policy changes that crossed some important political 'Rubicons'. One such change was the abandonment (in England, Wales, and Northern Ireland at least) of the former system of free university education and state subsidization of most students' living costs, significantly shifting the state's role from funder to regulator in an important policy sector. Another comprised the 'raids' on pension funds (and the effective abandonment of the principle that retirement savings should only be taxed once), beginning with Norman Lamont's reduction of tax credits for pension funds in 1993 and Gordon Brown's more dramatic removal of such credits four years later. A third was a further shift towards 'workfare' (that is, measures to compel benefit claimants to seek work or undergo training or work experience, as with the changes to lone parent benefit announced in 1997), and a fourth was the 1994 decision to raise the age of pension entitlement for women in the future, the first increase in pension entitlement age since state retirement pensions had been introduced in 1908. These fiscal squeezes certainly did not disappear without leaving their mark on public policy.

# 10

# After the 2008 Financial Crash

## The Early 2010s

### 10.1 Background: The Period in Perspective

The politics of the final fiscal squeeze episode we identified in Chapter Two—under a Conservative–Liberal Democrat coalition, though partially planned by the preceding Labour Government and continued for a time under the subsequent Conservative Government—differs from earlier episodes in several ways. First, although there is already a large literature on the austerity politics of this period and the financial crisis associated with it (for example Kickert and Randma-Liiv 2015; Gamble 2012), there is no archival material yet available for this period and only a few memoirs by the leading participants. So this chapter is based largely on media sources and official publications. Second, this episode was not definitely concluded at the time of writing, so the account given here covers only five years of a squeeze that was planned to extend over a longer period, though specific deficit-reduction plans were suspended in 2016. Third, this episode is too recent for any firm assessment of its long-term consequences.

Compared with the earlier episodes, this squeeze resembles 1931 in that it followed an international financial crisis of once-in-a-generation severity that plunged the UK and many other countries into their deepest recession since the 1930s. It also resembles 1931 in that it features a government taking office expressly to correct the public finances. But it resembles the early 1920s episode in some ways too, in that: it took place under a Conservative–Liberal (Democrat) coalition; fiscal squeeze (specifically, cutting spending) was, for some time at least, seen across much of the political spectrum as the only way to respond to the economic challenges of the day; outline plans for fiscal squeeze drawn up by one government were pursued (albeit in a modified form) by its successor; and the general election following the squeeze produced an outright if narrow victory for the Conservatives, with their coalition partners, the Liberal Democrats, reduced to a handful of MPs.

In other ways, though, this episode resembles those of the 1980s and 1990s in that a tax-raising budget that was attacked by the government's opponents as exacerbating recession was followed by an economic recovery in which revenues eventually began to rise in constant-price terms but not relative to growing GDP, while government spending fell relative to GDP but not in constant-price terms. It also resembles the 1970s in that, in contrast to the 1980s and 1990s, revenue from oil production taxes dropped heavily ('fell off a cliff', as one of our interviewees put it). And while, as with the 1980s and 1990s, asset sales played a part in the squeeze, that part was smaller than in those earlier episodes, with less 'low-hanging fruit' in the form of readily saleable public assets available by that time. About £2bn was realized in asset sales between 2010 and 2015, massively outweighed by huge asset purchases in the form of bank stocks bought by government during the financial crisis. So this episode was not simply a replay of any of the previous episodes we have discussed and at the least it represents a new combination of their features.

## 10.2 The Road to 2010

This squeeze followed a deep international financial crisis over bad loans, triggered by the sudden and unexpected collapse of a major US bank (Lehman Brothers) in 2008, but preceded a year earlier by the collapse, rescue, and nationalization of a small UK bank, Northern Rock. The 2008 crisis led the then UK Labour Government to mount what is said to have been the biggest bank bailout in history in rescuing the Royal Bank of Scotland and two other large British banks (Lloyds TSB and HBOS) through a £500bn package overall that included partial nationalization of those banks by share purchases—a bailout package that outweighed all the proceeds of asset sales through privatization over the previous three decades. The rescue was followed by efforts to reduce those banks' balance sheets by sums in the order of £1 trillion—an extraordinary and unprecedented financial operation.[1]

This huge bailout of insolvent banks by asset purchases (paralleled, albeit in somewhat different forms, in the USA and several other European countries) turned a private-sector financial crisis into a public debt crisis. The bailouts abruptly increased UK national debt by about one-third, raising it to roughly double the level relative to GDP that had been seen for four decades.

---

[1] (John Redwood) HC Deb 18 March 2015, c.796.

That huge sudden debt spike in turn greatly increased debt servicing costs and thereby pushed up the budget deficit, which was further increased by the deep recession following the financial crisis, as tax revenues plunged and welfare costs and other recession-related spending soared. The resulting deficit, some 11 per cent of GDP at the peak, was much higher than that associated with the IMF bailout in the 1976 crisis discussed in Chapter Seven, more than double what had been seen for over half a century and higher than the deficit of any other G7 country. The recession was also marked by plunging stock prices, falling GDP (which at almost 5 per cent turned into the biggest drop in peacetime since the 1930s, though much less than in some of the worst-hit eurozone countries), rising unemployment (which jumped from around 5 per cent to 8 per cent within a couple of years, albeit to a much lower peak than in the 1980s and 1990s recessions), and a balance of payments deficit that increased sharply as international trade slumped, particularly in the eurozone.

When the financial crisis struck, Britain's long-running Labour Government, first elected in 1997, was more than half way through its third electoral term. It had to face a general election not later than 2010 and could not plausibly blame its predecessors for the financial crash, the recession, or the fallout for the public finances. Gordon Brown had succeeded Tony Blair as prime minister barely a year earlier, after having been Chancellor for ten years and presided over a doubling of public spending on electorally salient public services (notably healthcare and education) that the Conservatives in opposition had promised the voters they would match. In late 2008 Brown took a leading role in coordinating the actions of different countries in bailing out stricken banks and in a synchronized cut in interest rates to near zero by central banks (Brown incautiously claimed he had 'saved the world' by such actions[2]). The Conservatives in opposition condemned the 'age of irresponsibility' that led to the financial crisis but supported the bank bailouts.

Shortly after the financial rescue, Brown helped to orchestrate a synchronized fiscal stimulus among G20 countries (part of a 'Keynesian moment' (Seccareccia 2012)). The UK government had increased spending and cut taxes in the face of ballooning debt and deficit some months before that, setting aside its 'golden rule' (of borrowing only to fund investment over an economic cycle, as discussed in Chapter Nine)[3] and enacting a fiscal stimulus package claimed to amount to £20bn, including a temporary cut in the

---

[2] HC Deb 10 December 2008, c.527.

[3] In November 2008, it replaced the 'golden rule' with a ponderously phrased 'temporary operating rule', to 'set policies to improve the cyclically-adjusted current budget each year, once the economy has emerged from the downturn, so it reaches balance and debt is falling as a proportion of GDP once the global shocks have worked their way through the economy in full' (HM Treasury 2008: 4, para 1.13).

standard rate of VAT from 17.5 to 15 per cent and bringing forward some £3bn of capital spending projects.

But this so-called 'Keynesian moment' soon passed, both in the UK and the eurozone, as political support for fiscal stimulus to counter recession gave way to alarm about the scale of public debt and deficit and risks of default. And the policy consensus among the two major parties broke down at the end of 2008, when the Conservatives moved from a strategy of promising to match Labour's plans for increased public spending to opposing the Labour Government's stimulus package and proposing spending cuts to correct the public finances.[4] For a time the Brown Government officially frowned on talk of 'cuts' evidently reflecting tensions between the Prime Minister and the Treasury (Darling 2011: 217), but political debate came to turn, not on *whether* a fiscal squeeze was needed to reduce debt and deficit, but on by how much, how soon, in what mix of tax rises and spending cuts—and on who was to blame for those levels of debt and deficit.

Politicians calling for a shift from fiscal stimulus to fiscal squeeze, in the UK and elsewhere, found their position conveniently supported by some respected economists. Those eminences included Carmen Reinhart and Kenneth Rogoff (2010), who in a paper much invoked at the time, though later discredited for errors (Herndon et al. 2014), claimed high debt levels were a 'drag on growth', and Alberto Alesina, who in comparative studies with colleagues showed that fiscal contraction in some cases had been followed by rapid output growth, particularly if contraction focused on spending cuts rather than tax increases. Alesina also claimed such policies in some cases could reap electoral dividends for incumbent politicians as well as fostering economic recovery (Alesina and Perotti 1997; Alesina and Ardagna 2010).

In the run-up to the 2010 general election, the Brown Government blamed the financial crisis on overseas forces beyond its control, while claiming credit for actions such as its 2008 stimulus package and tentative signs of economic recovery. It argued (much as did the 364 economists over the 1981 Conservative budget, discussed in Chapter Eight) that any fiscal squeeze should not start until recovery was well underway. But it put the standard rate of VAT back up to 17.5 per cent from the beginning of 2010, imposed a one-off 50 per cent tax on bankers' bonuses, announced a rise in compulsory National Insurance contributions to start the following year, and eventually went into the general election committed to a future revenue and spending squeeze.

Labour's deficit-reduction plan, presented by Chancellor Alasdair Darling in the Brown Government's final budget in March 2010, had a 'boiling frogs'

---

[4] HC Deb 24 November 2008, *c.*504–7. See also Darling (2011): 40–1.

character, in that it aimed to remove the 'structural deficit' over the course of two Parliaments (by 2016/17), and also involved delayed action in that it would not start until the year after the 2010 general election. The biggest reductions were scheduled in the final three years of the subsequent Parliament, at the end of which the structural deficit was expected to have fallen by more than two-thirds to 2.5 per cent of GDP.[5] A Fiscal Responsibility Act based on these plans and applying to the following four years was enacted shortly before the election.

The planned fall in future spending relative to GDP and corresponding increase in revenue rested on assumptions of years of steady economic growth after the recession—dismissed by the Opposition parties as wildly optimistic. The plan involved roughly 70 per cent of the deficit correction to come from reductions in planned spending and about 30 per cent from revenue increases. It comprised some £20bn reductions in overall planned spending (including a plan to cap public sector pay rises at not more than 1 per cent for two years) and approximately £20bn in asset sales, £16bn of which had already been announced. The figures implied reductions in planned spending of the order of 20 per cent in those policy domains not protected from cutbacks, but did not specify how those reductions would be achieved. The only exception was capital spending, where details of deep reductions were announced, amounting to cutting previous levels of spending by more than half over five years.

While Labour went into the 2010 general election with plans for a delayed-onset and slow-burn fiscal squeeze, the Conservatives proposed a swifter and earlier 'surgery without anaesthetics' approach. They claimed that, 'Gordon Brown's debt, waste and taxes have wrecked the economy and threaten to kill the recovery',[6] and that far from risking deeper recession, early spending cuts were essential for growth and for limiting debt servicing costs by retaining the UK's top rating by the international credit rating agencies. They therefore promised voters to eliminate the structural deficit more quickly, and by more emphasis on spending cuts, dismissing Labour's plans for an increase in compulsory National Insurance contributions from 2011 as a 'jobs tax' that would increase unemployment. The third main UK party, the Liberal Democrats, offered several proposals for tax increases and spending cuts and their election manifesto stressed the need for deficit reduction. But they were unspecific about the timetable and extent of fiscal squeeze, broadly implying they would match Labour's plans if they won government (Chote and Emmerson 2014).

---

[5] HC Deb 24 March 2010, c.255.
[6] 2010 Conservative Party manifesto, 'Invitation to Join the Government of Britain', p. 3, https://www.conservatives.com/~/media/files/activist%20centre/press%20and%20policy/manifestos/manifesto2010.

So while all major UK parties presented the voters with plans for fiscal squeeze in the 2010 general election, they differed over depth, balance, and timing. None offered specific plans for major cuts in programme spending, though much was made of the potential for large savings by greater operating efficiency. None mentioned higher VAT in their election manifestos, and indeed the Conservatives positively denied any plans to raise VAT.

In the run-up to the election, Labour ran well behind the Conservatives in the polls and did not expect to win an overall majority. At one point the Liberal Democrats moved ahead of Labour in the polls (and were not far short of the Conservatives) and the election result was widely predicted to be a hung parliament with minority government or a coalition. And as in 1997, the incumbent government laid some political traps for the Opposition parties. The most prominent one was a new top rate of income tax of 50 per cent for the approximately 300,000 UK taxpayers with taxable incomes over £150,000, introduced in the 2009 budget but only coming into force immediately before the 2010 election. That tax increase produced little if any extra revenue and indeed broke a pledge made in Labour's 2005 manifesto not to raise top rates of income tax, but was justified as a way of sharing extra tax burdens fairly during a crisis, and presented a subsequent government with a likely political challenge if it tried to repeal the tax.

In contrast to 1992, the pollsters' predictions of a hung parliament proved correct, but the polls over-estimated the Liberal Democrats' share of votes and seats. The Conservatives won the largest number of seats, but fell some twenty short of an absolute majority. Labour lost over ninety seats—a loss slightly worse than in 1979 (and far worse in vote share). The Liberal Democrats with fifty-seven seats (slightly fewer than before) held the balance, but attempts by Labour to form a coalition with them failed, since the two parties together would still fall ten seats short of a parliamentary majority. Instead a Conservative–Liberal Democrat coalition government was formed, but the election result meant there was no clear electoral mandate either for Labour's slower and more tax-focused fiscal squeeze plan or for the Conservatives' alternative plan for an earlier, shorter, and more spending-focused squeeze.

## 10.3 The Coalition's Plans for Fiscal Squeeze

The coalition formed in 2010 under the Conservative leader David Cameron presented itself from the outset as something of an emergency government centrally concerned with correcting the public finances. Its programme, following five days of post-election bargaining, heavily stressed the need for debt and deficit reduction to restore economic credibility: '...the most urgent task facing this coalition is to tackle our record debts...' Later in the document, the government announced it would 'significantly accelerate the reduction of the structural deficit over the course of a Parliament, with the main burden of deficit reduction borne by reduced spending rather than increased taxes'.[7]

A month after the election the new Chancellor (George Osborne) presented an 'emergency budget' that had been promised in the Conservative manifesto and foreshadowed in the coalition programme. Two-thirds of a five-year plan for fiscal squeeze announced in this budget followed what had been signalled in the pre-election Labour budget, as described earlier. But the coalition plan added roughly one-third to what Labour had proposed, in the form of an extra fiscal squeeze over 2010/11–2014/15 of about £40bn (about an extra 1.2 per cent of GDP on top of the Labour plan). It was intended to produce a fall in debt relative to GDP by 2015/16, and eliminate the structural deficit by the end of the Parliament in 2014/15, rather than cutting it by more than half by then, as Labour had planned to do (Emmerson Johnson and Joyce 2015).

That budget apparently reflected the overall plans announced by the Conservatives before the 2010 election and represented a notable change of stance by the Liberal Democrats from their previously announced opposition to early spending cuts. But (as with Alasdair Darling's plans), Osborne's plan for reducing debt and deficit rested on assumptions of above-average economic growth after the recession, to enable public spending to fall relative to GDP without falling substantially in constant-money terms (i.e. a 'soft' squeeze, in our language) and to boost revenue by some £175bn more than was raised in the last year of the Labour Government. The budget speech declared that the extra £40bn of fiscal squeeze should follow an 80:20 rule of thumb as between expenditure reductions and revenue increases, in contrast to the 70:30 split applying to the squeeze measures inherited from the Labour plan: 'The country has overspent; it has not been under-taxed.'[8] As already noted, the justification for an earlier, shorter, and deeper squeeze than Labour had planned stressed the need to reassure the financial markets, and thereby to reduce interest on UK borrowing to levels more likely to stimulate economic growth.[9]

On the revenue side, that post-election budget raised VAT from 17.5 per cent to 20 per cent—a change not mentioned by any of the major parties in the election campaign, but now claimed to be unavoidable, and expected to generate £13bn a year of extra revenue by the end of the Parliament. Also— recalling the bank windfall tax introduced by the Conservatives in 1981, discussed in Chapter Eight—the budget imposed a new tax on the balance sheets of UK banks and building societies, which differed from the 1981 tax

[7] *The Coalition: Our Programme for Government* (2010) London: HMSO, p. 7 and p. 15.
[8] HC Deb 22 June 2010, *c*.168.
[9] HC Deb 23 March 2011, *c*.951: 'We have a higher deficit than Portugal, Greece and Spain, but . . . virtually the same interest rate as Germany. This is our powerful monetary stimulus to our recovering economy.'

and the previous Labour Government's bank bonus tax in that it was intended to be permanent. The move was coordinated with the French and German Governments (which announced plans for similar taxes on the same day) and justified by blaming the banks for causing the 2008 financial crisis.

In addition, the tax threshold for higher rates of income tax was frozen for three years up to 2013/14, and indeed remained frozen until the eve of the following general election in 2015, with the effect that 1.5 million extra people became liable for higher rate tax (and consequently ineligible for some welfare payments) between 2010 and 2015. Inheritance tax thresholds, already frozen for four years by the previous government, remained frozen, and higher rate income taxpayers were also excluded in 2010/11 from an increased personal allowance for lower-rate taxpayers as well as being subjected to increased rates of capital gains tax. Several business tax offsets or allowances were reduced or removed, but the Corporation Tax rate was cut by 1 per cent, and it was announced that there would be four successive reductions to make the UK's Corporation Tax rate one of the lowest among the developed countries at 24 per cent in 2014/15. Income tax thresholds were also raised sharply for taxpayers at the lower end of the income scale, following the plan in the coalition agreement (itself reflecting one of the Liberal Democrats' major election promises) to raise the income tax threshold to £10,000 by the end of the Parliament.

The 2010 emergency budget also announced plans for an extra spending squeeze. Again reflecting 'red lines' in the coalition agreement, some spending domains, namely the National Health Service and overseas aid, were protected altogether from reductions in planned spending, but departments in non-protected areas faced an average real cut in their planned spending of about 25 per cent over four years (as against the 20 per cent implied in Labour's plans). The coalition government broadly followed its Labour predecessor's plans for big cuts in planned capital spending, but it chose not to impose further capital spending cutbacks (in contrast to what had happened in previous spending squeezes), such that the extra spending cutbacks imposed by the coalition mostly fell on current rather than capital spending.

Retirement pensioners—an electoral group especially important for the Conservatives but also to other parties given their higher-than-average voting turnout—were protected by a 'triple lock' on state retirement pensions (to be uprated annually in relation to inflation, earnings, or 2.5 per cent, whichever was the highest) that had been promised in the Liberal Democrats' manifesto. But other welfare spending figured prominently in the spending-squeeze plans, with extra cuts in welfare planned to comprise roughly one-third of the reductions in current spending. The post-election budget therefore announced cuts in welfare designed to save £11bn a year by 2014/15, including reductions of tax credits for higher income earners, stricter medical assessment for those claiming disability benefits, a cap on the level of benefit payable to support housing rental costs, a requirement that to be eligible for benefits, lone parents should look for work when their youngest child started school, and a three year freeze in child benefit payments, payable to mothers. The small print of the budget also announced a change in the inflation index (from the Retail Prices Index to the Consumer Prices Index) to be used from the following year in uprating retirement pensions and welfare benefits, which was expected to save over £6bn a year by the end of the Parliament.

Labour's pre-election budget had announced a two-year 1 per cent pay cap for public employees, but the coalition's post-election budget replaced that with a two-year pay freeze on all but the lowest incomes. Freezes or cuts in public sector pay were commonly applied in earlier spending squeezes, but this episode also saw an assault on public service pensions, in the form of a review of public service pensions chaired by a former Labour cabinet minister (Lord Hutton), that recommended raising the age of pension eligibility for public servants, raising employee contributions by several percentage points of their salary, and moving from pensions based on final salary to payments based on average pay over a career (Independent Public Service Pension Commission 2011). These recommendations were broadly enacted to take effect from 2015, subject to a 'grandfather' provision, that no public servants within ten years of their earlier pension age would be affected by the changes. So, as with the 1995 increase in the state pension age, these changes had little immediate effect on public spending, but were expected to limit the rise in spending on pensions by public service employers a decade or more into the future.

Arguably, the spending change representing the greatest political cost to the Liberal Democrats early in the government's life, not mentioned in the 2010 emergency budget, was a raising of the top-up tuition fees that universities were permitted to charge their students. It will be recalled that in the 1990s squeeze discussed in Chapter Nine, New Labour had scrapped the previous system of student maintenance grants. During its long post-election honeymoon it had replaced those grants entirely by loans and enabled universities to charge their students tuition fees of £1000 a year. Although as we saw in Chapter Nine, that move provoked New Labour's biggest backbench rebellion in its first term (and the fees were later abandoned for Scotland as a result of Liberal Democrat pressure in the Edinburgh Parliament), Labour had again later raised the fees to £3000 a year after the 2005 general election while promising no further increases before the next election. The fees were means-tested (and numbers of means-tested places were not capped) so the change did not directly bear on the poorest students, but the change affected aspirations even for those on low incomes and bore directly on those on middle and higher incomes.

The Liberal Democrats held parliamentary seats in several constituencies where student votes were important, and their 2010 manifesto promised to phase out tuition fees for all first-degree university students and immediately scrap fees for final-year undergraduates. But instead the 2010 coalition government followed a course similar to that charted by Labour in 1998 by accepting the recommendations of an independent report on university financing commissioned by their predecessor. It consequently legislated to triple tuition fees from their previous cap of £3000 per year, to be collected retrospectively from students through the tax system after they had graduated and their earnings were above a specified level. The legislation provoked a major parliamentary revolt by Liberal Democrat MPs (thirty-five of the Party's fifty-seven MPs either voted against or abstained) but the votes of the others sufficed to pass the legislation.

That violation of a central manifesto pledge—a key marker for high political effort or cost in our qualitative scale of fiscal squeeze in Chapter One—was repeatedly used by their political opponents to attack the Liberal Democrats, whose poll ratings never returned to their mid-2010 level over the rest of the Parliament. In part, that tuition fees hike seems comparable to the 'Geddes Axe' cuts in secondary education imposed by the Lloyd George coalition in 1922 (as discussed in Chapter Three), in that it struck at the aspirations of families who saw higher education as the route to social advancement. It was different in that no fees were payable upfront and the number of free places was not rationed, but its negative impact on electoral support for the Liberal Democrats seems to have been marked and lasting.

These policy changes early in the life of the coalition government were accompanied by changes in structures and procedures. Going well beyond the independent forecasters that Conservative Chancellor Norman Lamont had introduced into the Treasury in the early 1990s, the government 'outsourced' economic forecasting from the Treasury to a new semi-independent public body, the Office for Budget Responsibility, which had been promised in the Conservatives' election manifesto and was intended to offer greater credibility to official economic forecasting (and no doubt also to absorb some of the blame for forecasting errors as the OBR greatly over-estimated economic growth in the early 2010s). But the Liberal Democrats' manifesto proposal for a 'Council on Financial Stability' (comprising representatives of all political parties and other experts, such as the Governor of the Bank of England), did not see the light of day. The proposal—a probably unconscious echo of the 1931 May Committee, discussed in Chapter Four—was for this Council to recommend a deficit reduction framework for a comprehensive spending review—and presumably also spread the blame for unpopular tax increases and spending cutbacks.[10]

---

[10] Liberal Democrat Manifesto 2010: *Change that Works for You*, London: Chris Fox, p. 98, http://www.politicsresources.net/area/uk/ge10/man/parties/libdem_manifesto_2010.pdf.

Instead of that sharing-the-blame proposal, ministers made fiscal squeeze decisions directly, as had applied to every fiscal squeeze since 1931. But blame was shared among the parties in the coalition, with a Conservative Chancellor paired with a Liberal Democrat Chief Secretary in the Treasury and all major policy decisions going through a 'quartet' comprising the two party leaders and the two Treasury Cabinet ministers. A variant of the 'EDX' cabinet committee procedure described for the 1990s in Chapter Nine was adopted for spending-round decisions, with a similar rule that spending ministers could not join the committee to judge their fellow-ministers' claims until they had themselves agreed spending plans with the Treasury. But some interviewees reported that this arrangement proved less effective in deterring 'holdout' behaviour by spending ministers than in the early 1990s, perhaps because of different political conditions (such as coalition rather than single-party government and a smaller pool of long-serving, highly experienced ministers than two decades before).

## 10.4 Coalition Management, Labour Outcomes?

Some features of the fiscal squeeze introduced at the outset of the coalition government continued and developed over the following four years. For example, on the tax side, the raising of the threshold for basic rate income tax by stages every year to a figure slightly exceeding the Liberal Democrats' manifesto promise of £10,000 became a recurring feature of subsequent budgets and allowed the government to claim that 2.6 million working-age people had been taken out of income tax. But at the same time, as already mentioned, the threshold for the higher (40 per cent) income-tax rate stayed frozen until 2014, such that the government's opponents could equally claim that 1.5 million more people had been brought into that higher tax band during the 2010–15 Parliament and talk about a 'squeezed middle'.[11] The so-called 'jobs tax', the increase in National Insurance (social security) contributions from 2011 planned by the Brown Labour Government which the 2010 Conservative manifesto had promised to scrap and the Liberal Democrat manifesto had also opposed, went ahead in 2011, but with a higher threshold than Labour had planned.

On the spending side, within the category of non-cyclical expenditure, healthcare, schools, and overseas aid spending remained 'protected' and indeed spending on overseas aid rose by one-third in real terms over the period. Outside those domains, there were dramatic reductions in police numbers (a spending

---

[11] (Stuart Hosie) HC Deb 18 March 2015, c.815.

domain that was protected under the Thatcher Government and which the Brown Labour Government had also proposed to protect in its pre-election budget) and numerous changes to welfare eligibility designed to reduce the growth of welfare spending. As we saw earlier, child benefit was frozen in the post-election 2010 budget and two years later that benefit was removed altogether from any family that included a higher rate taxpayer. Tax credits that the Labour Government had introduced in the early 2000s were withdrawn from families with taxable incomes above £26,000 (well above the average wage). The government defended such changes on the grounds that it was important to limit benefits going to the better off (but did not apply the same principle to benefits for retirement pensioners) and to prevent benefit recipients from being better off than those in work at average wages, challenging the Labour Opposition to risk electoral unpopularity by defending welfare benefits above that level.

Amongst other changes in eligibility for welfare benefits, perhaps the most politically salient one was a change in housing benefit in 2012 that reduced the sums that welfare claimants could obtain for rental payments if they had one or more 'spare' bedrooms in their homes. That measure, officially titled 'the under occupancy charge', came to be dubbed by the government's critics as a 'bedroom tax' and a continuing stream of politically embarrassing hardship cases (for example, of disabled people or divorced fathers who wanted space to allow visits by their children) came to test the government's political cohesion.

Indeed, these tax and spending changes produced numerous political challenges. The slogan 'all in it together' (a perhaps unconscious echo of the 'equality of sacrifice theme' of the 1931 National Government, discussed in Chapter Four) that had featured prominently in the 2010 Conservative manifesto and reappeared in later budget speeches, was repeatedly used by the Opposition to attack the fiscal squeeze as unfairly bearing down hardest on the worst-off rather than those on the highest incomes. This charge became particularly marked after the 2012 budget, in which among other heavily criticized measures the government reduced the top income tax rate from the 50 per cent to which Labour had raised it in 2010 to 45 per cent. The Chancellor claimed that he had kept by a pledge announced in Opposition in 2009 not to cut the 50 per cent tax rate while there was a pay freeze on public sector workers, and that the estimated £100m a year of revenue lost by the rate reduction would be more than offset by an extra £500m a year from higher stamp duties on high-value real-estate purchases by wealthy individuals and corporate buyers. But the change allowed the Opposition to berate the coalition (and particularly the Liberal Democrats, whose leader had said only a few months before that a cut in the top tax rate was not a priority) for exempting the wealthy from the pain of fiscal squeeze, and challenge cabinet ministers to say whether they would benefit personally from the tax cut: 'The party that delivered the People's Budget of 1909 is supporting the Millionaires' Budget of 2012...'[12]

Although, as we have seen, the Conservatives and the coalition in general in 2010 had made much of the need for a shorter and sharper fiscal squeeze than Labour had planned, the result in financial outcome data at the end of the 2010–15 Parliament turned out to more closely reflect Labour's plan than that of the coalition. That is, by the end of the Parliament, overall debt was far above the levels envisaged in the 2010 plan. Actual revenue increases were less than had been planned under both Labour and coalition plans, while reductions in planned spending were more than had been planned in the coalition's first budget. Moreover, far from being eliminated by that time, the reported 'structural' (that is, cyclically adjusted) deficit was still running at well over 3 per cent of GDP. The government could certainly claim that the deficit as a proportion of GDP had more than halved between 2010 and 2015 (as had indeed been envisaged in Labour's 2010 plan), but it could not claim to have eliminated 'the bulk' of that deficit as its 2010 plan aimed to do.

So how and why did the coalition government come to deliver broadly what five years earlier the Conservatives had attacked as too modest in Labour's 2010 proposals? As noted earlier, it was on the revenue, not the spending side, where the squeeze fell short of what was planned in 2010. Revenue rose in constant-price terms (particularly due to the 2010 VAT increase and to a lesser extent by the tax on bank balance sheets and increased capital gains tax). But it did not rise relative to GDP and fell far short of the additional £175bn or so by 2015 that the 2010 deficit reduction plan was predicated on, such that the squeeze turned out to involve proportionately greater emphasis on reductions in planned spending than had been envisaged in 2010.

That tax shortfall stemmed in part from the fact that economic growth over the five years, and especially in the first three, fell far short of the assumptions that had underlain both the Labour and coalition deficit reduction plans. In 2010 the OBR had forecast GDP growth of 1.2 per cent in 2010–11, 2.3 per cent in 2011–12, and 2.8 per cent in 2012–13. But the reported outcomes were respectively 2.02, 1.62, and 0.72, such that, between 2010 and 2013, the OBR forecast that GDP would grow by 4 per cent more than it did. According to official financial outcome data, total managed expenditure fell relative to GDP and in constant-price terms between 2010/11 and 2014/15, while total current spending rose in current money terms over that period. Much of that reduction in total managed expenditure in constant prices seems to have come from reduced debt servicing costs (stemming in large part from

[12] (Ed Miliband) HC Deb 21 March 2012, c.809.

the massive economic-stimulus programme of quantitative easing involving purchase of extra government stock by the central bank that accompanied the fiscal squeeze)[13] and from the planned reductions in capital spending that the coalition government had largely inherited from its Labour predecessor in 2010.

But there was also a political aspect to that outcome. Since the coalition government had chosen to outsource economic forecasting to a quasi-independent body in 2010, it could partially sidestep political blame for forecasting errors in a way not open to governments in earlier episodes (for example, in the early 1990s when Treasury forecasts of economic recovery had proved embarrassingly over-optimistic). But the coalition government could not so easily escape the charge repeatedly made by its political opponents that it had itself hampered and slowed down economic recovery both by its 2010 rhetoric of severe fiscal crisis (which was claimed by its opponents to have damaged economic confidence) and by its efforts to start fiscal squeeze earlier than Labour had planned.

Just as the previous Labour Government had blamed the 2008 financial crisis on sub-prime lending in the United States rather than its own conduct, the coalition government began to blame the slow economic recovery on a continuing crisis in the eurozone, where the travails of the euro common currency and the austerity measures associated with its management depressed demand in the UK's largest export market. Since the coalition government had argued that reassuring the financial markets was a key reason for an extra squeeze on top of what Labour had planned, it faced further political embarrassment when early in 2013 two of the major credit ratings agencies (Moody's and later Fitch) downgraded the UK's credit rating for the first time since 1978, on the grounds that sluggish economic growth then forecast by the IMF for the UK would make debt reduction more difficult.

Further, the effect of that disparity between forecast economic growth and outcomes was filtered through political choice. That is—in contrast to what happened in 1931, as discussed in Chapter Four—the 2010 coalition government chose not to modify its plans for fiscal squeeze after 2010 in the light of lower than expected tax revenue (and higher than expected cyclical spending), for example, by pushing tax rates up further or imposing much deeper spending cuts to keep to the 2010 plan and timetable for debt and deficit reduction.

The decision to let the timetable of the deficit reduction plan slip in the early 2010s was never formally acknowledged, but Chancellor Osborne introduced both the 2011 and 2012 budgets by saying that they were intended to

---

[13] (Andrew Tyrie) HC Deb 19 March 2014, *c.*800 and 18 March 2015, *c.*786.

be fiscally neutral rather than to tighten further.[14] In his 2013 budget speech, he declared he would neither make more spending cuts to hit the original debt and deficit reduction target nor undertake extra borrowing to stimulate the economy, as some were urging,[15] though in fact he altered his borrowing plans at that point to borrow £48bn more than originally planned in 2013/14, £60bn in 2014/15, and £67bn in 2015/16.[16]

As a result of this unacknowledged change in its deficit reduction timetable, the coalition government could only claim that it had delivered the reduction in the structural deficit that Labour had planned in 2010. But a dramatic pick-up in UK economic growth in 2013 and 2014, accompanied by a sharp fall in world oil prices in 2014 and 2015, improved the prospects for increases in tax revenues and falls in cyclical spending. And in 2014 the Chancellor set new 'bear traps' for the Opposition parties by announcing an overall cap in welfare spending (excluding only the state pension and unemployment benefits) and announcing plans for further reductions in spending in the following Parliament, 'to lock in our country's commitment to the path of deficit reduction.'

That plan presented the Labour Opposition with a challenge similar to that posed by the Conservatives in 1997, putting it under pressure either to promise to match those spending cuts or to explain what extra taxes it would raise to fund the additional expenditure. In this case, Labour did not repeat its 1997 strategy of promising to match the previous government's plans for spending reductions. Rather, it chose to match part (some £30bn) of the further spending reductions planned by the coalition but still to spend some £50bn a year more than Osborne's 2014 plan allowed for, to be funded by extra taxes on the rich, including a restoration of the 50 per cent tax rate on the highest earners and a 'mansion tax' on the most expensive houses. So Labour went into the 2015 election offering an alternative style of fiscal squeeze with different distributional emphases, rather than no squeeze at all.

The 2015 election result was widely predicted as another hung Parliament with a minority government or coalition, but in the event produced a clear but narrow overall majority (of twelve) for the Conservatives. The Liberal Democrats were reduced to a handful of MPs and Labour experienced a further loss of vote and seat share. The election result was shaped by two other parties, namely the UK Independence Party, a right-of-centre populist party which won some 13 per cent of the vote even though it only won one parliamentary seat, and the SNP in Scotland. The latter had made much of its opposition to 'austerity'

---

[14] HC Deb 23 March 2011, c.951 and 21 March 2012, c.795. The IMF's chief economist (Olivier Blanchard) was reported to have criticized the UK government at that time for 'playing with fire' by its public spending restraint, though the following year the IMF approved the UK's fiscal adjustment plans and acknowledged it had previously underestimated UK economic growth (Armitstead 2014).
[15] HC Deb 20 March 2013, c.934.     [16] (John Redwood) HC Debs 20 March 2013, c.963.

imposed by Westminster and destroyed Labour's chances of a majority in the UK Parliament by winning all but one of Labour's former Scottish seats.

However, the new Conservative Government's pre-election plans for continuing fiscal squeeze were upset the following year when a narrow majority of voters in the June 2016 referendum on UK membership of the European Union unexpectedly chose the 'leave' option. That result led to consternation in the financial markets, the swift resignation of the prime minister, and the formation of a new government under his successor, the former Home Secretary Theresa May. May sacked George Osborne as Chancellor and Osborne's successor, Philip Hammond, announced the abandonment of the deficit reduction targets that had been set before the 2015 election.

## 10.5 Conclusions

As we noted at the outset, any discussion of consequences of this squeeze episode must be provisional, because it is so recent and not clearly finished at the time of writing. But, as with the previous seven chapters, we conclude with observations about how three issues in fiscal squeeze politics that were highlighted in Chapter One played out in this episode at least to date.

### 10.5.1 *Tax and Spending, Depth and Duration, Blame and Control*

In this episode, questions of what the balance should be between tax increases and spending reductions figured large in party political debate around the 2010 election, and so did the question of whether to follow a 'surgery without anaesthetics' or 'boiling frogs' approach to fiscal squeeze. While the George Osborne 'surgery without anaesthetics' approach won the battle in 2010, the outcome in deficit reduction five years later looked much more like the longer-drawn-out Labour timetable ostensibly rejected by the Conservatives. But as we have also seen, the deviation from plan seems to have come more on the revenue side than the spending side.

As for blame politics, this episode involved a combination of a government heavily blaming its predecessor for making fiscal squeeze necessary (failing to 'fix the roof while the sun was shining', in a catchphrase much used by George Osborne), and a coalition of parties formally sharing the blame for fiscal squeeze (while sending signals to voters implying that the other party was behind tax or spending measures unpopular with their own core voters). The Liberal Democrats' manifesto proposal for handling blame for fiscal squeeze through an all-party Council on Financial Stability was abandoned, but the outsourcing of blame for economic forecasting errors by creating an independent public body for forecasting was added to the previous Labour

Government's step of delegating monetary policy to a committee of 'econo-crats'. And, as we have also seen, blame politics in this case involved some notable 'heresthetic' moves too, notably over welfare cuts designed to prevent claimants from receiving more in welfare benefits than those in work on (roughly) median incomes—pitting so-called 'strivers' against 'shirkers' and challenging Labour to oppose such changes.

### 10.5.2 Loss, Cost, and Effort Involved in This Squeeze

As in previous chapters, Table 10.1 summarizes our assessment of the loss, cost, and effort associated with this squeeze episode. In this case we have not included the Brown Labour Government in the analysis since (unlike the Lloyd George coalition in 1922) it had not proceeded to implement any of its planned squeeze during its tenure; and we have also scored political costs separately for the Conservatives and Liberal Democrats since (again unlike the Lloyd George coalition) the two parties had campaigned on different manifestos in the preceding general election.

As we have seen, imposed losses in this episode were variable, hitting some non-median voters hard (such as the welfare benefit changes and the freeze on higher rate income tax thresholds), but much of those losses seem to fall into the 'moderate' category of Table 1.2 in Chapter One, as 'stealth taxes' outside the headline rates of income tax, or 'stealth' benefit changes such as the change in indexation of benefit payments. Moreover, far from non-fiscal austerity being added to the mix, monetary policy was far from restrained over this episode, with interest rates approaching zero, benefiting voters with mortgages while hitting savers.

There was much debate over who faced the greatest losses from this squeeze episode. Many of the government's opponents claimed the squeeze bore down hardest on the poor.[17] Some, including Ed Miliband, the Labour leader,

**Table 10.1.** A qualitative classification of imposed loss, political cost, and state effort associated with 2010–15 fiscal squeeze

| | Low | Moderate | High | Overall classification |
|---|---|---|---|---|
| Conservatives/Liberal Democrats | | | | |
| Loss | [3] | [1], [2] | [1] | Moderate |
| Cost (Cons) | [4] | [1], [2], [3] | | Moderate |
| Cost (Lib Dems) | [4] | [2], [3] | [1] | High |
| Effort | | [2], [3] | [1], [2] | High/Moderate |

Note: Numbers in square brackets refer to categories in Table 1.2, Chapter One.

[17] 'We are…punishing the poor for the bankers' errors…cuts are hitting the poor hardest' (Geraint Davies), HC Deb 20 March 2013, c.1017.

also argued that those in the middle of the income scale were squeezed, by measures such as extra means-testing of benefits and the freezing of the higher tax threshold. The incumbents claimed that after five years of squeeze, officially reported levels of inequality,[18] child poverty, and youth unemployment all showed decreases, while the share of income tax paid by the top 1 per cent of taxpayers rose from 25 per cent in 2010 to 27 per cent in 2015 (a higher proportion than had been achieved by the previous Labour Government in thirteen years), and by 2015 the lower-paid 50 per cent of taxpayers likewise paid a smaller proportion of income tax than they had done under the previous government.[19] Those asserting that fiscal squeeze had increased inequality tended to focus on pre- rather than post-tax inequality and on the relative share of total income taken by the top 1 per cent (rather than the top 10 or 20 per cent) which did increase after a sharp drop at the start of the recession, but had also done so since the 1970s, both in times of fiscal expansion and fiscal squeeze (Chu 2015).

As for political cost to incumbents, we have already noted that this case differs from the Liberal–Conservative coalition of the early 1920s in that, whereas the Lloyd George coalition campaigned on a common programme in the 1918 election, the Conservatives and Liberal Democrats campaigned under separate and different manifestos in 2010 and therefore the squeeze involved different political costs to them as incumbents, shown in separate entries in Table 10.1. Whereas for the Liberal Democrats the squeeze involved ditching black-letter manifesto promises, notably on student tuition fees (a high-cost move in our analysis in Chapter One), for the Conservatives it was more a case of unpopular measures not mentioned in their 2010 manifesto, notably the VAT hike and welfare cuts such as the 'bedroom tax'.

As for state effort, more was certainly required of the state machine in fiscal policy over this period than minor adaptation of established routines (for example, in wholesale changes to the benefit system and restructuring public sector pensions, something not undertaken even in the crises of 1931 or 1976). While the effort arguably fell well short of that involved in measures such as the development of a new system of mass income taxation in World War II, it seems to be at the upper levels, and so we class it as High to Moderate here.

---

[18] The UK's GINI index of post-tax inequality fell slightly over this episode (from 34.2 per cent in 2008/09 to 32 per cent in 2014/15) and other official measures of inequality (such as the ratio of the incomes of the top 10 per cent as against the bottom 10 per cent) pointed to inequality flatlining rather than soaring.

[19] (George Osborne) HC Deb 18 March 2015, *c.*771.

### 10.5.3 *Electoral and Other Consequences*

As mentioned earlier, because this squeeze episode was so recent, we comment here only on electoral effects. And compared to our earlier cases, there were multiple electoral events during this squeeze episode—not just local, central, and European elections, but also elections to the UK's post-1999 devolved parliaments and assemblies in 2011 and 2016, and three referendums, one on the electoral system in 2011 (part of the coalition agreement between the Conservatives and Liberal Democrats the previous year), a second, in Scotland only, on Scottish independence in 2014, and a third on the UK's membership of the European Union in 2016.

As for general election results, the 2015 election outcome perhaps most closely resembles that of 1922 (discussed in Chapter Three), at least in England and Wales, in that the Conservatives were rewarded by the voters with a higher vote and seat share, while their coalition partners, the Liberal Democrats, were heavily punished and reduced to a handful of seats. That outcome is consistent with the idea of 'asymmetric punishment' for spending squeezes (as between left-of-centre and right-of-centre parties) that we discussed in Chapter One.

But the parallel between the 2015 and 1922 general election outcomes did not extend to Scotland. In that case, the outcome resembles the 1918 election in which in one part of the country (the twenty-six counties of Ireland in 1918, Scotland in 2015) the result was an overwhelming victory for a nationalist party (Sinn Féin in 1918, the SNP in 2015) opposed to Westminster rule, and corresponding defeat for Labour and Liberal Democrats as left-of-centre unionist parties, each reduced to only one Scottish seat in the Westminster Parliament. The SNP also retained its dominance in the devolved Scottish Parliament in the Scottish elections the following year. What remains unclear at the time of writing is whether this dramatic weakening of support for the Union in Scotland should be attributed to this particular fiscal squeeze (in the same way that the Thatcher squeeze of the 1980s, discussed in Chapter Eight, was commonly said to have built up support for devolution two decades before) or whether it has other or longer-term causes.

Equally elusive is any link between fiscal squeeze and the outcome of the 2016 referendum on the UK's position in the European Union (which, unlike the 2011 'Alternative Vote' referendum and the 2014 Scottish independence referendum, did not produce a majority for the status quo but a narrow majority for 'Brexit', at least in England and Wales). Some commentators attributed that result to the numbers in which working-class voters in traditionally safe Labour seats, particularly in the North of England, turned out to vote for the 'Leave' option, contrary to what Labour and the Liberal Democrats campaigned for. But again, the link between fiscal squeeze and that outcome is tenuous, especially given that the two other referendums over the period produced majorities for the status quo.

Still, two things do seem to be clear. One is that in this case, unlike most of the other fiscal squeezes we have discussed, major constitutional issues relating to two levels of 'union' were broached during the fiscal squeeze, with effects on the structure and even continuing existence of the UK as a state that cannot yet be assessed. The other is that those political commentators (such as Legrain 2010) who saw the 2010 general election as an election that it would be best to lose (on the grounds that the austerity policies the winners would have to enact would thereafter condemn them to electoral perdition for years to come) were at most only half correct. While the electoral fate of the Liberal Democrats in 2015 is consistent with those prophecies, that of the Conservatives is decidedly not.

# Part III
# Patterns and Lessons

# 11

# Conclusions

## From the Past to the Future of Fiscal Squeeze

After eight chapters examining the particularities of the politics of fiscal squeeze episodes—the stories that lie behind the reported financial outcomes we compared in Chapter Two—this chapter begins with a qualitative comparison of those episodes, considered in terms of loss imposition, political costs to incumbents, and effort by the state.

This comparison builds on our analysis in Chapter One (Table 1.2) and our summary assessments at the end of each of the 'episode' chapters. It reviews the intensity of fiscal squeezes in terms of the three qualitative dimensions of squeeze intensity that we identified in Chapter One and rated for each squeeze episode in the previous eight chapters.

When we compare our fiscal squeeze episodes in that way, bringing together our summary assessments at the end of the previous eight chapters, we find the 'loss imposition' element broadly corresponds to the intensity of squeeze as measured by hardness or softness on reported financial outcome measures in Chapter Two, but not necessarily with other financial outcome indicators commonly used in the 'consolidation' literature, notably of reductions in debt and deficit. The other two elements, the amount of political capital staked or reputation risked by incumbent politicians and the degree of effort expended by the state, do not seem to correspond very closely with intensity of squeezes measured in terms of financial outcome indicators.

This chapter then draws on the qualitative accounts of the previous eight chapters to explore how the fiscal squeeze 'game' seems to have changed over the century, going beyond the two trends that showed up in the statistical analysis in Chapter Two—that is, a certain shift (on the measures we used) to the more gradualist 'boiling frogs' approach away from 'surgery without anaesthetics' and an apparent shift away from hard revenue-led squeezes. In this section, drawing on the qualitative accounts of how blame was managed for fiscal squeeze in the last eight chapters, we point to the absence of moves towards outsourcing unpopular squeeze decisions to technocrats and experts, explore what might have changed in the factors triggering fiscal squeezes, and discuss what might be new about squeeze-related tactics such as 'stealth taxes', 'stealth' spending cuts or creative accounting, and 'bear traps' left by outgoing governments to constrain or embarrass their political opponents.

Third, bringing together the analysis of Chapter Two and the accounts given in the eight 'episode' chapters, we return to the issue of the consequences of fiscal squeeze that was raised in Chapter One. As we have seen in earlier chapters, fiscal squeezes commonly seem to have left noticeable political scars and memories that shape later actions. Each squeeze left something behind it in policy or procedural change, a few led to long-term abandonment of previous state activities (as opposed to temporary pauses or retreats) and one or two in the course of the hundred years might be seen as having constitutional consequences.

Further, we explore the electoral aftermath of fiscal squeeze. We noted in Chapter One that the general electoral consequences of 'austerity' are not clear in the fiscal consolidation literature. We do not dispute the conclusion of Alberto Alesina and his colleagues (2012), drawn from comparative research covering a period since the 1970s, that there is no clear correlation between incumbent loss of office and fiscal consolidation measured in terms of deficit and debt reduction, but we reach a different conclusion on the basis of our qualitative and quantitative indicators of squeeze intensity. When we look at fiscal squeeze on the basis of those indicators rather than debt and deficit reduction, we find that hard squeezes did indeed tend to be electorally toxic for incumbent parties over the century considered here. But they were not invariably so, and we comment on the few exceptions where incumbents survived hard squeezes.

Finally, having reviewed a century of fiscal squeeze politics, we look to the future. What will future fiscal squeezes look like if past trends continue? What would have to happen for those trends to be reversed? Can we expect the squeezes of the 2020s to resemble more closely those of the 1920s and 1930s or those of the last three decades?

## 11.1 Squeeze Intensity and Reported Financial Outcomes Compared

Building on the tables at the end of each of the previous eight chapters, Table 11.1 brings those analyses together into a summary comparative assessment of the fiscal squeezes identified in Chapter Two in terms of loss imposition, political cost or risk to incumbents, and state effort involved in fiscal

**Table 11.1.** Fiscal squeeze episodes compared: quantitative type and qualitative evaluation of loss, cost, and effort involved

| Overall episode (ratio method) | Sub-episode (ratio method) | Quantitative type | Qualitative evaluation of degree of voter loss, political cost to incumbent parties, and state effort | | |
|---|---|---|---|---|---|
| | | | Imposed loss | Political cost to incumbent parties | State effort |
| 1916–18 WW1 | 1916–18 | Hard Revenue | High | Low | High |
| 1919–25 Post-WW1 | 1919–21 | Hard Spending/Hard Revenue | Low/Moderate | Moderate | Low |
| | 1923–25 | Hard Spending | High | Moderate (Nat. Lib); Low (Cons., Labour) | Moderate |
| 1931–35 Financial crisis | 1931–32 | Hard Revenue | High | High (Labour); Low (later National Govt) | High |
| | 1933–35 | Hard Spending | Moderate/High | Low | Low |
| 1941–45 WW2 | 1941–45 | Hard Revenue | High | Low | High |
| 1946–49 Post-WW2 | 1946–49 | Hard Spending/Soft Revenue | Moderate | Moderate | Moderate |
| | 1953–55 | Soft Spending/Soft Revenue | Moderate | Moderate | Moderate |
| | 1960–61 | Hard Revenue | High | High | Moderate |
| | 1964–67 | Hard Revenue | High/Moderate | Moderate | High/Moderate |
| | 1968–69 | Soft Spending/Hard Revenue | High | High | Moderate |
| 1973–79 Stagflation | 1973–75 | Hard Revenue | High/Moderate | Moderate | High/Moderate |
| | 1976 | Hard Spending/Soft Revenue | High/Moderate | Moderate | Moderate |
| | 1977–78 | Hard Spending | High | High | High |
| 1980–88 Thatcherism | 1980–81 | Hard Revenue | High | High | High |
| | 1983–88 | Soft Spending/Soft Revenue | Moderate | Moderate | Moderate/High |
| 1993–2000 | 1993–00 | Soft Spending/Soft Revenue | Moderate | Moderate (Cons.); Low (Labour) | Moderate |
| 2010–15 | 2010–15 | Soft Spending/Soft Revenue | Moderate | Moderate (Cons.); High (Lib. Dems) | High/Moderate |

squeezes. We have shown that such an analysis necessarily involves tricky judgement calls and some episodes are easier to classify than others on some or all of those dimensions. That is why we avoid aggregating the qualitative dimensions into a single measure of squeeze intensity and restrict the rating to a high/moderate/low judgement in each case.

Limited as this qualitative assessment is, Table 11.1 clearly demonstrates three points. First, only three of the eighteen squeeze episodes analysed in Table 11.1 rated high on this assessment on all three of the qualitative dimensions of squeeze intensity. They were: the 1931/32–1932/33 squeeze (showing up only as a revenue squeeze on the financial outcome data in Chapter Two[1]) that broke Ramsay MacDonald's minority Labour Government and subsequently led to an electoral landslide never matched before or since in modern UK election history; the 1977/78–1978/79 revenue and spending squeeze that followed the 1976 currency crisis amid deep internal conflict between right and left in the Labour Government led by Harold Wilson and then James Callaghan; and the 1980/81–1981/82 revenue squeeze in the early embattled years of Margaret Thatcher's Conservative Government.

A second and related point about Table 11.1 is that the intensity of fiscal squeeze when rated in terms of 'hardness' or 'softness' on financial outcome indicators (as set out in Chapter Two, Table 2.1) broadly corresponds with our qualitative assessments of the amount of loss inflicted on voters or citizens (summarized as 'imposed loss' in Table 11.1, column 4). That correspondence is perhaps not very surprising, since the basis of the qualitative assessment overlaps somewhat with the quantitative analysis. But there was only a weak, indeed, sometimes negative, association between periods of sustained deficit reduction relative to GDP (the measure conventionally used in the econometric literature) and fiscal squeeze episodes classified as 'high' on the three dimensions shown in Table 11.1. We showed in Chapter Two that deficit reduction by no means corresponds exactly with fiscal squeeze as measured by hardness or softness of spending or revenue changes, and the correspondence is even weaker for the qualitative assessments of squeeze intensity. And, as we shall show later, that divergence between different ways of identifying episodes and measuring the intensity of 'austerity' is really important when it comes to identifying the consequences and particularly the electoral outcomes of fiscal squeeze.

The other two qualitative elements of squeeze intensity identified in Chapter One seem to be rather less closely linked to our hardness and softness

---

[1] As noted earlier, that outcome may reflect the fact that efforts to squeeze spending tend to show up with more lag than revenue squeezes in financial outcomes data. And in this case, Middleton's (1996) historic spending data, following calendar rather than fiscal years, does indicate a spending squeeze in 1932.

measures, perhaps particularly the second element, that of political cost to incumbent politicians. That means that some politically crucial elements of fiscal squeeze intensity do not seem to be satisfactorily captured either by deficit reduction or by our 'hardness' and 'softness' metrics of changes in spending and revenue. For example, the most severe revenue squeezes observed in the whole century (those imposed in the two twentieth-century world wars, particularly World War II) cannot be rated as involving especially high political cost or risk to incumbents, because although those squeezes undoubtedly involved high state effort to raise revenue (again, particularly in World War II), they were undertaken by grand coalition governments, with overt party competition suspended by the mainstream parties.

It is also notable that the only case of a double hard squeeze on spending and revenue in the whole century (the 1919/20–1921/22 episode), does not rate especially high on our qualitative measures of squeeze intensity. That is because, although direct taxes on middle-class voters and firms remained very high (disappointing expectations of relaxation after World War I), the over-whelming bulk of the spending cuts at that time were on defence demobiliza-tion, did not break election promises about post-war reconstruction, and state activity related to fiscal matters does not appear to have been particularly frenetic either. Certainly, as we showed in Chapter Three, there were related challenges for the state machine, for example in handling major strikes over pay and industrial working conditions and indeed military action involving some 10,000 troops to suppress the rioting associated with strikes over work-ing hours in Glasgow in January 1919. But as far as specifically fiscal matters were concerned, it seems hard to rate that episode as involving markedly greater effort than many of the other cases we have discussed in this book.

A third feature is a certain apparent shift to 'fiscal squeeze without tears' over the most recent episodes of the century considered here (as reflected in Table 11.1, column 5). 'Fiscal squeeze without tears' is perhaps too strong a description; but it is notable that for the second qualitative dimension of squeeze intensity, namely the risk or cost to incumbent political parties in imposing squeezes, the degree of political effort put into fiscal squeezes broadly seems to have been lower in the last third of the period considered here than in a number of earlier episodes.

Over that final thirty years or so, fiscal tightening was not supplemented by other types of austerity in the form of rationing, conscription, wage caps, exchange controls, or especially tight money policies (indeed, quite the reverse on that last item over 2010–15). With the important and electorally costly exception of the Liberal Democrats' 2010 manifesto pledge to cut university tuition fees, those squeezes broadly did not involve outright breaches of election promises over spending and taxation, although as we have seen, there were numerous tax increases, new taxes, or removals of tax offsets that had not been mentioned in election campaigns (such as the Conservatives' 1993 tax 'raid' on retirement pension funds, described in Chapter Nine, which provided the precursor for New Labour's dramatic and unexpected follow-up in 1997).

Moreover, in the most recent three episodes, squeezing on the expenditure side tended to rely heavily on slowing the rate of growth of public spending while the economy grew rather than cutting spending in constant-price terms—a process obscured by the catch-all language of 'cuts' used both by political opponents and on a few occasions by governments themselves when it suited them to portray themselves as bearing down hard on public spending. Whether that 'fiscal squeeze without tears' formula—involving relative rather than absolute spending reductions and arguably less electoral risk than in some of the earlier dramatic episodes—can be continued in the future is an issue we comment on later.

## 11.2 How Did the Fiscal Squeeze Game Change Over Time?

While all of the squeezes explored in this book involved loss imposition of some kind to increase revenue or rein in spending, we noted two changes over time from our analysis in Chapter Two, namely an apparent move away from revenue-led squeezes in the final third of the period, and an apparent move from more emphasis on 'short sharp' squeezes (the 'surgery without anaesthetics' approach) in the early part of the period to more long-drawn out 'boiling frogs'-type squeezes in the final three episodes. But as we also noted, those episodes included individual years of hard squeeze sandwiched within longer periods of soft squeeze.

Looking more qualitatively at each of the squeeze episodes over the past eight chapters, other accompanying changes over time are noticeable. One, relating to 'blame politics', is the apparent (and in some ways curious) absence of delegation strategies for fiscal squeeze since the 1930s. A second relates to changing triggers for fiscal squeeze over time, and a third consists of changes in the way the spending and revenue game was played over the hundred years considered here.

### 11.2.1 Blame Politics

When it comes to the 'blame politics' of fiscal squeeze, as discussed in Chapter One, Kent Weaver's (1986) classic account of limiting blame from loss imposition, mentioned in Chapter One, notes strategies that include delaying or diffusing losses, delegating decisions, finding scapegoats, and diffusing blame by sharing it out. We saw plenty of instances of all those strategies in the preceding chapters, and indeed delaying or diffusing losses might be said to be at the heart of the 'boiling frogs' approach to longer-drawn out fiscal squeezes.

But the 'heresthetic' approach (discussed in Chapter One) of finding new dividing lines, notably in welfare provision in drawing new lines between 'strivers and shirkers', but also stretching back at least to the Conservatives' unsuccessful attempt to make the 1923 election a contest over free trade or protectionism as well as over fiscal squeeze, represents a rather different approach to handling blame. And the strategy of delegating decisions only seems to have been partially applied in this case. Economic forecasting—a notoriously error-prone process, with high accompanying blame risks—was not 'outsourced' from the Treasury until surprisingly late in the period considered here. The setting of interest rates, another potential 'blame magnet', was outsourced to external bodies at both ends of our time period but not in the middle. And it is particularly notable that most of the fiscal squeezes were handled through 'normal' governmental decision procedures, and that emergency coalition governments set up specifically to carry out fiscal squeezes were very rare (1931 and perhaps 2010).

We have shown that the UK moved away from using expert commissions to propose spending cuts since the May Committee of 1931, which as we saw in Chapter Four was itself a modified version of the Geddes Committee of ten years earlier, as a special high-level committee outside the normal government decision-making machinery to propose measures for spending cuts and extra charges on a tight timetable, with those decisions subsequently being filtered by cabinet committees for political acceptability. That absence of such bodies in recent decades contrasts with practice in Australia, where 'audit commissions' have been given such a role by incoming right-of-centre governments since the late 1980s (mostly at state level, but also at Commonwealth government level in 1996 and 2014), or with even more dramatic cases in the eurozone, for example in Italy or Greece, where established party politicians made way for ostensibly non-political governments of 'technocrats' to handle fiscal squeezes.

On the face of it, that long absence seems odd, contrasting with the proliferation of quangos and delegated decision arrangements in many other policy areas, and moreover in a policy domain where pressures for blame-avoidance through delegation might be expected to be particularly high. It is perhaps not difficult to see why the post-World War II Labour Government chose not to repeat the strategy of its 1930s predecessor, which in any case had been acting under pressure from the other parties. After all, in the late 1940s Labour memories were still fresh about the way the 1931 May Committee had played into the political debacle of the collapse of the Ramsay MacDonald Labour Government. But the Attlee Government's Conservative successor also explicitly rejected the idea of a version of the Geddes or May Committee to find expenditure savings, though it set up the Guillebaud Committee on the National Health Service in 1953 in the hope—not realized in that case—that it would recommend ways of cutting NHS costs. And since then there have been numerous cases of governments using outside or technocrat committees to recommend ways of reining in spending in specific fields, for instance, over university fees in the 1990s and 2010s and over the cost of public-sector pensions in the review by ex-Labour minister Lord Hutton, commissioned by the Conservative–Liberal Democrat Government in 2010.

But it is not so obvious why the government-wide 'expert commission' approach to a public spending–wide review continued to be off the table for so long after direct memories of the fiscal politics of the 1920s and 1930s had faded, and it is notable that the Liberal Democrats' proposal for an all-party 'Council on Financial Stability' (in the Party's 2010 election manifesto) was not taken up in the coalition agreement when the Party went into government with the Conservatives in 2010.

Against that 'dog that didn't bark' (or stopped barking) in blame management politics, a development in the blame politics of fiscal squeeze that seems to have become more prominent in the later decades of our period is the phenomenon, noted in Chapters Nine and Ten, of so-called 'bear traps' set by incumbents ahead of elections. As we saw there, that term was used by some commentators to label a tactic used by outgoing governments to force challenger political parties to commit to continuing spending restraints or new taxes, or else to explain what other taxes they would impose to avoid such restraints. In effect, such political tactics are designed to have the effect of increasing the electoral risk to parties of *not* squeezing relative to that of squeezing, at least on the spending side.

To some extent such issues have always been raised in general election campaigns, but the tactic seems to have been sharpened since 1992, when Labour Shadow Chancellor John Smith's careful attempt to demonstrate the affordability of his party's proposals for higher public spending led the Party into the 'Labour's tax bombshell' trap described in Chapter Nine. The same tactic was duly repeated by the Conservatives in 1997 (this time resulting in an electoral pledge by the New Labour opposition to match the outgoing Conservative Government's announced plans for continuing spending restraint for the first two years of the subsequent Parliament). It was used by the Brown Labour Government in 2010, by introducing a new top income tax rate shortly before the election, and again by the Conservative–Liberal Democrat coalition in the run-up to the 2015 election, when it announced plans for a soft spending squeeze extending into the following Parliament, thereby drawing Labour into a debate over what new charges or taxes would be required to fund its plans for a somewhat more modest austerity programme in the mid- and late 2010s.

### 11.2.2 *Triggers for Squeeze*

Another changing aspect of the fiscal squeeze game over the period considered here relates to what triggered fiscal squeezes.

As we have seen in earlier chapters, two of the revenue squeezes were specifically driven by the pressures of war finance, particularly in World War II, when politicians who had lived through the 1920s were anxious to avoid the massive post-war debt management problems caused by the decision to fund World War I largely by borrowing. And as we have seen, financial market pressures are arguably always in the background as triggers for fiscal change in any capitalist democracy like the UK, whose debt and currency is traded on international financial markets and risk-assessed by ratings agencies.

Indeed, dramatic currency crises and post-crisis devaluations seem to have been the trigger for several of the fiscal squeezes considered here (notably in 1931, 1967, 1976, and to some extent 1992) and three of the squeezes in the middle of our period, all involving Labour governments, involved direct (or more or less direct) bargaining with outside lenders. They were: the so-called 'bankers' ramp' (the pejorative term used to denote the discussions with international bankers in the 1931 fiscal squeeze), the negotiations at prime ministerial level over bailout loans from Canada and the United States in the late 1940s, and the 'letter of intent' conditions attached to the 1976 IMF bailout. Those episodes thus had something of the character of 'negotiated bailouts', but recent decades have witnessed a remarkably long bailout-free period, in sharp contrast to what happened to several of the smaller eurozone economies in the 2010s.

Similarly, an episode of revenue squeeze intended to fund extra public spending has not been seen since the mid-1970s. The opposite of that, namely spending squeezes intended to facilitate tax cuts (as in the Lloyd George Government's response to the electoral threat posed by the 'Anti-Waste League' in 1922, and in the Conservatives' efforts to squeeze spending in the 1950s) did seem to play a part in the 1980s and 1990s squeezes, but budget deficit reduction seems to have been the main trigger for the more recent squeeze episodes. Whether the earlier triggers for fiscal squeeze—currency crisis linked to balance of payments, war finance, pressures to finance tax cuts, or spending increases—have gone for good is obviously debatable.

### 11.2.3 *Taxing and Spending*

As far as taxation is concerned, whereas the early part of that period had featured special and explicit war taxes (notably on excess profits) in the two world wars, there have been no such taxes since the 1950s, despite overseas military operations such as the Falklands, the Gulf War, Bosnia, Iraq, Afghanistan, Libya.

Nor were there increases in regular taxes that were specifically justified by the need to finance wars, although war sometimes featured as a reason given for not cutting taxes, for example in the 1990s.

But there seems to have been some increase in the later part of the period in 'stealth taxes'—a term rather drained of meaning in recent political debates, but used in this book broadly to denote less visible taxes and charges, and 'small print' tax increases outside headline rates of income tax and VAT. Examples include stamp taxes or parking charges, the 'regulator' power to vary key indirect taxes outside the traditional budget procedure (a measure first introduced in 1961, as described in Chapter Six) and a number of sudden 'windfall' raids on politically unpopular groups or institutions. Cases of the latter include the Conservatives' 1981 bank windfall tax, Labour's 1997 windfall tax on the privatized utilities—in that case, foreshadowed in its election manifesto—and the Conservative–Liberal Democrats' 2010 tax on bank balance sheets, following a previous Labour tax on bankers' bonuses. Just as budget airlines over recent decades have built their businesses by combining (at least apparently) low basic charges with less immediately visible supplements, changes in government revenue, on the direct tax side at least, seems to have had some of those characteristics.

Indeed, at the intersection of revenue and expenditure (since it was commonly counted as 'negative expenditure' in public accounts), the resort to asset sales in the later decades of the century beginning with Labour's sale of BP stock in the late 1970s, might also be considered as a kind of intergenerational 'stealth tax' under certain assumptions. That is, unless such asset sales produced sufficiently higher taxable profits through higher productivity associated with the shift to private ownership, those sales could have the effect of depriving future taxpayers of revenue streams they would otherwise enjoy for the purpose of lowering the financial demands on current taxpayers. Of course, asset sales were far from unknown in earlier parts of the century (indeed, as we have seen, they figured large in the demobilization periods after the two world wars), but such sales seem to have received more emphasis since the 1970s than in the 1930s or in the 1950s and 1960s.

Those changes on the revenue side might possibly be linked to Martin Daunton's (2002: 361–2) account of changes in the UK tax regime between 1914 and the late 1970s. At the beginning of that period, Daunton claims that a relatively autonomous Treasury and revenue departments prioritized the revenue-raising function of taxes, promoted a culture of tax compliance, equity, and 'balance', and resisted political pressures for changes to the tax system that might undermine tax compliance by threatening the apparent equity of the fiscal system. By the late 1970s Daunton argues that the system had changed into one in which there was more emphasis on using taxation for social or economic micro-management or for short-term benefits to politically favoured groups, though he does not discuss the 'budget airline' approach to revenue raising mentioned earlier. But to the extent that there was indeed such a change in the administrative culture of the tax regime over that period, it is hard to distinguish its effects from other major changes, such as the shift from the position in the 1910s when the income of the median voter was below the income tax threshold, to that of the 1970s when the median voter had become an income tax payer (Daunton 2002: 368), and other social changes such as large-scale immigration which may also have undermined voters' willingness to pay higher taxes to support other groups.

On the spending side, we showed in Chapter Two how the changing composition of public spending over the century meant that defence expenditure (traditionally advocated by the left as the proper target of public spending cuts) amounted to a steadily smaller part of overall public spending, even though it did not fall in constant-price terms. That change meant that major efforts to rein in public expenditure on the part of any political party in government could not leave 'welfare state' spending untouched and hence led to the application of 'heresthetic' within welfare state politics, characterized by the development of new political dividing lines over precisely which elements of 'welfare state' spending were to be 'red-lined' for protection and which were not. Those dividing lines not only reflected older distinctions between the 'deserving' and 'undeserving' poor (or 'strivers and shirkers', in the media language of the 2010s) but involved other cleavages too, for example, between state spending on higher education as against earlier years' education, between spending on welfare benefits for retirement pensioners as against benefits for those of working age, between spending on healthcare as against social care. Some of those new welfare dividing lines were reflected in formal 'ring-fencing' arrangements that separated politically favoured domains of spending from the unprotected domains that were subject to cuts.

The implication of a changing composition of public spending for fiscal squeeze may also account for two notable cases involving an element of 'stealth' in welfare state spending restraints, in the sense of changes to future entitlements rather than current ones, or small-print changes in current entitlements over the last three decades or so of the period considered here. One case is the raising of entitlement ages for state pensions and other age-related benefits (a decision taken for the first time in 1994) to take effect well beyond the following general election or the expected term in office of the responsible ministers. The other is the switch from one price index to another (RPI to CPI) as the basis for uprating retirement pensions and other benefits in 2010, with little immediate effect but calculated to produce large savings in the medium to long term.

## 11.3 Consequences: What Did Fiscal Squeezes Leave Behind?

What did the fiscal squeezes we identified in Chapter Two leave behind? What happened afterwards? Were the leaders or parties doing the 'squeezing' systematically punished or rewarded by the voters; applauded or condemned by policy analysts as providing 'lessons' for what to do or what not to do in managing the public finances; were there constitutional or other major social developments that can clearly be attributable to those squeezes?

We here divide the consequences of fiscal squeeze into two categories: financial and economic outcomes, and political and constitutional/institutional outcomes, and we also consider fiscal squeezes both in terms of the amount of change taking place on reported financial outcomes and of qualitative assessment of squeeze intensity, as shown in Table 11.1 earlier.

For financial and economic outcomes, we explored whether debt and/or deficit significantly fell in the three years after the squeeze, what happened to other economic indicators such as unemployment or currency exchange rates, whether there were major long-term changes in policy direction, and the extent to which the episode came to be widely seen as a model to be emulated elsewhere or an example of egregious policy error to be avoided by later governments in the UK or in other countries.

For political and constitutional/institutional outcomes, we explored whether and how far governments handled the squeezes without collapse or major party splits, how incumbents initiating or carrying out the squeezes fared at the polls after those squeezes, and what if any constitutional or major institutional effects the squeezes had. Other possible consequences of squeeze episodes might include significant social disorder or protest (riots, demonstrations, or strikes or mutinies by police, armed forces, or other significant arms of the state).

Table 11.2 shows some readily measurable financial and economic outcomes of the eighteen fiscal squeezes considered in this book. What is striking is the variety of outcomes shown there. Anyone who believes either that fiscal squeeze is always a certain route to economic/financial improvement or disaster will find it hard to reconcile such beliefs with what is shown in Table 11.2. It is true there were cases where deficits came down, debt reduced, and unemployment fell after episodes of fiscal squeeze—but there were roughly the same number of episodes where those indicators moved in the opposite direction. There was only one case out of the eighteen where all three of those indicators moved in a positive direction after a squeeze (the episode of 1953–55), and there were only two episodes where all three of those indicators moved in a negative direction (1976 and 1980–81).

That variety of outcome may in part be explained by the different goals that have underlain the fiscal squeezes explored in this book. As we noted in section 11.2, not all fiscal squeeze efforts over the century were triggered by

**Table 11.2.** UK fiscal squeeze episodes 1900–2015: economic aftermath

| Overall episode | Sub-periods | Type of overall squeeze | | 'Substantial' deficit reduction[a] | 'Substantial' debt reduction[b] | Fall in unemployment rate?[c] |
|---|---|---|---|---|---|---|
| | | Quantitative: R= revenue, E=Expenditure | Political loss, cost, effort (H=High, M=Moderate, L=Low) | | | |
| 1916–18 | 1916–18 | Hard R | H, L, H | Yes | No | No |
| 1919–25 | 1919–21 | Hard R/Hard E | L/M, M, L | Yes | No | No |
| | 1923–25 | Hard E | H, M/L, M | No | Yes | Yes |
| 1931–35 | 1931–32 | Hard R | H, H/L, H | No | Yes | No |
| | 1933–35 | Hard E | M/H, L, L | No | Yes | Yes |
| 1941–45 | 1941–45 | Hard R | H, L, H | Yes | No | Yes |
| 1946–49 | 1946–49 | Hard E/Soft R | M, M, M | Yes | Yes | No |
| 1953–55 | 1953–55 | Soft E/Soft R | M, M, M | Yes | Yes | Yes |
| 1960–61 | 1960–61 | Hard R | H, H, M | No | Yes | Yes |
| 1964–67 | 1964–67 | Hard R | H/M, M, H/M | Yes | Yes | No |
| | 1968–69 | Soft E/Hard R | H, H, M | Yes | Yes | No |
| 1973–78 | 1973–75 | Hard R | H/M, M, H/M | No | Yes | No |
| | 1976 | Hard E/Soft R | H/M, M, M | No | No | No |
| | 1977–78 | Hard E | H, H, H | Yes | No | Yes |
| 1980–88 | 1980–81 | Hard R | H, H, H | No | No | No |
| | 1983–88 | Soft E/Soft R | M, M, M/H | No | Yes | Yes |
| 1993–00 | 1993–00 | Soft E/Soft R | M, M/L, M | Yes | No | Yes |
| 2010–15 | 2010–15 | Soft E/Soft R | M, M/H, H/M | n.a. | n.a. | n.a. |

*Notes:* [a] 'Substantial' if primary deficit/GDP three years after the end of the episode was at least two percentage points below level at the start. [b] 'Substantial' if debt/GDP three years after the end of the episode was at least five percentage points below level at the start. [c] Coded yes if the unemployment rate in the year after the squeeze ended was less than the rate the year before the squeeze started.

determination to reduce budget deficits, and a few were even undertaken at times when the budget was approximately balanced. That is one of the reasons we set out in Chapter One in arguing that the degree of reduction in deficit, although the favoured metric of numerous 'budget consolidation' studies in the econometric style, is a far from reliable or valid measure of political effort put into fiscal squeeze. But as we have also already noted in the previous section, the more recent episodes seem to have been mainly driven by the goal of reducing deficit, and those squeezes mostly do seem to have been followed by deficit reduction.

We also see variety in the policy changes that accompanied or followed fiscal squeezes, and in their perceived significance in international perspective. As we have seen in previous chapters, in every case fiscal squeeze episodes left something behind them in policy change—such as the shelving of some of the more ambitious post-World War I 'reconstruction' plans for extending secondary education in the 1920s, the abandonment of the gold standard after the Invergordon naval mutiny provoked by naval pay cuts in 1931, the beginning of user charges for the NHS and abandonment of elaborate civil defence and protection in the 1950s, the abandonment of 'East of Suez' military bases in the late 1960s, the beginning of the modern era of privatization in the squeezes of the 1970s and 1980s, the ending of mandatory grants for university students, abandonment of the principle that savings for retirement should only be taxed once and the first decision to raise the age of eligibility for retirement pensions in the 1990s, and the tripling of university tuition fees (outside Scotland) in the 2010s. But those policy changes were themselves highly varied and their relative significance is not easy to show. Some had a certain once-for-all character, like the abandonment of civil defence, while others were later partially or fully reversed, like the charges for prescription medicines in the NHS, and the extent to which they were 'mould-breaking' is debatable in many cases.

Similarly, the squeezes seem to vary in terms of the extent of international attention they attracted as models to be imitated (or avoided) elsewhere. Only two of the squeeze episodes up to 2010, namely the 1920s Geddes Axe and the 1980s Thatcher 'cuts', seem to be plausibly countable as cases attracting significant international attention as 'models', and in both cases, they sharply divided international opinion as to whether the model was an example to be followed or avoided. It is still too early to say whether the 'boiling frogs' squeeze of the 2010s will come to be seen internationally as a model or an awful warning, or neither, but as we noted in Chapter Ten, during its lifetime it attracted in fairly short order both condemnation from IMF economists for being too fast and deep, and subsequent praise as a successful route to fiscal consolidation and economic recovery.

Turning from the economic, financial, and policy consequences of fiscal squeeze to electoral, political, and constitutional/institutional consequences, the pattern also looks varied, at first sight at least. In general, constitutional or major institutional change directly linked to fiscal squeeze seem to have been the exception rather than the rule. The only unambiguous case is that of 1931, when King George V's role in putting together an emergency National Government to implement fiscal squeeze attracted continuing party-political criticism in a way that almost certainly had a restraining impact on later monarchs' behaviour. Another instance is that of the often-argued effects of the Thatcher Government's 1980s squeezes on later pressures for Scottish devolution and indeed independence, but in that case it is harder to separate the effects of fiscal squeeze from those of other causal factors (such as the long-term decline of religious sectarianism as a primary cleavage in Scottish society). And as we noted in Chapter 10, the same goes for any link between the 2010–15 squeeze and the subsequent 'Brexit' vote in the 2016 referendum on the UK's membership of the European Union. The direct effect of fiscal squeeze is hard to separate from other factors.

Turning to electoral effects and party splits following fiscal squeezes, the pattern shown in Table 11.3 appears varied, at first sight at least. The table shows how each episode is classed according to our measures drawn from reported financial outcomes and those reflecting our assessments of qualitative severity as discussed earlier. It also reports electoral outcomes for incumbent parties in the general elections following each squeeze, and the incidence of government collapses or major party splits over squeezes. As we have seen, there is only one clear case in the century of a government collapsing as a result of conflicts over how to conduct a squeeze (1931), though there are several cases of significant party splits, in all cases on the left and in all cases over spending rather than revenue.

When it comes to the relationship between 'austerity' policies and the likelihood of incumbent parties losing office, we noticed in Chapter One that welfare state retrenchment studies as well as some econometric studies have analysed comparative electoral data for OECD countries since the 1970s, related electoral outcomes to measures of fiscal outcomes expressed as falls in deficit relative to GDP, and reported erratic electoral punishment for fiscal correction policies measured in those terms (see in particular Alesina et al. 2012). Such findings challenge the expectations of the simpler variants of 'economic' retrospective voting theory that we discussed in Chapter One, in which electoral punishment follows policies that impose losses on key interest groups and voters (Wenzelburger 2014).

But such results may depend on precisely how we define the slippery concept of 'austerity' or 'fiscal correction', and as we showed in Chapter Two, there are numerous cases out of the eighteen considered here in which fiscal squeeze was not accompanied by deficit reduction. Indeed, when we look at the case of the UK over a century and measure 'austerity' in terms of the intensity of fiscal squeeze in terms of hardness or softness (which, as we have seen, broadly corresponds to our qualitative indicator of the degree of loss imposed on voters), we reach a conclusion different from that arising from the work of Alesina and his colleagues.

When we look at fiscal squeeze in that way, 'high loss' squeezes look more electorally toxic. The overall casualty rate for incumbent parties partially or wholly losing office at elections over the whole century from 1900 to 2015,[2] whether or not a fiscal squeeze had been applied, was just over 62 per cent (eighteen out of twenty-nine cases), or 50 per cent in the case of single-party governments. The incumbency casualty rate for the seven elections over that period that were not preceded by a fiscal squeeze (in all cases involving single-party governments) was some 42 per cent.

---

[2] Excluding the 1901 election in this analysis.

**Table 11.3.** UK fiscal squeeze episodes 1900–2015: the political and constitutional aftermath

| Overall episode | Sub-episode[a] | Type of overall squeeze | | General election outcome for incumbent | | | Government collapse or major party split? |
|---|---|---|---|---|---|---|---|
| | | Quantitative: R= Revenue, E=Expenditure | Political loss, cost, effort (H=High, M=Moderate, L=Low) | Lost office? (election year[b]) | Swing in vote share[c] | Difference in seat share[d] | |
| 1916–18 | 1916–18 | Hard R | H, L, H | Partly (1918) | n/a | n/a | No—war coalition |
| 1919–25 | 1919–21 | Hard R/Hard E | L/M, M, L | Partly (1922) | n/a | n/a | No |
| | 1923–25 | Hard E | H, M/L, M | Yes (1923) | −0.5 | 0.1 | Not over squeeze |
| | | | | Yes (1924) | 2.6 | −0.42 | No |
| 1931–35 | 1931–32 | Hard R | H, H/L, H | Partly (1931) | n/a | n/a | Collapse and split |
| | 1933–35 | Hard E | M/H, L, L | Partly (1935) | n/a | n/a | No |
| 1941–45 | 1941–45 | Hard R | H, L, H | Partly (1945) | n/a | n/a | No—war coalition |
| 1946–49 | 1946–49 | Hard E/Soft R | M, M, M | No (1950) | −1.6 | 0.03 | Internal party split |
| | | | | Yes (1951) | 2.7 | −0.04 | Internal party split |
| 1953–55 | 1953–55 | Soft E/Soft R | M, M, M | No (1955) | 1.7 | 0.11 | No |
| 1964–69 | 1964–67 | Hard R | H/M, M, H/M | Yes (1964) | −6.0 | −0.02 | No |
| | | | | No (1966) | 3.9 | 0.18 | No |
| | 1968–69 | Soft E/Hard R | H, H, M | Yes (1970) | −4.9 | −0.07 | No |
| 1973–78 | 1973–75 | Hard R | H/M, M, H/M | Yes (1974a) | −8.5 | −0.01 | No |
| | | | | No (1974b) | 2 | 0.03 | No |
| | 1977–78 | Hard E | H, H, H | Yes (1979) | −2.3 | −0.11 | Internal party split |
| 1980–88 | 1983–88 | Soft R/Soft E | M,M, M/H | No (1983) | −1.5 | 0.29 | No |
| | | | | No (1987) | −0.2 | 0.23 | No |
| 1993–00 | 1993–00 | Soft R/Soft E | M, M/L, M | Yes (1997) | −11.2 | −0.38 | No |
| | | | | No (2001) | −2.5 | 0.37 | No |
| 2010–15 | 2010–15 | Soft R/Soft E | M, M/H, H/M | Partly (2015) | n/a | n/a | No |

*Notes:* [a] 1960–61, 1976, and 1980–81 sub-episodes excluded as there was no general election held during or two years after squeeze ended. [b] The 1906, 1/1910, 12/1910, 1929, 1959, 1992, 2005, and 2010 elections excluded as they did not occur during or within two years of episode end. [c] Difference between vote share at current and previous elections for single party incumbent. [d] Difference in parliamentary seat share between incumbent and closest competitor. Only single-party incumbent governments are considered.

Against that background casualty rate, Table 11.3 shows that during or immediately after a hard revenue squeeze, the incumbent parties in government lost office partly or wholly at a general election 77 per cent of the time (seven out of nine elections), whereas during or after a soft revenue squeeze they lost office 38 per cent of the time (three out of eight elections). Likewise, a hard spending squeeze was associated with incumbents wholly or partly losing office 86 per cent of the time (six out of seven elections), whereas during or after a soft spending squeeze they lost office 42 per cent of the time (three out of seven elections).

If we ignore the complications that arise over scoring what happened to incumbents in general elections when there were two or more parties in coalition and look only at fiscal squeezes carried out by single-party governments (that is, excluding the 1916–18, 1919–21, 1931–32, 1933–35, 1941–45, and 2010–15 squeezes) we find a similar pattern. Hard revenue or spending squeezes were associated with a higher probability of the incumbent losing office at subsequent general elections (at roughly 60 and 80 per cent respectively), compared to soft revenue and spending squeezes (where the incidence was roughly 37 and 42 per cent, respectively). Moreover, soft revenue or spending squeezes are not associated with a casualty rate markedly above that observable in elections not preceded by fiscal squeeze.

As already noted, hardness and softness as we defined it in Chapter Two broadly corresponds with our first qualitative indicator of the effort put into squeeze, namely the degree of loss or pain imposed on core or mainstream voters. We found some differences in the relationship between electoral outcomes and the other two qualitative indicators, namely political cost to incumbents and effort on the part of the state machine. On the second indicator, most (66 per cent) of the single-party government squeezes involved low or moderate reputational risk or related political costs and were associated with mixed electoral outcomes, with the incumbent party losing office in seven out of twelve elections. The few single-party government cases of squeezes involving high political cost were always associated with electoral defeat for incumbents.

The same broadly applies to the third indicator, that of effort exerted by the state machinery. Most of the single-party government squeezes involved moderate effort on this indicator, and were associated with a roughly fifty per cent incidence of subsequent electoral defeat that was not clearly distinguishable from the incidence of defeat by incumbents whether or not there was a squeeze. But for the single-party government cases, high-effort squeezes were always associated with electoral defeat for incumbents.

These findings do not necessarily invalidate the claims of scholars such as Alberto Alesina, who base their analyses on different ways of identifying episodes and intensity of austerity, and compare different countries rather than looking at one country over time. But what they do show is that different—and we have argued, possibly more meaningful ways—of identifying episodes and measuring the intensity of fiscal squeeze—lead to very different conclusions, indicating that, on those measures, fiscal squeezes can be highly consequential for election outcomes.

Two other points can be noted from the electoral and party outcomes summarized in Table 11.3. One is that while, in general, hard or high-effort squeezes seem to have been toxic for incumbents in subsequent elections, there are one or two notable exceptions of incumbents securing re-election after hard squeezes, all on the left. That is, the Labour Party was re-elected in 1950 after imposing a hard spending squeeze, and was re-elected in 1966 and 1974 (October) after imposing hard revenue squeezes. The first is scarcely an exception, since the Party was undoubtedly punished by the voters as retrospective voting theory might predict (as we noted in Chapter Five, the Party suffered an adverse vote swing of some 3.6 per cent, lost seventy-eight parliamentary seats and saw its previous 146-seat majority cut to a mere five). But in the other two cases of elections following hard revenue squeezes (the swingeing tax increases, including increases in the standard rate of income tax, introduced in the post-election budgets of 1964 and 1974) the Party saw an increase in its electoral support, particularly in 1966. Those episodes indicate that in some conditions a party on the left has been able to benefit electorally from a hard revenue squeeze to support higher public spending, and are consistent with the 'asymmetrical punishment theory' that was mentioned in Chapter One.

Second, electoral outcomes following a coalition that imposed a squeeze indicate no cases in which both or all the political parties forming the coalition were equally punished by the voters. In all such cases one of the parties in the coalition was rewarded by the voters in the subsequent election, while another (in all cases the party on the left, unless we count the Conservatives following the World War II tax squeeze) was punished. That suggests that during fiscal squeeze, coalition has not so much been about sharing the subsequent blame as a zero-sum competition for post-squeeze blame and credit among the incumbent parties.

## 11.4 The Future of Fiscal Squeeze Politics: Can We Extrapolate?

What can we extrapolate from the history of fiscal squeeze in the UK, from the past to the future, or from the UK to other states or political systems?

Starting with the first type of extrapolation, if the history of fiscal squeeze, as examined in this book, is any guide to the future, there is no reason to expect fiscal squeeze to be a thing of the past. As we have seen, over the century explored in this book, fiscal squeeze episodes of one kind or another tended to occur at least once a decade on the financial outcomes data we explored in Chapter Two. The main exceptions to that were the decades of the 1900s and the 2000s, the second of which happened to be sandwiched between the long-drawn-out but 'soft' spending squeeze of the 1990s initiated by the Conservatives and followed by New Labour in its first two years, and the spending squeeze initiated by the Conservative–Liberal Democrat coalition in 2010 after a short-lived fiscal stimulus immediately following the 2008 financial crash. Given that record, the question is when, not whether, fiscal squeeze will be back. And projecting the historical pattern into the future, the odds are that there will be further episodes of fiscal squeeze in the 2020s if not before that.

So what is the nature of those future fiscal squeezes likely to be? If we simply extrapolate the trends we identified in Chapter Two, we could expect those future episodes to continue to bite harder on the spending than on the revenue side (albeit with a few hard revenue spikes associated with crisis years or sudden raids on politically unpopular industries or groups). We could expect the pain of spending restraint to be spread over longer periods with lower annual falls relative to growing GDP, rather than in sudden steep cuts in constant-price terms. We could expect to find further development of the 'budget airline' approach to increasing revenue (stealth taxes, windfall taxes, user charges) and the 'heresthetic' drawing of new dividing lines over welfare spending, for example, within groupings of welfare beneficiaries (such as pensioners). We could expect fiscal squeeze to be accompanied by loose monetary policy, and for the fiscal measures to be orchestrated and planned within the central administrative apparatus of executive government rather than by outside commissions.

Some of those developments (such as further division of voters over welfare spending) seem very likely. But there are well-known dangers in basing forecasts about the future on what we can see in the rear-view mirror. And as we have seen in this book, some fiscal squeezes have taken the form of conscious political rejection of what had been done (or not done) in a previous episode. In particular, for the Labour Party, the trauma and deep party split occasioned by the decision over whether to cut unemployment benefits in the middle of a deep recession in 1931 meant that cuts in social security benefits were avoided by Labour governments right up to the 1970s, as we saw in Chapter Seven. For the Conservatives, a squeeze that did not happen (the failure of Chancellor Peter Thorneycroft, together with his fellow Treasury ministers Enoch Powell and Nigel Birch, to secure the agreement of Prime Minister Harold Macmillan and their cabinet colleagues to significant spending cuts in 1958) has also been said to cast its shadow forward to the Thatcher Government some two decades later, as we noted in Chapter Six.

Similarly, as well as processes of political reaction against earlier choices that were perceived as politically erroneous, the circumstances that underlay some of those trends are not necessarily immutable either. Tax toleration can alter abruptly, as happened with the fuel tax revolt by road tanker drivers in 2000 that struck hard at the fuel tax accelerator that had hitherto been a standby of both Conservative and Labour governments in the 1990s. Sources of taxation can dry up as well. For example, the North Sea oil that came on stream as a taxable resource in the 1980s and to some extent acted as a substitute for rises in mainstream taxes that would have been more visible during the squeezes of the Thatcher, Major, and Blair Governments, was a finite resource that may or may not be replaced in the future by other revenue sources such as shale gasfields. The same goes for the supply of readily privatizable public-sector enterprises or assets that also served as a partial substitute for tax increases or spending cuts over the same era. It is far from clear that those assets remaining in public ownership will be capable of realizing the sums raised during the privatization booms of the 1980s and 1990s.

Other background factors that could be different for future fiscal squeezes include changes in debt levels, the value of money, and the rate of economic growth. The next fiscal squeeze could be very different from those of the past few decades if it starts with a debt wall more comparable to that of the 1920s and 1930s, when governments' room for fiscal manoeuvre was sharply limited by their predecessors' decision to fund the huge costs of World War I largely by borrowing rather than by taxes. As for the value of money, we noted in Chapters Seven and Eight on the 1970s and 1980s that high rates of inflation provide opportunities for fiscal squeeze tactics such as the use of 'fiscal drag' to increase revenue in constant-price terms by not fully indexing all tax thresholds and allowances, and also to restrain spending through similar expedients. But a rate of low or nil inflation undermines such strategies, and a background of falling prices means that squeeze has to be undertaken in more visible ways, by reducing tax thresholds or allowances, or absolute cuts in public service wages. As for economic growth, we noted in Chapters Eight, Nine, and Ten that that was what underpinned the recipe applied to reducing public spending relative to GDP over the past three episodes—namely of keeping overall public spending growing, but at a lower rate than the rate of growth in GDP over successive years. But if those who believe that an economic background of 'secular stagnation' is here to stay as some sort of 'new normal' are correct,[3] that spending-squeeze strategy may also be less easy to deploy in the future than in the past.

---

[3] 'Secular stagnation' is the idea, normally attributed to Alvin Hansen (1939) who argued in the 1930s that slowing population growth and technological progress would reduce opportunities for investment, causing savings to pile up unused and economic growth to fall unless governments borrowed and spent more to boost demand. More recently the idea has been taken up by the leading Harvard economist Larry Summers (2016).

In short, it is far from impossible to identify possible future changes of circumstances that might undermine the foundations of the fiscal squeeze approaches of the past three decades, such that the economic and political future might turn out to be more like that of the 1920s and 1930s than that of more recent decades, and if that did indeed prove to be the case, some of those apparently discarded approaches to fiscal squeeze might turn out to make a reappearance.

As for the second type of extrapolation—from the UK to other states or political systems rather than from the past to the future—recent fiscal squeezes in the harder-hit eurozone countries have indeed more closely resembled the UK squeezes of the 1920s and 1930s than those of the more recent past, in the sense that they took place against a background of recession or slow growth, stable or falling prices, and sluggish tax revenues, and in many cases also in the context of multiparty political systems rather than the predominance of two alternating parties in government that was more typical of UK politics in the decades after World War II. By contrast, some of the much-lauded fiscal consolidations in other developed countries in the 1990s—such as Canada, Sweden, and New Zealand—were more like the most recent three UK episodes in that they took place against a background of economic growth with more buoyant tax revenue and to that extent shared something of the 'fiscal squeeze without tears' characteristics.

Whether the British record of three fiscal squeezes in a century at a high qualitative level of intensity (in terms of loss, political stress, and state effort) is typical or exceptional in international context would merit more investigation, and that would require more scholars to supplement readily accessible reports of financial outcomes with more hard-won qualitative comparative judgements of such intensity. The same goes for the time pattern of fiscal squeezes identified in Chapter Two: as we have seen, in the British case those episodes occurred often enough in the course of a century for some political and bureaucratic memory to shape the process in one way or another in most episodes, but not so often as to turn squeezing into a continuous routine for bureaucracies or a blame arena in which the next fiscal squeeze would regularly arrive before those who handled the last one had given way to a new set of incumbents. Those conditions did not always apply even in the British case (for example, they did not apply to the Conservatives in the 1990s), they are not guaranteed to continue in the future, and such a pattern cannot be expected to apply everywhere. But more generally, it could be argued that the development of modern capitalist democracy combined with maturing or ageing welfare states is likely to make non-trivial fiscal squeeze a recurring feature of democratic politics across the world.

# Appendix

**Table A1.** Defining expenditure-based episodes using alternative data sources and definitions of spending

| | Mitchell & ONS[a] | | Middleton[b] | | Peacock & Wiseman[c] | | OECD[d] | | White & Chapman[e] | |
|---|---|---|---|---|---|---|---|---|---|---|
| | Ratio[f] | Con. Pr.[g] | Ratio[f] | Con. Pr.[g] | Ratio[f] | Con. Pr.[g] | Ratio[f] | Con. Pr.[g] | Ratio[f] | Con. Pr.[g] |
| Period | 1919–21 | 1919–21 | 1919–20 | 1918–20 | 1918–20 | 1918–20 | n.a. | n.a. | n.a. | n.a. |
| Depth | −20.6 | −65.5 | −23.1 | −62.1 | −25.5 | −53.7 | n.a. | n.a. | n.a. | n.a. |
| Period | 1923–25 | 1923–24 | 1922–24, | 1923 | 1922–24 | 1921–23 | n.a. | n.a. | 1922–25 | n.a. |
| Depth | −9.0 | −19.0 | −4.0 | −3.2 | −5.7 | −11.7 | n.a. | n.a. | −5.0 | n.a. |
| Period | 1933–35 | 1933–34 | 1932–34 | 1932–33 | 1932–35 | 1932–33 | n.a. | n.a. | 1932–34 | n.a. |
| Depth | −4.2 | −3.6 | −3.1 | −4.8 | −4.4 | −5.8 | n.a. | n.a. | −3.4 | n.a. |
| Period | 1946–49 | 1946–49 | 1945–48 | 1944–48 | 1944–50 | 1944–48 | n.a. | n.a. | 1945–50 | n.a. |
| Depth | −33.5 | −45.1 | −23.4 | −45.4 | −34.9 | −32.7 | n.a. | n.a. | −27.6 | n.a. |
| Period | 1953–55 | 1955 | 1954–57 | 1954 | 1953–55 | 1954–55 | n.a. | n.a. | 1953–55 | 1954 |
| Depth | −5.0 | −2.4 | −3.6 | −2.4 | −4.9 | −4.1 | n.a. | n.a. | −4.2 | −2.9 |
| Period | 1968–69 | | | | | | | | | |
| Depth | −2.1 | | | | | | | | | |
| Period | 1976–78 | 1976–77 | 1976–79 | 1977 | n.a. | n.a. | 1976–79 | 1977 | 1976–77 | 1976–77 |
| Depth | −4.6 | −3.6 | −4.1 | −4.0 | n.a. | n.a. | −4.8 | −3.5 | −6.3 | −8.3 |
| Period | 1983–88 | 1988 | n.a. | n.a. | n.a. | n.a. | 1985–89 | – | n.a. | n.a. |
| Depth | −9.4 | −2.1 | | | | | −7.7 | | | |
| Period | 1993–00 | 1996–97 | n.a. | n.a. | n.a. | n.a. | 1993–00 | 1996–97 | n.a. | n.a. |
| Depth | −8.8 | −2.4 | | | | | −10.5 | −2.2, −7.4 | . | |
| Period | 2010–15 | – | n.a. | n.a. | n.a. | n.a. | 2010–13 | 2010–13 | n.a. | n.a. |
| Depth | −6.4 | – | | | | | −3.7 | −2.5 | | |

*Notes and Sources:* [a] 1900–48: Total government expenditure (general government and postoffice), fiscal year, approximated using Mitchell (1988: 569–645); GDP–Mitchell (1988: 832–5). 1949–2015: Total Managed Expenditure (TME), GDP– ONS (2014). There is a break in the data in 1949 and the two series are not equivalent. [b] 1900–79: Middleton (1996), Appendix 1, Total Public Expenditure and Revenue, calendar years. [c] Derived from Peacock and Wiseman (1961) data for Total Government Expenditure as a percentage of GNP. [d] Refers to General Government expenditure, a narrower measure of government spending compared to TME. Actual outcome data available until 2013. OECD (2014). [e] Derived from White and Chapman (1987). [f] Ratio Method: Columns show squeeze years followed by 'depth' indicating the total percentage point fall in spending relative to GDP during the episode. [g] Constant price method: Columns show years followed by 'depth', indicating total percentage fall in spending in constant price terms (2008 = 100).

**Table A2.** Defining revenue-based episodes using alternative data sources and definitions of revenue

| | Mitchell & ONS[a] | | Feinstein[b] | | Middleton[c] | | OECD[d] | |
|---|---|---|---|---|---|---|---|---|
| | Ratio[e] | Con. Pr.[f] | Ratio[e] | Con. Pr.[f] | Ratio[e] | Con. Pr.[f] | Ratio[e] | Con. Pr.[f] |
| Period | 1916–21 | 1916–21 | 1916–21 | 1909–19,1921–23 | 1914–22 | 1909–19, 1921–23 | n.a. | n.a. |
| Depth | 23.8 | 114.5 | 11.8 | 121.9,14.9 | 13.3 | 111.0, 20.1 | n.a. | n.a. |
| Period | – | 1926–28 | – | 1925–32 | – | 1924–28 | n.a. | n.a. |
| Depth | | 22.2 | | 24.8 | | 13.5 | | |
| Period | 1931–32 | 1931–32 | 1931–32 | – | 1930–32 | 1931–32 | n.a. | n.a. |
| Depth | 3.6 | 8 | 3.3 | | 3.6 | 8.4 | | |
| Period | 1941–48 | 1936–39, 1941–50 | 1939–45 | 1934–43 | 1939–45 | 1934–43 | n.a. | n.a. |
| Depth | 19.62 | 16.4, 89.7 | 14.7 | 117 | 14.5 | 111.7 | | |
| Period | 1960–61 | 1953–58 | n.a. | | 1961–2 | 1957–70 | n.a. | n.a. |
| Depth | 2.1 | 7.7 | | | 3.0 | 96.7 | | |
| Period | 1964–69 | 1960–70 | n.a. | | 1967–70 | | n.a. | n.a. |
| Depth | 8.8 | 77.8 | | | 7.14 | | | |
| Period | 1973–76 | 1973–76 | 1974–75 | n.a. | 1974–75 | 1973–74 | 1974–75 | 1973–76 |
| Depth | 5.2 | 18.4 | 4.1 | | 4.1 | 14.7 | 4.6 | 14.6 |
| Period | 1980–81 | 1979–88 | n.a. | n.a. | n.a. | n.a. | 1980–82 | 1979–89 |
| Depth | 4.4 | 27.4 | | | | | 5.5 | 34.6 |
| Period | – | 1993–01 | n.a. | n.a. | n.a. | n.a. | – | 1994–01 |
| Depth | | 41.3 | | | | | | 44.6 |
| Period | – | 2003–07 | n.a. | n.a. | n.a. | n.a. | – | 2003–8 |
| Depth | | 22.5 | | | | | | 25.8 |
| Period | – | 2010–15 | n.a. | n.a. | n.a. | n.a. | – | 2010–12 |
| Depth | | 18.0 | | | | | | 8.9 |

*Notes and Sources:* [a] 1900–48: Total current revenue and GDP approximated using Mitchell (1988: 569–645; 832–5). 1949 onwards public sector current receipts and GDP taken from ONS (2014); fiscal years. There is a break in the data in 1949 and the two series are not equivalent. [b] Feinstein (1972) Table 14. [c] Middleton (1996) Appendix 1, public sector receipts. [d] General Government revenue OECD (2014) [e] Ratio Method: Columns show squeeze years followed by percentage point rise in Revenue/GDP over the episode. [f] Constant-price method: Columns show years followed by percentage rise in expenditure in constant prices over the episode.

**Table A3.** Economic conditions at the start of spending squeezes 1900–2015[a]

| Squeeze episode (ratio method) | Spending (% GDP) | Revenue/GDP rises prior to squeeze | | National debt (% GDP) | Current acc. deficit (% GDP) | Budget deficit (% GDP) | Inflation rate | Unemployment rate | % Change in nominal effective exch. rate[b] |
|---|---|---|---|---|---|---|---|---|---|
| | | Average increase % point | Years the increase persisted | | | | | | |
| 1919–1921 | 53.3 | 1.2 | 3 | 114 | –5.1 | –37 | 15.0 | 1 | –0.1 |
| 1923–1925 | 35.4 | 3.9 | 6 | 170 | 3.8 | 0.2 | –18.7 | 9.8 | 9.5 |
| 1933–1935 | 32.7 | 1.8 | 2 | 177 | –2.4 | –1.6 | –2.1 | 15.6 | –19.7 |
| 1946–1949 | 70.9 | 4.3 | 4 | 232 | –8.6 | –30.4 | 2.0 | 0.5 | –0.1 |
| 1953–1955 | 40.6 | – | – | 154 | 1.3 | –1.3 | 9.2 | 1.6 | –0.2 |
| 1968–1969 | 44.3 | 1.2 | 4 | 84 | –0.7 | –4.1 | 2.6 | 2.2 | –11.5 |
| 1976–1978 | 48.9 | – | – | 50 | –1.6 | –6.7 | 24.2 | 3.3 | –13.3 |
| 1983–1988 | 48.1 | – | – | 43 | 0.6 | –2.8 | 8.6 | 10.5 | –6.9 |
| 1993–2000 | 43.1 | – | – | 40 | –1.6 | –6.9 | 3.7 | 9.7 | –8.9 |
| 2010–2015 | 49.5 | – | – | 87 | –2.7 | –10.2 | –0.5 | 7.7 | –11.5 |

*Notes:* [a] Spending, National debt, Current account deficit, budget (or fiscal) deficit, inflation, and unemployment values reported pertain to year before squeeze started. Public Sector Primary Deficit (–)/Surplus (+) for the year before the squeeze for 1918, 1922, 1932, 1945, 1952, 1967, 1975, 1982, 1992, and 2009 were, –20.9, 7.9, 7.6, –12.8, 3.1, 1.1, –2.1, 2.7, –3.2, and –5.4, respectively. [b] Change to nominal effective exchange rate for the year before the squeeze commenced, compared to the previous year. For the 1968–69, 1973–75, and 1993–2000 squeezes the change is between the start year of the squeeze compared to year before, as the fluctuation was more dramatic.

*Sources:* Spending: See Table A1 note a; Revenue: See Table A2 note a; National debt: National Archives UK Historical National debt data. http://webarchive.nationalarchives.gov.uk/20080630092159/http://dmo.gov.uk/reportview.aspx?rptcode=d4a&rptname=20886580&reportpage=national_debt; current account deficit and nominal effective exchange rate: Hills, Thomas, and Dimsdale (2015); inflation rate: Williamson (2014).

**Table A4.** Economic conditions at the start of the revenue squeeze and spending rises during the squeeze 1900–2015[a]

| Squeeze episode (ratio method) | Revenue (% GDP) | Spending/GDP rises during squeeze | | National debt (% GDP) | Current account deficit (% GDP) | Budget deficit (% GDP)[b] | Inflation rate | Unemployment rate | % Change in nominal effective exchange rate[c] |
|---|---|---|---|---|---|---|---|---|---|
| | | Average rise % point | Number of years the increase persisted | | | | | | |
| 1916–21 | 12.6 | 1.5 | 6 | 36 | –1.7 | –11 | 19.8 | 1 | –0.1 |
| 1931–32 | 27.5 | 1.9 | 2 | 162 | 2 | –1.3 | –3.8 | 11.2 | 2.2 |
| 1941–45 | 22.9 | 8.5 | 5 | 121 | –10.6 | –5.5 | 13.5 | 3.3 | –19.7 |
| 1960–61 | 34.2 | 0.7 | 2 | 117 | –0.7 | –2.3 | 1.4 | 1.9 | 2.6 |
| 1964–69 | 35.6 | 0.7 | 6 | 101 | 0.4 | –2.9 | 1.9 | 2.1 | 0.02 |
| 1973–75 | 39 | 2.6 | 3 | 58 | 0.3 | –3 | 7.1 | 3.1 | –10.31 |
| 1980–81 | 40 | 1.5 | 2 | 49 | 0.6 | –5 | 8.3 | 5.2 | 5.5 |

*Notes:* [a] Revenue, National debt, Current account deficit, budget (or fiscal) deficit, inflation, and unemployment values reported pertain to year before squeeze started. [b] Public Sector Primary Deficit (–)/Surplus (+) for the year before the squeeze, for 1915, 1930, 1940, 1959, 1963, 1972, and 1979 were –24.9, 6.5, –22.3, 2.2, 2.4, 1.6, and 0.2, respectively. [c] Change to nominal effective exchange rate for the year before the squeeze commenced, compared to the previous year.

*Sources:* Spending: See Table A1 note a; Revenue: See Table A2 note a; National debt: National Archives UK Historical National debt data. http://webarchive.nationalarchives.gov.uk/20080630092159/http://dmo.gov.uk/reportview.aspx?rptcode=d4a&rptname=20886580&reportpage=national_debt; current account deficit and nominal effective exchange rate: Thomas, Hills and Dimsdale (2010); inflation rate: Williamson (2014).

**Table A5.** Change in expenditure disaggregated by policy domain as percentage of fall in total spending

| | Selected current expenditure categories | | | | | | Public sector gross investment |
|---|---|---|---|---|---|---|---|
| | Defence | Education | Social security | Health | Public safety | Transport | |
| 1919–21 | −187.3 | 7.6 | 17.2 | 6.0 | 2.8 | −0.0 | 6.6 |
| 1923–25 | −18.5 | −5.8 | −20.3 | −2.8 | −3.4 | 0.9 | −23.2 |
| 1933–35 | −2.4 | −12.2 | −9.3 | −9.3 | −2.2 | −0.2 | −35.9 |
| 1946–49 | −139.2 | 5.1 | 7.3 | 1.9 | 0.6 | 3.7 | 21.7 |
| 1953–55 | 8.3 | 1.4 | −16.8 | −3.8 | 0.8 | −3.2 | −33.3 |
| 1968–69 | −46.4 | 5.8 | 19.8 | −1.5 | 1.9 | 114.5 | −57.1 |
| 1976–78 | −0.1 | −17.0 | 21.2 | −4.9 | 1.4 | −12.5 | −64.7 |
| 1983–88 | −13.3 | −7.5 | −19.3 | −3.1 | 0.2 | −5.1 | −28.7 |
| 1993–2000 | −13.3 | −7.2 | −16.9 | 0.3 | −2.5 | −9.1 | −26.1 |
| 2010–15[a] | −6.6 | −11. | 0 | −5.0 | −8.3 | −6.6 | −31.6 |

*Note:* [a] Reported falls in current spending categories based on data up to 2013/14.

*Source:* Health, Public Safety, Transport (1900–79); Social Security (1900–49) Education, Defence (1900–1953): Mitchell, B. R (1988), Chapter XI, Table 4, 12, 13, 15, and 16. Public Sector Gross Investment (1900–49) Middleton (1996: 648). Health, Public Safety, Transport (1980–2013); Social Security, Public Sector Gross Investment (1950–2013), Education, Defence (1953–2013): IFS (2014). Defence costs after 1998 include non-cash costs.

**Table A6.** Revenue changes in three sources of revenue as percentage of total revenue increases

| Timing of revenue squeeze (ratio method) | Change in revenue category as a percentage of total rise in revenue[a] | | |
|---|---|---|---|
| | Income and capital | Tax on expenditure | Compulsory contributions |
| 1916–21 | 61.6 | 30.1 | 2.1 |
| 1931–32 | 53.2 | 53.9 | 10.7 |
| 1941–49 | 49.6 | 28.4 | 13.3 |
| 1960–61 | 46.3 | 11.2 | 20.2 |
| 1964–69 | 39.5 | 48.4 | 7.3 |
| 1973–75 | 54.6 | −15.7 | 35.7 |
| 1980–81 | 33.3 | 9.8 | 30.7 |

*Note:* [a] Total revenue data pertains to central and local government expenditure but excludes public corporations. Post Office is treated as a part of central government until 1961, and after that as a public corporation. Apart from the categories in the table, other main revenue categories include gross trading surplus, rent, interest and dividends, and current grants from abroad.

*Source:* 1900–78 derived from Middleton (1996: 650–1). 1979 onwards ONS (2014), series NMZJ, HZS7, AllH, and NMYE. Given the break in sources in 1979, the 1980–81 figures are not directly comparable with figures for previous episodes, especially for the tax on expenditure category.

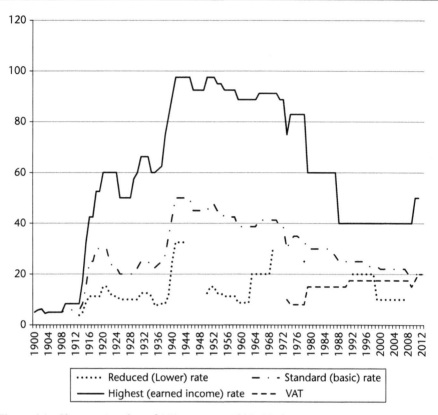

**Figure A1.** Changes in selected UK tax rates, 1900–2012

*Source*: Roger Middleton, data provided by author.

# References

Adamthwaite, A (1992) 'Overstretched and Overstrung: Eden, the Foreign Office and the Making of Policy' in Nolfo, E (ed.) *Power in Europe II: Great Britain, France, Germany and Italy and the Origins of the EEC 1952–57*, Berlin: de Gruyter.

Alesina, A, and Ardagna, S (2010) 'Large Changes in Fiscal Policy: Taxes versus Spending' in Brown, J R (ed.) *Tax Policy and the Economy*, Volume 24, Chicago: University of Chicago Press: 35–68.

Alesina, A, Barbiero, O, Favero, C, Giavazzi, F, and Paradisi, M (2015) 'Austerity in 2009–2013', *Economic Policy* 30 (83): 383–437.

Alesina, A, Carloni, D, and Lecce, G (2012) 'The Electoral Consequences of Large Fiscal Adjustments' in *Fiscal Policy after the Financial Crisis*, Chicago: University of Chicago Press: 531–70.

Alesina, A, and Giavazzi, F (2013) *Fiscal Policy After the Financial Crisis*, Chicago: Chicago University Press.

Alesina, A, and Perotti, R (1997) 'Fiscal Adjustments in OECD Countries: Composition and Macroeconomic Effects', *International Monetary Fund Staff Papers* 44 (2 June): 210–48.

Alesina, A, Perotti, R, Tavares, J, Obstfeld, M, and Eichengreen, B (1998) 'The Political Economy of Fiscal Adjustments', *Brookings Papers on Economic Activity* (1): 197–266.

Allport, A (2009) *Demobbed: Coming Home After World War Two*, New Haven: Yale University Press.

Anderson, C J (2000) 'Economic Voting and Political Context: A Comparative Perspective', *Electoral Studies* 19 (2/3): 151–70.

Ansell, B W, and Samuels, D J (2010) 'Democracy and Redistribution, 1880–1930: Reassessing the Evidence', *APSA 2010 Annual Meeting Paper*, SSRN, http://ssrn.com/abstract=1643055.

Armingeon, K, and Giger, N (2008) 'Conditional Punishment: A Comparative Analysis of the Electoral Consequences of Welfare State Retrenchment in OECD Nations, 1980–2003', *West European Politics* 31 (3): 558–80.

Armitstead, L (2014) 'IMF Accepts it Was Wrong on George Osborne's Austerity', *Telegraph*, 6 June 2014, http://www.telegraph.co.uk/finance/economics/10881540/IMF-accepts-it-was-wrong-on-George-Osbornes-austerity.html.

Ban, C (2015) 'Austerity versus Stimulus? Understanding Fiscal Policy Change at the International Monetary Fund since the Great Recession', *Governance* 28 (2): 167–83.

Barnard, H C (1947) *A Short History of English Education, 1760–1944*, London: University of London Press.

# References

Barnett, C (1970) *Britain and her Army, 1509–1970: A Military, Political and Social Survey*, London: Allen Lane.

Barnett, J (1982) *Inside the Treasury*, London: Deutsch.

Bartels, L, and Bermeo, N (eds) (2013) *Mass Politics in Tough Times: Opinions, Votes and Protest in the Great RecessionI*, Oxford: Oxford University Press.

Bassett, R (1958) *1931: Political Crisis*, London: Macmillan.

Black, D (1958) *The Theory of Committees and Elections*, Cambridge: Cambridge University Press.

Blyth, M (2013) *Austerity: The History of a Dangerous Idea*, New York: Oxford University Press.

Bogdanor, V (1991) '1931 Revisited: The Constitutional Aspects', *Twentieth Century British History* 2 (1): 1–25.

Booth, A (2004) 'Brittain, Sir Herbert (1894–1961)', *Oxford Dictionary of National Biography*, Oxford: Oxford University Press.

Booth, A, and Glyn, S (1975) 'Unemployment in the Interwar Period', *Journal of Contemporary History* 10: 611–36.

Brittan, S (1976) *The Economic Consequences of Democracy*, London: Temple Smith.

Brown, C (1997) 'Politics: Labour Revolt Threatened over Cut in Lone-Parent Benefit', *The Independent*, 21 November 1997.

Budd, A (2004) 'Black Wednesday: A Re-Examination of Britain's Experience in the Exchange Rate Mechanism', 34th Wincott Lecture, London, Institute of Economic Affairs.

Burk, K, and Cairncross, A (1992) *Good-bye Great Britain: The 1976 IMF Crisis*, New Haven: Yale University Press.

Burns, P F, and Thomas, M O (2015) *Reforming New Orleans: The Contentious Politics of Change in the Big Easy*, Ithaca: Cornell University Press.

Butler, D, and Kavanagh, D (1997) *The British General Election of 1997*, London: Palgrave Macmillan.

Butler, D, Travers, T, and Adonis, A (1994) *Failure in British Government: The Politics of the Poll Tax*, Oxford: Oxford University Press.

Butler, R A (1971) *The Art of the Possible*, London: Hamish Hamilton.

Cairncross, A (1985) *Years of Recovery: British Economic Policy 1945–51*, London: Methuen.

Cairncross, A (1985) *Years of Recovery: British Economic Policy 1945–51*, London: Taylor and Francis.

Callaghan, J (1987) *Time and Chance*, London: Politico's.

Castle, S (1992) 'Would the Real Norman Lamont Please Stand Up?', *The Independent*, 4 October 1992.

Chote, R, Emmerson, C, and Simpson, H (2003) *The IFS Green Budget*, London: Institute for Fiscal Studies.

Chote, R, and Emmerson, E (2014) 'The Liberal Democrats: Tighter or Looser?' Institute for Fiscal Studies 'Observations', Blog, 14 April 2010, http://www.ifs.org.uk/publica tions/4819, accessed October 2015.

Chu, B (2015) 'It's Official, Inequality in the UK Isn't Really on the Increase (or Is It?)', *The Independent*, 29 October 2015.

Clark, C (1945) 'Public Finance and the Value of Money', *Economic Journal* 55 (Dec 1945): 371–89.

Committee on National Expenditure (1921) *First Interim Report of the Committee on National Expenditure*, London: HMSO, Cmd 1581.

Committee on National Expenditure (1922) *Third Report of the Committee on National Expenditure*, London: HMSO Cmd 1589.

Committee on National Expenditure (1931) *Report*, London: HMSO Cmd 3952.

Cooper, C (2011) 'Little Local Difficulties Revisited: Peter Thorneycroft, the 1958 Treasury Resignations and the Origins of Thatcherism', *Contemporary British History* 25 (2): 227–50.

Crafts, N, and Fearon, P (2010) 'Lessons from the 1930s Great Depression', *Oxford Review of Economic Policy* 26 (3): 285–317.

Crawford, R, Emmerson, C, and Tetlow, G (2009) 'A survey of Public Spending in the UK', IFS Briefing Note BN43, London: Institute of Fiscal Studies.

Cukierman, A, and Tommasi, M (1998) 'Why Does it Take a Nixon to Go to China?' *American Economic Review* 88 (1): 180–97.

Curtis, S J (1948) *History of Education in Great Britain*, London: University of London Press.

Darling, A (2011) *Back from the Brink*, London: Atlantic Books.

Dassonneville, R, and Hooghe, M (2015) 'Economic Indicators and Electoral Volatility: Economic Effects on Electoral Volatility in Western Europe, 1950–2013', *Comparative European Politics* advance online publication; doi: 10.1057/cep.2015.3.

Daunton, M (2002) *Just Taxes: The Politics of Taxation in Britain 1914–1979*, Cambridge: Cambridge University Press.

Davies, A (2012) 'The Evolution of British Monetarism 1968–1979', *University of Oxford Discussion Papers in Economic and Social History* No. 104, October 2012.

Dell, E (1991) *A Hard Pounding: Politics and Economic Crisis 1974–1976*, Oxford: Oxford University Press.

Devries, P, Guajardo, J, Leigh, D, and Pescatori, A (2011) 'A New Action-Based Dataset of Fiscal Consolidation', *IMF Working Paper* No. 11/128.

Donoughue, B (1987) *Prime Minister: The Conduct of Policy under Harold Wilson and James Callaghan*, London: Cape.

Dransfield, R and Dransfield, D (2003) *Key Ideas in Economics*, Cheltenham: Nelson Thomas.

Dunleavy, P J (1991) *Democracy, Bureaucracy and Public Choice: Economic Explanations in Political Science*, London: Harvester Wheatsheaf.

Dunsire, A, and Hood, C (1989) *Cutback Management in Public Bureaucracies*, Cambridge: Cambridge University Press.

Eichengreen, B (2015) *Hall of Mirrors: The Great Depression, the Great Recession and the Uses—and Misuses—of History*, New York: Oxford University Press.

Emmerson, C, Johnson, P, and Joyce, R (eds) (2015) *The IFS Green Budget 2015*, London: Institute for Fiscal Studies.

Evans, B, and Taylor, A (1996) *From Salisbury to Major: Continuity and Change in Conservative Politics*, Manchester: Manchester University Press.

Fay, S, and Young, H (1978) 'The Day the £ Nearly Died', *Sunday Times*, 14 May 1978: 33–5.

Feinstein, C H (1972) *National Income, Expenditure and Output of the United Kingdom 1855–1965*, Cambridge: Cambridge University Press.

Ferguson, T (1994) *Golden Rule: The Investment Theory of Party Competition and the Logic of Money-Driven Political Systems*, Chicago: Chicago University Press.

Fiorina, M P (1978) 'Economic Retrospective Voting in American National Elections: A Micro-Analysis', *American Journal of Political Science* 22 (2): 426–43.

Gamble, A (2012) 'The United Kingdom: The Triumph of Fiscal Realism', Ch 3 in Grant, W, and Wilson G K (eds), *The Consequences of Global Financial Crisis: The Rhetoric of Reform and Regulation*, Oxford: Oxford University Press: 34–50.

Giavazzi, F, and Pagano, M (1990) 'Can Severe Fiscal Contractions be Expansionary? Tales of Two Small European Countries', Cambridge, MA, National Bureau of Economic Research, NBER Macroeconomics Annual 1990, Volume 5: 75–122.

Green, J, and Jennings, W (2016) *The Politics of Competence: Parties, Public Opinion and Voters*, Cambridge: Cambridge University Press.

Grigg, P J (1948) *Prejudice and Judgement*, London: Jonathan Cape.

Guajardo, J, Leigh, D, and Pescatori, A (2014) 'Expansionary Austerity? International Evidence', *Journal of the European Economic Association* 12 (4): 949–68.

Hansen, A (1939) 'Economic Progress and Declining Population Growth', *American Economic Review* 29 (1): 1–15.

Hansen, R (2000) *Citizenship and Immigration in Post-War Britain*, Oxford: Oxford University Press.

Hayek, F A (1949) *Individualism and Economic Order*, London: Routledge and Kegan Paul.

Healey, D (1990) *The Time of My Life*, London: Penguin Books.

Hendry, D F (2001) 'Modelling UK Inflation, 1875–1991', *Journal of Applied Econometrics* 16 (3): 255–75.

Herndon, T, Ash, M, and Pollin, R (2014) 'Does High Public Debt Consistently Stifle Economic Growth? A Critique of Reinhart and Rogoff', *Cambridge Journal of Economics* 38 (2): 257–79.

Hickson, K (2005) *The IMF Crisis of 1976 and British Politics*, London: Taurus Academic Studies, International Library of Political Studies 3.

Higgs, H (1922) 'The Geddes Reports and the Budget', *Economic Journal* 32 (126): 251–64.

Hills, S, Thomas, R, and Dimsdale, N (2010) 'Three Centuries of Data—Version 2.1', Bank of England, http://www.bankofengland.co.uk/research/Pages/onebank/threecenturies.aspx, accessed March 2014.

Hills, S, Thomas, R, and Dimsdale, N (2015) 'Three Centuries of Data—Version 2.1', Bank of England, http://www.bankofengland.co.uk/research/Pages/onebank/threecenturies.aspx.

Himaz, R (2015) SN851814 The Politics of Austerity in Public Services: UK Public Finance and Political Variables Data 1900–2015, https://www.ukdataservice.ac.uk/.

Hirst, F W (1915) *The Political Economy of War*, London: J.M. Dent.

HM Treasury (1994) *Public Expenditure Statistical Supplement to the Financial Statement and Budget Report 1994–95*, London: HMSO.

HM Treasury (2008) *Pre-Budget Report 2008: Facing Global Challenges, Supporting People Through Difficult Times*, Cm 7484, London: HMSO.

Hood, C (2011) *The Blame Game: Spin, Bureaucracy and Self-Preservation in Government*, Princeton: Princeton University Press.

Hood, C, and Dixon, R (2015) *A Government that Worked Better and Cost Less? Evaluating Three Decades of Reform and Change in UK Central Government*, Oxford: Oxford University Press.

Hood, C, Heald, D, and Himaz, R (eds) (2014) *When the Party's Over: The Politics of Fiscal Squeeze in Perspective*, Oxford: Oxford University Press and British Academy.

Hood, C, and Himaz, R (2014) 'The UK Geddes Axe of the 1920s in Perspective' in Hood, C, Heald, D, and Himaz, R (eds) *When the Party's Over: The Politics of Fiscal Squeeze in Perspective*, Oxford: Oxford University Press and British Academy, Chapter 4: 73–92.

Houghton, D (1979) 'The Futility of Taxation by Menaces' in A Seldon (ed.) *Tax Avoision: The Economic, Legal and Moral Inter-Relationship between Avoidance and Evasion*, London: Institute of Economic Affairs.

Howe, G (1994) *Conflict of Loyalty*, London: Pan Books.

IMF (2010) 'Chapter 3', *World Economic Outlook*, Washington, DC: International Monetary Fund.

Independent Public Service Pensions Commission (2011) *Final Report*, London: HMSO.

Institute of Fiscal Studies (IFS) (2014) LR_Spending_Autumn_Statement_2014, dataset, http://www.ifs.org.uk/uploads/publications/ff/lr_spending_Autumn_Statement_2014.xls.

James, S (1997) *British Government: A Reader in Policy-Making*, London: Routledge.

Jones, T J (1969) *Whitehall Diary*, ed K. Morgan, 1 (1916–1925), London: Oxford University Press.

Kempley, J (2010) 'How Far Was the Falklands War the Main Reason for Thatcher's 1983 General Election Victory?', *Conservative History Journal* 8 (Winter 2009/10): 38–40.

Kickert, W, and Randma-Liiv, T (2015) *Europe Managing the Crisis: The Politics of Fiscal Consolidation*, Oxford: Routledge.

König, P D, and Wenzelburger, G (2014) 'Toward a Theory of Political Strategy in Policy Analysis', *Politics and Policy* 42 (3): 400–30.

Konishi, H (2006) 'Spending Cuts or Tax Increases? The Composition of Fiscal Adjustments as a Signal', *European Economic Review* 50 (6): 1441–69.

Konzelmann, S J (2014) 'The Political Economics of Austerity', *Cambridge Journal of Economics* 38 (4): 701–41.

Laffer, A (2004) 'The Laffer Curve: Past, Present, and Future' Backgrounder #1765 on Taxes, The Heritage Foundation, http://www.heritage.org/research/reports/2004/06/the-laffer-curve-past-present-and-future, accessed December 2014.

Lamont, N (1999) *In Office*, London: Little, Brown and Co.

Latham, R and Prowie, M (2012) *Public Services and Financial Austerity: Getting out of the Hole?*, Basingstoke: Palgrave Macmillan.

Lawson, N (1992) *The View from No.11: Memoirs of a Tory Radical*, London: Bantam Press.

Legrain, P (2010) 'A Good Election to Lose?', *The Guardian*, 9 March 2010.

Leigh, D (1988) *The Wilson Plot: How the Spycatchers and Their American Allies Tried to Overthrow the British Government*, London: Pantheon Books.

# References

Lewin, L (1991) *Self-Interest and Public Interest in Western Politics*, Oxford: Oxford University Press.

Lowe, R (1989) 'Resignation at the Treasury: The Social Services Committee and the Failure to Reform the Welfare State 1955–57', *Journal of Social Policy* 18: 505–26.

Lowe, R (1997) Milestone or Millstone? The 1959–1961 Plowden Committee and its Impact on British Welfare Policy', *The Historical Journal* 40 (2): 463–91.

McDonald, A (1989) 'The Geddes Committee and the Formulation of Public Expenditure Policy, 1921–22', *The Historical Journal* 32 (2): 643–74.

Mackenzie, W J M (1963) 'The Plowden Report: A Translation', *Australian Journal of Public Administration* 22 (2): 155–63.

Major, J (2000) *The Autobiography*, London: HarperCollins.

Marr, A (2007) *A History of Modern Britain*, London: Pan Macmillan.

Marshall, G, and Moodie, G C (1964), *Some Problems of the Constitution*, 3rd edn, London: Hutchison.

Mauro, P (2011) *Chipping Away at Public Debt: Sources of Failure and Keys to Success in Fiscal Adjustment*, Hoboken, NJ: Wiley.

McCombie, J S, Thirlwall, A P, and Thompson, P (1994) *Economic Growth and the Balance-of-Payments Constraint*, New York: St Martin's Press.

McKibbin, R (1975) 'The Economic Policy of the Second Labour Government 1929–31', *Past and Present* 68: 95–123.

McKibbin, R (1990) *The Ideologies of Class: Social Relations in Britain 1880–1950*, Oxford: Oxford University Press.

McLean, I (2002) 'Review Article: William H. Riker and the Invention of Heresthetic(s)', *British Journal of Political Science* 32: 535–58.

Middleton, R (1982) 'The Treasury in the 1930s', *Oxford Economic Papers* 34: 48–77.

Middleton, R (1996) *Government vs the Market: The Growth of the Public Sector, Economic Management and British Economic Performance, c.1890–1979*, Cheltenham: Edward Elgar.

Middleton, R (2010) 'British Monetary Policy in the 1930s', *Oxford Review of Economic Policy* 26 (3): 414–41.

Miller, M (1981) 'The Medium Term Financial Strategy: An Experiment in Co-ordinating Monetary and Fiscal Policy', *Fiscal Studies* 2 (2): 50–60.

Mitchell, B R (1988) *British Historical Statistics*, Cambridge: Cambridge University Press.

Moodie, G C (1957) 'The Monarch and the Selection of a Prime Minister: A Re-Examination of the Crisis of 1931', *Political Studies* 5 (1): 1–20.

Morgan, K (1984) *Labour in Power, 1945–51*, Oxford: Clarendon.

Mowat, C L (1968) *Britain Between the Wars*, London: Methuen.

Nagel, J H (1993) 'Populism, Heresthetics and Political Stability: Richard Seddon and the Art of Majority Rule', *British Journal of Political Science* 23 (2): 139–74.

Nason, J M, and Vahey, S P (2007) 'The McKenna Rule and UK World War I Finance', *American Economic Review*, 97 (2): 290–4.

Needham, D, and Hotson, A (eds) (2014) *Expansionary Fiscal Contraction: The Thatcher Government's 1981 Budget in Perspective*, Cambridge: Cambridge University Press.

Nield, R (2012) 'The "1981 Statement by 364 Economists" Revisited', *Royal Economic Society Newsletter* No 159, October 2012: 11–14.

Office of National Statistics (ONS) (2014) Public Sector Finances, supplementary data February 2014, http://www.ons.gov.uk/ons/rel/psa/public-sector-finances, accessed March 2014.

Organization for Economic Coordination and Development (OECD) (2014) OECD Economic Outlook No. 96. November 2014, https://stats.oecd.org/Index.aspx?DataSetCode=EO96_INTERNET.

Peacock, A T and Wiseman, J (1961) *The Growth of Public Expenditure in the United Kingdom*, Princeton, NJ: Princeton University Press.

Peck, J (1998) 'Making space for welfare-to-work: Assessing the prospects for Labour's New Deal', paper for 'Reinventing the State', ESRC Labour Studies Seminar, Centre for Comparative Labour Studies, University of Warwick, 27 November 1998, https://web.warwick.ac.uk/fac/soc/complabstuds/confsem/Peck.htm, accessed September 2015.

Peden, G (1979) *British Rearmament and the Treasury: 1932–1939*, Edinburgh: Scottish Academic Press.

Peden, G (2000) *The Treasury and British Public Policy, 1906–1959*, Oxford: Oxford University Press.

Peltzman, S (1992) 'Voters as Fiscal Conservatives', *Quarterly Journal of Economics* 107 (2): 327–61.

Pensions Policy Institute (2005) 'Is £5 Billion Being Taken Every Year from Pension Funds?', PPI Briefing Note 22, https://www.pensionspolicyinstitute.org.uk/, accessed June 2016.

Pierson, P (1994) *Dismantling the Welfare State? Reagan, Thatcher and the Politics of Retrenchment*, Cambridge: Cambridge University Press.

Pierson, P (1996) 'The New Politics of the Welfare State', *World Politics* 48 (2): 143–79.

Raya, S (1999) *Britain Disarmed: The Ending of National Service*, London: Sinar Raya.

Reinhart, C, and Rogoff, K (2010) 'Growth in a Time of Debt', *American Economic Review* 100 (2): 573–8.

Riddell, P (1987) *The Thatcher Government*, 2nd edn, London: Basil Blackwell.

Riker, W H (1986) *The Art of Political Manipulation*, New Haven: Yale University Press.

Rollings, N, and Middleton, R (2002) 'British Economic Policy in the 1950s and 1960s', Economic History Society Annual Conference, University of Birmingham (Vol 6, April 2002).

Romer, C (2015) 'The Aftermath of Financial Crises: Each Time Really is Different' text of 2015 Sir John Hicks Lecture in Economic History, Oxford University, 28 April 2015, http://eml.berkeley.edu/~cromer/Romer%20Hicks%20Lecture%20Written%20Version.pdf, accessed March 2015.

Rose, R (1980) 'Misperceiving Public Expenditure: Feelings about "Cuts"', Ch 9 in Levine, C H, and Rubin, I (eds) *Fiscal Stress and Public Policy*, Beverly Hills, CA: Sage: 203–30.

Rose, R, and Karran, T (1987) *Taxation by Political Inertia: Financing the Growth of Government in Britain*, London: Allen and Unwin.

Rose, R, and Peters, B G (1978) *Can Government Go Bankrupt?* New York: Basic Books.

Sanders, D, Ward, H, and Marsh, D (1991) *Economics and Politics, the Calculus of Support—Macroeconomics, The Falklands War and the Thatcher Government: A Contrary View*, 2nd edn, Michigan: University of Michigan Press.

Sanders, D, Ward, H, Marsh, D, and Fletcher, T (1987) 'Government Popularity and the Falklands War: A Reassessment', *British Journal of Political Science* 17 (3): 281–313.

Schumacher, G, Vis, B, and van Kersbergen, K (2012) 'Political Parties' Welfare Image, Electoral Punishment and Welfare State Retrenchment', *Comparative European Politics* 11 (1): 1–21.

Seccareccia M (2012) 'The Role of Public Investment as Principal Macroeconomic Tool to Promote Long-Term Growth: Keynes's Legacy', *International Journal of Political Economy* 40 (4): 62–82.

Skidelsky, R (1967) *Politicians and the Slump: The Labour Government of 1929–31*, London: Macmillan.

Stephens, P (1997) *Politics and the Pound: The Tories, the Economy and Europe*, London: Papermac.

Stevenson, F (1971) *Lloyd George: A Diary*, ed. A.J.P. Taylor, London: Harper and Row.

Streeck, W, and Shäfer, A (2013) *Politics in the Age of Austerity*, London: Polity.

Summers, L (2016) 'The Age of Secular Stagnation: What It Is and What to Do About It' *Foreign Affairs*, March/April 2016, https://www.foreignaffairs.com/articles/united-states/2016-02-15/age-secular-stagnation, accessed December 2016.

Swenarton, M (1981) *Homes Fit for Heroes*, London: Heinemann.

t'Hart, P, and Tindall, K (2009) *Framing the Global Economic Downturn: Crisis Rhetoric and the Politics of Recessions*, Canberra: ANU E Press.

Tanzi, M V (ed.) (1993) *Transition to Market: Studies in Fiscal Reform*. Washington, DC: International Monetary Fund.

Temin, P (1976) *Did Monetary Forces Cause the Great Depression?*, New York: W.W. Norton.

Thain, C (2010) 'Budget Reform in the United Kingdom: The Rocky Road to "Controlled Discretion"', in Wanna, J, Jensen, L, and de Vries, L (eds), *The Reality of Budgetary Reform in OECD Nations: Trajectories and Consequences*, Cheltenham: Edward Elgar.

Thain, C, and Wright, M (1995) *The Treasury and Whitehall: The Planning and Control of Public Expenditure, 1976–1993*, Oxford: Clarendon.

Thomas, R, Hills, S, and Dimsdale, N (2010) 'The UK Recession in Context—What do Three Centuries of Data Tell Us?', *Bank of England Quarterly Bulletin*, Q4, 2010.

Wanniski, J (1978) 'Taxes, Revenues and the "Laffer Curve"', *The Public Interest* (Winter): 3–16.

Wass, D (2008) *Decline to Fall: The Making of British Macro-Economic Policy and the 1976 IMF Crisis*, Oxford: Oxford University Press.

Weaver, R K (1986) 'The Politics of Blame Avoidance', *Journal of Public Policy* 6 (4): 371–98.

Wenzelburger, G (2014) 'Blame Avoidance, Electoral Punishment and the Perceptions of Risk', *Journal of European Social Policy* 24 (1): 80–91.

Wheeler-Bennett, Sir J (1948) *Munich: Prologue to Tragedy*, London: Macmillan.

White, G, and Chapman, H (1987) 'Long Term Trends in Public Expenditure', *Economic Trends* 408 (October): 124–8.

Wildavsky, A (1964) *The Politics of the Budgetary Process*, Boston: Little, Brown.

Wildavsky, A (1980) 'The Logic of Public Sector Growth', in Lane, J-E (ed.) *State and Market*, London: Macmillan: 231–70.

Williamson, P (1984) ' "A Bankers' Ramp"? Financiers and the British Political Crisis of August 1931', *English Historical Review* 99 (393): 770–806.

Williamson, P (1992) *National Crisis and National Government: British Politics, the Economy and Empire 1926–32*, Cambridge: Cambridge University Press.

Williamson, S H (2014) 'What was the US GDP Then?', *Measuring Worth*, https://www.measuringworth.com/ukgdp/, accessed Dec 2016.

Wilson, J Q (1980) *The Politics of Regulation*, New York: Basic Books: 357–94.

Wright, P (1987) *Spycatcher*, London: Heinemann.

Wrigley, C (2013) 'The Fall of the Second MacDonald Government 1931', Ch 3 in Heppell, T, and Theakston, K (eds), *How Labour Governments Fall: From Ramsay MacDonald to Gordon Brown*, London: Palgrave Macmillan.

Zweiniger-Bargielowska, I (2002) *Austerity in Britain: Rationing, Controls and Consumption, 1939–1955*, Oxford: Oxford University Press.

# Index

Note: Unless otherwise stated references are to UK

2008 financial crash 3–5, 9, 19, 221
'accelerator' 170, 173, 177, 222
accounting, creative 14, 133, 204
  rules 158
Accounting Officers 95
Aden 111
Admiralty 49, 58
agency strategies 10, 14
Air Passenger Duty 170
airlines, budget 212–13, 221
Aitken, Jonathan 168
Alesina, Alberto 9, 183, 204, 217, 219–20
Amory, Derek Heathcote 109, 115, 118
Anderson, Sir John 83
Anti-Waste League 46–7, 57, 59, 99, 104, 211
Argentina 149–50, 157
Armstrong, William 101
Asquith, Herbert 42
asset purchases *see* nationalization
asset sales *see* privatization
asymmetrical punishment 12–13, 55, 57, 118,
  138, 158, 178, 198, 220
Attlee, Clement 81, 84–9, 91, 105, 209–10
audit commissions 209
austerity 3–6, 12, 15–18, 20–2, 28, 84, 89, 180,
  193, 199, 204–6, 217
  non-fiscal 15, 42, 54, 76, 80–2, 89, 96–7,
  110, 117, 121, 135–6, 142, 166, 176,
  196, 207
Australia 209
Austria 61
automatic stabilizer effects 31n
automation 19, 79

bailouts 3, 21, 92, 126–31, 135, 211
balance of payments 81, 84–6, 89, 96, 100,
  109, 110–14, 119, 122, 133, 182
balanced budgets 45–6, 142, 151, 153, 160–1,
  172, 215
Baldwin, Stanley 50–2, 56, 65, 67
Bank of England 15, 60, 68, 79, 126, 175,
  189, 193
Bank Rate 109, 117
bankers' bonuses 183, 212

'bankers' ramp' 60, 68, 79, 211
banks:
  bailouts 181–2
  tax 186–7, 192
Barber, Anthony 122
Barnett, Joel 124–5, 131n, 132–3, 135–6
bear traps 171–4, 204, 210
'bedroom tax' 191, 197
Belarus 131
Benn, Tony 127, 128–9, 131
Bevan, Aneurin 95
Bevanites 99, 138, 142–3
Beveridge Plan 82–3, 86
Bevin, Ernest 89
Biffen, John 146n
Birch, Nigel 108, 221
Black, Duncan 11–12
Blair, Tony 95, 161–2, 171–5, 182, 222
blame 5, 10, 14, 56, 68–71, 116, 119, 167–8,
  195–6, 203–4, 223
blame avoidance 8–9, 21–2, 136, 175,
  189–90, 193
blame game 64, 121, 149
blame politics 208–10
Blunkett, David 174
'boiling frogs' 13–14, 159, 167–8, 175, 183–4,
  195, 203, 208–9, 216
borrowing (public sector) 30, 42, 59, 131, 161,
  168, 211
Boyd-Carpenter, John 101, 106
BP 131, 133, 139, 141, 158, 167, 212
Bretton Woods 100, 115, 120
Brexit 198, 216
'bribes budget' 155
Bridges, Sir Edward 91, 92n, 93n, 101,
  103n, 105n
British National Oil Corporation 131
Brittain, Sir Herbert 87, 98
Brockway, Fenner 68
Brown, George 111
Brown, Gordon 171–9, 182–4, 190–1, 196, 210
budget deficit 7, 24, 43–4, 60, 70, 81–2, 100,
  147, 150, 161, 164, 166, 182, 211, 214–15
  US 11

budget surplus 52, 81
budgetary process 6–7
Bush, George H. W. 162
business tax credits 88, 187
Butler, Richard (Rab) 100, 101–7, 115–19, 146
Butler Education Act 1944 *see* Education Act 1944
by-elections 10, 46–7, 50, 57, 84, 104, 111, 124, 127, 134, 143, 166

cabinet 52, 61, 64, 95, 103, 108, 130, 132, 145–8, 164–7, 221
  committees 47–50, 105–6, 164–5, 190, 209
Callaghan, James 110–13, 118, 128–9, 130, 138, 148n, 166, 206
Cameron, David 185
Canada 86, 89, 91, 97, 162, 211, 223
Capital Gains Tax 111, 117, 187, 192
capital levy 43, 88–9
capital spending 32–4, 51, 105, 112–13, 123–5, 131–2, 147, 166, 168, 183–4, 187, 193
Capital Transfer Tax 153
capitalist democracy 12, 223
Carloni, Dorian 9
cash limits regime 138–9
Chamberlain, Austen 44–5, 50, 59, 102
Chamberlain, Neville 88
Chanak crisis 50
Chancellor of the Exchequer 42, 47–8, 52, 65, 69, 113, 124, 127, 130, 152, 162, 164–5, 190–1, 194–5
Chief Economic Advisers to the Government 143
child benefit 134, 147, 151, 173, 188, 191
  Tax Charge 119
child poverty 197
China 12
Churchill, Winston 49, 63, 80, 83, 101, 104, 107
civil defence 107, 113, 216
Civil List 71
civil service 51, 68, 73, 96
  staffing 102, 107, 123, 133, 144, 159
civil service bonus 64
Clarke, Kenneth 168–9
Clynes, John Richard 69
coal shortage 89
coalition governments 10, 19, 30, 42, 53, 80, 178, 180–94, 196, 207–10, 220–1
Cold War 106, 161
Committee on National Expenditure 47–50, 57–8, 63, 70, 97, 104, 116, 175, 209–10
Communist International 56
comprehensive spending review 174, 177, 189
'confidence and supply' arrangement 121n, 133
conscription 42, 80, 82, 85, 88, 108, 207

Conservative Government 30, 52, 178, 180–1, 185–6, 192, 194, 196–8, 220–1
Conservative Party 31, 57, 145, 151, 155, 158, 160, 165–6, 170, 171–2, 176
  Conference 103–4
constitutional consequences 10, 57, 204
constitutional crisis 61, 76
consumer boom 153, 155
Consumer Prices Index 188, 213
Corporation Profits Tax 44, 45, 52
Corporation Tax 113–14, 117, 124, 153, 172–3, 187
Council on Financial Stability 189, 195, 210
'coupon' general election (1918) 43
Crafts, Nicholas 76
credit rating agencies 184, 193, 211
Crimean Wars 42
Cripps, Stafford 89–94, 112
Crosland, Anthony 127–8
currency 31, 60, 115, 119, 120, 126, 211
  crisis 112, 161, 165, 206
Customs and Excise 106
  duties 110, 124–5, 151, 153

*Daily Express, The* 95–6
Dalton, Hugh 86–9, 108
Darling, Alastair 183–4, 186
Daunton, Martin 81, 88–9, 97, 212–13
De Valera, Éamon 84
debt:
  national 15, 42–6, 51, 59, 81, 142, 153, 161, 181–5, 192–3, 203, 211, 214, 222
  personal 142, 155
Defence, Ministry of 58
defence spending 32, 34–5, 43–5, 48–9, 51, 58, 72, 75, 80–5, 90, 93, 98, 101–2, 108, 111–12, 123, 125, 132, 137, 144–9, 151, 161, 169, 207, 213
deficit reduction 19, 24, 172, 180, 183–6, 189, 192–5, 203, 206, 214–15
deflation 21, 43, 70, 78, 87
depression *see* recession
Deutschmark 165
devaluation 66, 85, 91, 99, 117, 165–6, 211
  (1967) 100, 112, 122, 131
Development Land Tax 153
devolution 129, 198
  Scotland 134, 158, 216
diesel *see* road fuel
direct labour organizations 141
direct taxes 36, 41, 71, 123–4, 145, 170, 207
disability benefits 174, 187–8
'Doctor's Mandate' 61, 66
doctors 82
Driberg, Tom 84
'drift' 78

economic cycle 172, 182–3
economic forecasting 22, 138, 175, 189, 193,
    195–6, 209
economic growth 16, 19, 21, 128, 135, 140,
    152–6, 160, 164, 176, 186, 189, 192–4, 208,
    222–3
economic policy 165
Economic Policy Committee 92–3
economic recovery 11, 193, 216
economists 69, 87, 143, 154, 183
economy drive (1949) 91–2, 97
Eden, Sir Anthony 107–8
Education, Board of 49–50
    Department of 174
    Ministry of 92
Education Act 1918 49–50
    1944 59, 83
education spending 32, 43–5, 49–51, 72, 75–6,
    86, 101, 115, 132–3, 144, 169, 172, 174,
    189–90, 213
EDX 165, 168, 177–8, 190
egalitarian attitudes 5
electoral competition 53, 55, 80, 98, 169
electoral consequences 6, 22, 55–9, 77–8,
    118–19, 137–9, 206, 214, 216–20
    punishment 9, 12, 84, 99, 146, 149–50, 155,
    158, 177–8, 204
    reward 151, 183
electoral cycles 13–18, 117–18, 151–2, 158,
    171, 175, 177
electoral politics 8–10
employment measures 141, 144, 169, 172,
    174, 177, 179
energy, VAT 167–8, 170–2
energy supplies 123, 154
English National Party 129
equal sacrifice 14, 71, 73
'escalator' see 'accelerator'
euro 46, 163, 165, 193
European Economic Community (EEC) see
    European Union
European Exchange Rate Mechanism
    (ERM) 165–6, 176, 178
European Union 19, 31, 121–3, 129, 149, 160,
    163, 172, 178, 194
eurozone 3, 61–2, 143, 182–3, 193, 209,
    211, 223
Excess Profits Tax 42, 44–5, 55, 81–2, 87–8,
    102, 104, 117, 211
exchange rates 31, 42, 59, 62, 66, 100, 110,
    115, 120, 165, 214
    controls 207
Excise see Customs and Excise
exogenous forces 115, 118, 126, 135, 143, 149
expansionary fiscal contraction 3, 59, 143, 183
expenditure squeeze see spending squeeze
export credits 133

F111 113
Falkland Islands 149–50, 154, 157–8, 211
family allowance 82–3, 86–7, 113, 119
Far East 113, 119, 216
Ferguson, Thomas 12
Festival of Britain 92–3
Finance Act 1977 148
financial crises 19, 70, 180
    Europe 61
    US 4
financial markets 31, 41, 60–2, 75, 140, 186,
    193, 195, 211
financial outcomes 21, 203, 204–8,
    214–17, 221
fiscal consolidation 7, 15, 25, 28, 31, 37, 45,
    203, 204, 215–16, 223
fiscal constitution 81
fiscal drag 124, 127, 137, 147–8, 158, 222
fiscal policy 149, 156–8, 163, 165
Fiscal Responsibility Act 184
fiscal squeeze:
    consequences 11–14
    definition 6–10
    depth 13–14, 31
    double hard 28, 29, 37, 43–5, 207
    double soft 30, 101–7
    hard 15, 21, 24–5, 29–31, 96, 121–5, 141–51,
    168–71, 204
    soft 15, 21, 24–5, 30–1, 97, 151–6, 164–8
    triggers 32–7, 46, 62–8, 211
'fiscal squeeze without tears' 207–8, 223
fiscal stimulus 182–3, 193, 221
Fisher, Herbert A. L. 49–50
Fitch 193
Food, Ministry of 107
food banks 5
food subsidies 81, 86, 88, 90, 93, 95, 98, 102–3,
    107, 119, 125, 132, 137
Foot, Michael 128–9
Ford, Gerald 130
Foreign Office 106
France 172, 187
Freeman, John 95
Fyfe, Sir David Maxwell 101

G20 countries 182–3
Gaitskell, Hugh 85, 94–5, 102, 108–9, 112–13
Gaitskellites 99, 138, 142–3
Gallup polls 165–6
Geddes, Sir Eric 47–50
Geddes Axe 28, 47–50, 54–5, 61, 66, 69, 115,
    119, 132, 189, 216
Geddes Committee see Committee on National
    Expenditure
general elections 52, 56, 80, 198, 210, 214,
    217–20
    landslides 61–3, 67, 77, 80–4, 160, 172, 206

general strike 1921  43
General Strike 1926  62, 74
George V  64–5, 68, 76, 216
Germany  58, 131, 135, 172, 187
Gilbert, Sir Bernard  90
'Gnomes of Zurich'  111, 118–19
gold standard  42–3, 46, 61–2, 66–7, 68, 215
'golden rule'  172, 182–3
Great Depression  4, 7, 9, 28
Greater London Council  154
Greece  3, 209
Gross Domestic Product (GDP)  15, 24–5, 41,
    45, 51, 110, 122, 126, 128, 141, 145, 150–2,
    156, 159, 160–1, 164, 169, 176, 181–4, 186,
    206, 217, 222
group pressures  12
Guillebaud Committee  105, 210

Hammond, Philip  195
Hansen, Alvin  222n
Hayek, Friedrich  8
HBOS Halifax Bank of Scotland  181
Healey, Dennis  123–4, 125, 128, 130–1, 133–4,
    135, 139, 167
health insurance  58
Heath, Edward  113, 121–3, 125, 135–7, 142
Henderson, Arthur  64, 66
Henderson, Hubert  87
heresthetic  10, 12, 56, 77, 149, 158, 196, 209,
    213, 221
higher education fees *see* university tuition fees
Hirst, Francis Wrigley  4
Home Affairs Committee  103
Home Office  74
'homes for heroes'  51
Horne, Sir Robert  45, 48, 50, 52
hospitals  82, 86
House of Commons  155
housing, social  34, 43, 45, 51, 63, 82, 84, 86,
    93–4, 113, 115, 122–3, 132
Housing Act 1930  78
housing benefit  188, 191
Howe, Geoffrey  140, 145, 167
Hungary  131
Hutton, Lord  188, 210

Iceland  131
immigration  19, 114, 213
import restrictions  129, 131, 139
imports  153
income support  173
income tax  31, 114, 121, 142, 212
    rates  42, 43, 50, 52, 59, 63, 71, 87, 103, 107,
        122, 124, 134, 145–6, 150–3, 155–6, 159,
        170, 172, 185, 194, 220
    thresholds  63, 87, 107, 114, 122, 133–4,
        146–7, 150, 157, 170, 187

incomes policy  110, 117
incumbents  8–10, 55–6, 89, 115, 126, 136–7,
    157–8, 160, 176–7, 183–5, 197, 203–4, 207,
    210, 214, 217–20, 223
Independent Public Service Pension
    Commission  188
independent tribunals  102
indexation  21, 124, 127, 144, 147–8, 196, 222
indirect taxes  21, 36, 50, 52, 63, 71, 75, 80–1,
    89, 95, 109–10, 114, 123, 125, 145, 147,
    159, 173, 177, 212
inequality  197
'inertia strategies'  16, 98, 101, 145, 147, 177
inflation  21, 42–3, 87–8, 100, 107, 109, 120,
    122–4, 126–7, 134–6, 144–50, 152, 161–2,
    169, 172–3, 175, 222
inheritance tax  42, 44, 63, 88, 98, 153, 167,
    170, 187
insurance premium payments tax  170
interest rates  15, 22, 46, 59, 121, 126, 135, 142,
    165, 175, 182, 196, 209
International Monetary Fund (IMF)  11, 25, 91,
    144, 193–4, 216
    loan 1967  110–12
    loan 1976  30, 121, 126, 127–31, 138, 147,
        165, 182, 211
Invergordon  66, 72, 74, 215
investment taxes  89–90, 153, 172, 182–3
investment theory of politics  12
IPSOS-Mori poll  148
Ireland  19, 43, 55, 198
Iron Lady *see* Thatcher, Margaret
Italy  165, 209

Japan  85, 135, 172
Jay, Peter  131
Jenkins, Roy  113–18, 128, 137
jobseeker's allowance  174
Joseph, Sir Keith  142, 174

Keynes, John Maynard  42
Keynesian economics  10, 59, 78, 127, 148,
    182–3
Khaki election 1918  55
Kinnock, Neil  155, 171
Korean War  81, 85, 94, 99, 101–2, 107,
    117, 161

Labour Government  4, 7, 37, 52, 60, 62–5,
    80, 84–5
Labour Party  31, 61, 65–9, 85, 95–6, 118–19,
    128–31, 138–9, 142–3, 149–51, 165–6,
    171–3, 176–8, 185–6, 192–4, 198, 220
Laffer curve effects  31, 153–4
Lamont, Norman  162, 164, 166–7, 173, 175,
    177–9, 189
land values tax  63, 64, 76

Landfill Tax 170
Lansbury, George 65, 79
Latham, Charles 70
Law, Andrew Bonar 43n, 52
law and order spending 144, 169, 190–1
  *see also* police
Lawson, Nigel 140, 144–8, 152, 159, 161–2,
  163n
Legal Aid scheme 93
Lecce, Giampaolo 9
Lehmann Brothers 181
'Lend-Lease' scheme 82, 86
'letter of intent' 112, 127n, 130n, 144, 211
'levels' method 25–6, 30n
Lever, Harold 133
Lib–Lab pact 134
Liberal Democrats 138, 172, 180–1, 184–90,
  194–8, 207, 210
Liberal Government 41–2
Liberal Party 57, 138
life insurance 153
Lloyd, (John) Selwyn 109, 115, 118
Lloyd George, David 42–3, 45–7, 50–1, 57–9,
  62, 78, 98, 189, 196–7, 211
Lloyds TSB 181
local government 91, 138, 141, 154
  elections 83, 103, 111, 148, 198
  spending 51, 73, 102–3, 132–3, 169
lone parent benefits 173, 177, 179, 188
Lord President of the Council 83
Lord Privy Seal 67
Loss imposition 7–8, 15–17, 21, 54–5, 76, 97–8,
  116–17, 136–7, 157–8, 175–6, 196–7,
  203–6, 208, 219

Maastricht rules 46
  Treaty 163
MacDonald, Ramsay 52, 60–1, 64–9, 71, 77–8,
  106, 206, 209
McIntyre, Robert 84
McKenna, Reginald 42n
'McKenna Rule' 45
McKibbin, Ross 78
Macmillan, Harold 108, 221
Macmillan Committee 69
Major, John 161–3, 164–8, 171–2,
  175–8, 222
*Manchester Guardian, The* 92
'mansion tax' 194
Marr, Andrew 149
Maudling, Reginald 110
May, Sir George 63–4, 70
May, Theresa 195
May Committee 63–4, 69–72, 75, 97, 104, 116,
  175, 189, 209–10
means testing 72, 92, 119, 174, 188, 197
median voter theorem 11–12, 213

median voters 16–17, 150, 157–8
Medium Term Financial Strategy 144–5,
  152, 164
Middle East 48, 113, 119, 211
Miliband, Ed 192n, 196–7
military spending *see* defence spending
Millionaires' Budget 192
Mitchell, Brian 26, 50
Monck, Nicholas 132
monetarism 10, 59, 142–3, 150
monetary policy 15, 21, 76, 148, 156–7, 196,
  207, 221
Monetary Policy Committee 175
money supply 142, 207
Moody's 193
Morrison, Herbert 89
mortgages 112, 196
  tax relief 151, 167, 170, 172
motoring 44
  government 96
  tax 102, 125, 133
motorways, electronic charging 170
Mulroney, Brian 162

Napoleonic Wars 19, 42
National Assistance Board 92
National Economy Bill 65
National Government 6, 14, 19, 60–1, 62,
  65–8, 106, 191, 216
National Health Insurance Scheme 73
National Health Service 73, 82–3, 85–7, 90–3,
  101–2, 105, 144, 155, 169, 174, 187,
  190, 210
National Insurance 31, 36, 64, 72, 75, 83, 87,
  90, 93, 102, 105, 109–12, 114, 117, 122,
  130, 147, 150, 153, 155, 163, 167, 183, 190
national output 128
National Registration system (identity
  card) 93, 107
National Union of General and Municipal
  Workers 69
nationalization 60, 67, 79, 123, 181
  land 141
NATO 146
naval mutiny 66, 72, 74, 215
Nazi Germany 58
negativity bias 9
Neild, Robert 150
New Control Total 165, 177, 178
New Deal 174
New Labour 30, 162, 171–7, 188, 208, 210, 221
New Zealand 223
Nixon, Richard 12
Norfolk, Duke of 146
North Sea oil 11, 19, 120–1, 127, 133, 141, 143,
  147, 153–8, 176, 181, 222
  tax 150

Northern Rock 181
nuclear weapons 104, 107, 113
  disarmament 149

Office for Budget Responsibility (OBR) 189, 192
Office of National Statistics (ONS) 25, 34
oil 120–1, 123–4, 127, 135, 140, 143, 150,
  154, 194
OPEC 123, 127, 157
opinion polls 21, 55–6, 77, 81, 89, 114, 134,
  148, 150, 163, 165–6, 171, 178, 185
Orders-in-Council 65–6
Osborne, George 186, 193–4, 195
overseas aid 131, 144, 187, 190

Pay as You Earn (PAYE) 82, 98
Plaid Cymru 129
'peace dividend' 117
Peden, George 49–50
pension funds 153, 167, 173, 178–9, 208
pensioners 88, 101, 155, 170, 187, 191,
  213, 221
pensioners' tobacco tokens 88, 108
pensions (state) 5, 48, 78, 83, 92, 109, 111, 114,
  125, 134, 144–7, 151–2, 174, 177, 188, 194
  age 88, 105, 107, 169–70, 179, 188, 213, 216
  double lock 144–5, 216
  triple lock 187
Pensions, Ministry of 92
Pensions Policy Institute 173
petrocurrency 141
petrol *see* road fuel
Petroleum Revenue Tax 146
Pierson, Paul 8, 10, 11, 13–14
Plowden Report (1961) 125
'Plowden' expenditure planning system 138
police 73–4, 214
  public order 154
policy strategies 10, 14, 78
political business cycles 13, 118
political cost 15–18, 24, 54–5, 75–6, 97–8,
  116–17, 136–7, 147, 157–8, 175–7, 196–7,
  203–7, 219
poll tax 162–3
post-war credits 82, 87, 88
Powell, Enoch 108, 114, 221
presentational strategies 10, 14
privatization 34, 38, 78, 133, 139, 141, 146,
  152, 155–8, 172, 176, 181, 184, 212,
  216, 222
profits 42, 43, 82, 172
Profits Tax 59, 109
property tax (rates) 148, 155, 162–3
protectionism 10, 51–2, 56, 62, 66–7, 77, 209
Public Accounts Committee 96
Public Assistance Authority 73
Public Sector Borrowing Requirement 133

public sector pay 58, 64, 66–8, 72–6, 102, 110,
  117, 134, 142, 166, 176, 184, 188, 207, 222
public sector pensions 188, 197, 210
public sector spending 32–5, 43, 80, 85, 123,
  128, 130, 150, 161, 164, 168–9, 171–2, 213
  cuts 45, 125, 140–7, 152, 183, 184, 187, 192,
  194, 208
public spending:
  cyclical 164–9, 171, 178, 193, 194
  non–cyclical 164–9, 178, 190
public venture capital 131
public works programmes 78
Pugh, Arthur 70
Purchase Tax 81, 95, 104, 109, 114, 122

quangos 209
quantitative easing v, 15, 193

ratio method 25–6, 37
rationing 3n, 21, 80, 84, 88–9, 98, 117,
  176, 207
Reagan administration 8, 11
recession 7, 10, 21, 45, 48, 62–3, 78, 140, 143,
  148, 150, 160–6, 180–2, 186, 197, 221
recesso-petroflation 120
reconstruction, post-World War I 7, 43–9,
  207, 215
referendum:
  'Alternative Vote' 2011 198
  EU 2016 123, 195, 198, 216
  Scottish Independence 2014 198
Reinhart, Carmen 183
Renton, Tim 147
Retail Prices Index 188, 213
retrenchment, welfare state 8–9, 11, 217
retrospective voting 9, 56–7, 67, 77, 151, 217
revenue squeeze 24–6, 29–31, 41–2, 43–5,
  60–8, 71, 81–4, 96–7, 101–7, 108–10,
  110–15, 121–5, 141–51, 151–6, 168–71
Riker, William 10
'ring-fencing' 14, 125, 132, 190, 213
riots 214
  1919 207
  1981 148–9
  poll tax 162
road fuel 64, 80, 84, 111, 124, 133, 137, 146,
  148, 153, 161, 167, 170, 173, 222
road traffic accident victims 144, 146
roads 48, 72, 80, 82–3, 113, 132, 169
Rogoff, Kenneth 183
Romer, Christina 19
Rooker-Wise amendment 148
Rose, Richard 10n, 24
Rothermere, Lord 46
Royal Bank of Scotland 181
Royal Economic Society 143
Royal Yacht, *Victoria and Albert* 71

running costs 160, 169
Russian Revolution 1917 4, 43

Sanders, David 150
schools 82, 86, 215
  transport 146
Scotland 120–1, 132, 134, 155, 158, 195, 198, 216
  Parliament 188, 198
Scottish Nationalist Party 10, 19, 84, 129, 130, 134, 194–5, 198
sectarianism, religious 216
secular stagnation 222
Selective Employment Tax 112, 114, 117, 121, 122
'shirkers' 196, 209, 213
Shore, Peter 129, 131
Simon, Sir John 67, 88
single parent see lone parent
Sinn Féin 10, 19, 84, 198
Skidelsky, Robert 4, 78
'sleaze' 178
slum clearance 78
Smith, John 163, 210
Snowden, Philip 52–3, 60–7, 75–6
'social contract' 127, 135
Social Democratic Party (SDP) 138, 143, 148–9, 151, 158
social housing see housing, social
social security:
  benefits 102, 111, 113, 144, 152, 169, 191, 196
  spending 32–5, 51, 64, 70, 75, 81, 93–4, 101, 125, 131–2, 141, 147, 170–1, 173, 187, 194–6, 213, 221
  taxes see National Insurance
  see also welfare state
'socialist reconstruction' 67
South East Asia 113, 119
Soviet Union 43, 56, 161, 166
spending cuts 5, 11–13, 64, 81, 102
'spending-led adjustments' 11
spending squeeze 24–6, 29–30, 31, 32, 43–53, 65–8, 71–4, 84–96, 101–7, 108, 110–15, 125–7, 127–33, 151–6, 164–8, 185–90
'squeezed middle' 190, 197
stagflation 21
stamp duty 44, 173, 191, 212
'Star Chamber' 164–5
state effort 16–18, 25n, 54–5, 77, 97–8, 116–18, 136–7, 157–8, 175–7, 196–7, 203–7, 219–20
statistical series 24
statutory control 122, 127, 135, 136
stealth taxes 14, 21, 159, 173, 196, 204, 212–13, 221 see also fiscal drag

stock market:
  crash 61, 63, 154, 173
  prices 182
Straw, Jack 148n
stress test 8
strikes 55, 134–7, 207, 214
  coal miners' 43, 123–4, 154
  police 74
'strivers' 196, 209, 213
'structural deficit' 184, 186, 192, 194
student finance 174, 178, 188, 216
sub-prime lending 193
Suez Canal 108
Summers, Larry 222
supertax see surtax
'surgery without anaesthetics' 13–14, 41, 195, 203, 208
surtax 44, 63, 81, 88, 112, 114, 136, 142
Sweden 223
Swinton, Lord 106
Swinton Committee 143–4

tax revolt 1921 45–50, 62
  fuel 2000 161, 173, 222
taxation 4, 7, 63, 81, 84, 87, 96, 102–3, 122, 207–8, 211–13, 220, 222
  allowances 147–8, 150–1, 153, 156, 170, 172–3, 187, 222
  avoidance 153
  'bombshell' 31, 163, 166, 171, 210
  credits 187–8, 191
  cuts 29–30, 85, 90, 94, 101
  hikes 4–5, 10–13, 42, 81–2, 89, 123, 145, 167
  revenue 141, 147, 150, 223
  squeeze see revenue squeeze
  structure 31, 35–7, 81, 90, 97, 145–6
  thresholds 21, 42
  wedge 167, 176, 177–8
technical education 49, 58–9
Thatcher, Margaret 8, 11, 28, 106, 129–30, 134, 138, 142–9, 153–9, 160–2, 168–9, 174–6, 191, 198, 206, 216, 221–2
Thatcherism 108, 140
Thorneycroft, Peter 103–4, 108–9, 221
three-day week 123
town and country planning 83
trade, international 43, 46, 62, 182, 209
trade unions 68, 120–4, 127, 135–6, 141, 148, 154
Trades Union Congress 64, 70, 129
traffic lights 79
Treasury 19, 45–6, 48, 52, 65, 74, 78–9, 83, 86–7, 90, 92–3, 96, 102, 127, 130–2, 143n, 145–6, 160–1, 164–5, 175, 189, 190, 193, 209, 212–13, 221
Tribune Group 128
TSR-2 111

UK Independence Party 194
Ulster Unionists 114, 121n
unemployment 43–6, 51–2, 56–9, 61–6, 100,
    108, 114, 120, 133, 136, 141–3, 147–9,
    152–4, 160–2, 171, 182–4, 214
  benefits 72–3, 76, 98, 169, 194, 221
  youth 197
United States 11, 12, 46, 82, 86, 89, 91, 97, 107,
    121, 127, 130–1, 162, 172, 181, 193, 211
  Embassy 92
university funding 174
  tuition fees 49, 95, 177–8, 188–9, 197, 207,
    210, 216
urbanization 5
US dollar 129
user charges (NHS) 93–5, 99, 102, 106–7, 111,
    113, 119, 122–3, 138, 144–6, 216, 221
USSR *see* Soviet Union
utilities 124, 172, 174
  regulation 157

Value Added Tax (VAT) 31, 122–5, 140, 145–6,
    153–5, 161, 163, 167–8, 170, 172, 177,
    183–6, 192, 197, 212
'Votes of Credit' 86n

Wales 129, 132, 155
War Department 68–9

Wass, Douglas 126, 133
waste disposal 170
Waterhouse, Captain 96, 101, 103
Waterhouse Committee 103–4
wealth tax 43–4, 88, 151–2
Weaver, Kent 8, 208
welfare–to–work programme *see* employment
  measures
welfare state 82–3, 86–92, 101, 107, 223
Wilson, Harold 26, 95, 110, 112, 123,
    127–8, 206
Wilson, Sir Horace 87
windfall taxes 212, 221
  bank 147, 150, 157, 186–7
  utilities 161, 172, 174, 176–7
Woolton, Lord 103
workfare *see* employment measures
World War I 18–19, 20–1, 29, 46, 51, 53, 59,
    80, 161, 207, 211, 222
World War II 20–1, 30–1, 38, 53, 58, 107,
    122, 140, 158, 175, 197, 207, 211,
    220, 223
world wars 9–10, 36

*Yorkshire Post, The* 92
Yom Kippur War 123

Zinoviev letter 56